D1599447

CADETS IN GRAY

The Story of
the Cadets of the
South Carolina Military Academy
and the Cadet Rangers
in the Civil War

by
Gary R. Baker

Palmetto  Bookworks

Columbia, South Carolina

ISBN 0-9623065-0-9
Library of Congress Catalog Card Number 89-061483

To

The Corps of Cadets

and Alumni

of The Citadel,

the Military College of South Carolina

ACKNOWLEDGEMENTS

August 31, 1989

As a teenager, I, along with some high school buddies, nurtured an interest in the Civil War, acquiring a very small collection of books and relics. Our interest was stimulated by a handful of bicycle trips to the battlefields in proximity to my Maryland home. Gettysburg, Sharpsburg, Harpers Ferry, Ball's Bluff, Manassas, Fredericksburg, Wilderness, Chancellorsville, and Spotsylvania Court House were toured as only a group of pedalling high schoolers could.

This interest in the Civil War period probably had a major impact on my eventual matriculation at The Citadel, the Military College of South Carolina. During my four years there, I was aware of the tradition of the Cadets' firing on the *Star of the West*, however, I never really took the time to seriously research the activities of the Cadets during the war period. Almost ten years ago, I happened to be visiting The Citadel Museum with the intent of obtaining some information on the subject and was informed that, except for some newspaper articles and some citations in histories of The Citadel, no major research had been done. The speaker then challenged me to do that research. I took it seriously and have spent many hours searching through libraries, archives, cemeteries, and talking to many folks about what has become an exciting avocation. This book, a labor of love, is the result of that conversation some ten years ago.

It is difficult to remember or thank each and every person who has contributed to this effort. Two people who have provided invaluable assistance, guidance, and friendship to me deserve special attention. Several years ago, I became acquainted with Jim Moody, Citadel '65, who has an incredible knowledge of the Civil War period and the Cadets of the war and pre-war period. He and I have shared a large amount of information for a project he has undertaken to publish biographical information on the Cadets who attended The Citadel and Arsenal from 1842 to 1865. Jim has edited, offered suggestions, provided valuable research citations, helped immeasurably with the biographies contained in the appendices, and provided editorial expertise. Finally, I am greatly indebted to one of my bike-riding high school buddies, Tom Low, who did the illustrations and maps. Tom and I were soaked in our trip to Gettysburg, spent a cold night in a warehouse in Sharpsburg, nearly fell off Ball's Bluff in the dead of night, and camped on the grounds of Ferry Farm, George Washington's boyhood home, in Fredericksburg. Tom edited and provided other valuable advice. To these two friends, I salute you!

Mike Story did an excellent job with the dustjacket. Ms. Jane Yates of The Citadel Archives/Museum has been patient with me and provided research materials, photographs, and much valuable assistance. Herb Hartsook and the rest of the staff at the South Caroliniana Library, and Robert Mackintosh and the remainder of the research staff at the South Carolina Archives Department also deserve my thanks. The fine ladies of the United Daughters of the Confederacy gave me access to their scrapbooks. I would be remiss if I failed to thank the staff of the Confederate Relic Room, the South Carolina State Library, the South Carolina Historical Society, and the Confederate Museum in Charleston.

I must also express my appreciation to the alumni and friends who responded to my appeals for information and gave me needed encouragement. They responded and their efforts are graciously noted.

But a special group of people need also to be acknowledged. My parents Harry and Freda Baker and my brother Dan have long tolerated my interest in the Civil War and have encouraged me in my endeavors. My wife, Judy, has felt neglected at times as I have devoted much of my time to this project. Her love and encouragement have led me to the completion of this book. I thank her for her patience.

I also must mention my children who, like Judy, have had to tolerate my penchant for long hours engaged in research, banging away on my computer, talking on the phone, or traipsing through cemeteries. Mark, Gara, Marshall, Hamp, and Theresa have all provided encouragement to me. Mark begins his senior year at The Citadel this fall, soon to also wear the ring I have cherished and, hopefully, to share my interest and pride in the exploits of our predecessors.

To all who have given input, assistance, or encouragement, I can only say Thank You.

Gary R. Baker
'66

NOTE: Considerable research has been done to verify the facts as contained herein but, due to the type of records, there are bound to be errors. Errors are quite possible in the biographical section where cemetery records, unit rosters, family records, or other sources have been consulted. Many of the extant records contain initials or misspellings. While the author has been careful to obtain the best information available, he apologizes for any errors which may occur. Any such errors should be brought to his attention for correction.

Abbreviations:

    Citadel '62   Refers to the year of graduation

    ex-'62   Refers to the class year the person was supposed to graduate but left, withdrew, resigned, etc. before graduation.

TABLE OF CONTENTS

ILLUSTRATIONS

PROLOGUE

The history of the Citadel emanates from an 1822 slave insurrection in Charleston, South Carolina, led by a free black, Denmark Vesey. The unrest was inspired by antislavery propaganda and fueled by a successful, bloody revolt in Santo Domingo. Vesey and his fellow conspirators planned to take possession of the arsenals and public buildings. Once weapons were seized and distributed, the conspirators along with other negroes from the countryside would slaughter the local white population to follow Vesey's rather brutal interpretation of selected portions of the Old Testament.[1] Two slaves, included in the plot, revealed the details to authorities shortly before the time, June 16, 1822, at midnight, when the uprising was to begin. This disclosure resulted in the capture, trial, and subsequent hanging of Vesey and many of his co-conspirators. From this aborted insurrection, the authorities in Charleston realized their vulnerability and quickly established a Municipal Guard and the Citadel, an arsenal for arms and munitions. Another arsenal was also established in Columbia, the State capital.

A decade later, as the Nullification Crisis in 1830-32 raged, the State asserted its sovereignty and prepared

---

[1] Thomas, 12-18. Vesey's favorite Scriptures were: "Behold the day of the Lord cometh, and thy spoil shall be divided in the midst of thee. For I will gather all nations against Jerusalem to battle; and the city shall be taken, and the women ravished; and half of the city shall go forth into captivity; and the residue of the people shall not be cut off from the city. Then shall the Lord go forth, and fight against those nations, as when he fought in the day of battle." Zechariah 14:1-3. "And they utterly destroyed all that was in the city, both man and woman, young and old, and ox, and sheep, and ass, with the edge of the sword." Joshua 4:21.

to defend itself. Two hundred thousand dollars was appropriated for the purchase of arms, ordnance, and ammunition. The Citadel and the magazine were expanded. Although a compromise on the issue of nullification precluded any bloodshed after extensive debate in 1832, legislation was passed authorizing the employment of sixty officers and men to guard the Citadel. Four years later, an appropriation was made to erect a small magazine there.

The Arsenal evolved from an 1833 Act providing for establishment of an arsenal in Columbia's old jail. All State arms and munitions would be divided between the Arsenal and Citadel. Four years later, an appropriation was made to erect a magazine and barracks. The next year, an additional appropriation provided for another building.

After much debate, the General Assembly determined that these two arsenals could be more efficiently utilized by converting them into military academies, the students of which would then constitute the public guard of the Arsenal and Citadel while obtaining a military education. On December 20, 1842, the South Carolina General Assembly passed a bill creating the two schools, ultimately to become the South Carolina Military Academy. The school in Columbia, the Arsenal, was to be a preparatory school. After successfully completing one year of studies there, students would then transfer to the Citadel in Charleston to continue their education. The two academies were to operate under the same set of regulations and under a common regulatory Board of Visitors but were to be otherwise independent of one another.

Students to be admitted were to be at least fifteen but not over eighteen. The Cadets would receive instruction in South Carolina history, modern history, French, mathematics, bookkeeping, rhetoric, architectural and topographic drawing, moral philosophy, sciences, civil and military engineering, United States Constitutional law, and the law of nations. Military instruction, including infantry and artillery, rounded out the curriculum. Those students who could pass an examination involving the curriculum of the Arsenal could bypass the first year and directly enter the Citadel.

The original plans for the academies provided for fifty-four Cadets to man the Arsenal and Citadel. They were to be "maintained and educated at the public expense." These beneficiary, or State Cadets, were to be selected from the twenty-nine districts of the State in proportion to their population. They were further "selected from those not able to bear their own expenses." There were to be admitted in the same proportions an equal number of pay Cadets. These pay Cadets were charged $200 a year, a figure which was not changed until wartime inflation mandated it.

In 1842, the Citadel consisted of a rectangular two-story brick building with a wooden parapet located on Marion Square between King and Meeting Streets. The parade ground, the Citadel Green, adjoined to the south. In 1849, a third story was added while five years later, two wings were built. The buildings managed to survive the war and two fires to now serve as a county office building.

Two rectangular, detached brick structures comprised the Arsenal on Arsenal Hill at Richland Street. The adjoining square contained two small, circular magazines. In 1852, a three story brick structure was built connecting the two detached buildings. Then, three years later, a separate building housing the officers' quarters was constructed. This last facility was left standing at the end of the war and currently serves as the Governor's Mansion for the State of South Carolina.

On March 20, 1843, the first students entered the Academy, fourteen Cadets matriculating at the Arsenal and twenty at the Citadel. In 1846, the first class graduated from the Citadel. Charles Courtney Tew, the first honor graduate of that class, would later lose his life commanding the Second North Carolina Regiment at Sharpsburg, Maryland, in 1862. From that first graduating class in 1846 to the time of secession in 1860, the Citadel graduated 175 men, most of whom would serve in some capacity during the coming sectional conflict.[2]

With war fever at high pitch in early 1861, many alumni immediately offered their services to the State while many of the enrolled Cadets left the Academy to enter the army. The service of these men during this period in our history has established a proud tradition, with graduates serving and giving their lives in every American war since. The military and academic environment of the institution has prepared thousands of young men who have gone on to distinguish themselves in public life and private business, as well as the military.

The service of the alumni is chronicled to some extent in Thomas' *History of the South Carolina Military Academy* and individual unit histories. A comprehensive chronicle of their service is left for later publication. This book focuses upon the Cadets and their service during the war. It also focuses on the service of a group of high-spirited Cadets who left the Academy in mid-1862. These men played a role in this divisive conflict, and it is only appropriate that their names and story be recorded as fully as possible.

---

[2] Thomas, 18-94, 129-136, 246.

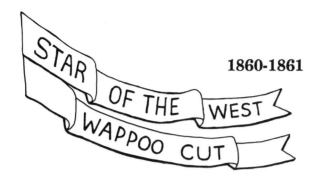

1860-1861

Maj. Stevens, the young Superintendent of the Citadel, was awakened by the Cadet Sergeant of the Guard. Wearily leaning over the side of the bed, he listened to the young Cadet explain that one of the battery's lanyards was unraveled and could not do its intended job. Then, while the Cadet held the unraveled lanyard, Stevens carefully wound it with thread. The repaired lanyard would be needed in a few hours to fire one of the howitzers in the battery. For come dawn of this clear January morning, the Major and the Cadets of his command would find themselves on the threshold of the greatest drama in American history.[3]

Just three weeks before, on December 20, 1860, Charleston had taken on the air of a carnival as bonfires crackled in the streets and rockets rose into the sky. Flags of every description flew from every conceivable location. Impromptu bands led parades through

---

[3] Law, 283. Thomas Hart Law (1838-1923) (Citadel '59) was a former roommate of S. Porcher Smith, the Sergeant of the Guard. He served as an Army chaplain after seminary graduation in 1862. Postwar, he was a pastor and an agent of the American Bible Society.

Peter Fayssoux Stevens (1830-1910) (Citadel honor graduate '49) served as professor at both the Arsenal and the Citadel, and subsequently as Superintendent in 1859-1861. He resigned and organized the Holcombe Legion, commanding it in service on the coast and in VA and was slightly wounded at Sharpsburg, MD. He resigned from the army and served as a minister and bishop of the Reformed Episcopal Church.

Samuel Porcher Smith (1842-1915) (Citadel '62) was 2nd Lt. and Capt. of Co. B (Horry Artillery), 18th Battalion SC Heavy Artillery and was wounded twice. Postwar, he was in the naval stores business and a planter in the Charleston area, then became Berkeley County Clerk of Court and US Commissioner.

the port city. Salvos from cannon at the Citadel and the clanging of church bells added to the cacaphony. The act of secession, so long awaited, was now a fact.[4]

Secession had been debated for years, the crowning blow coming with the November 1860 election of Abraham Lincoln. Dissatisfied with the politics of the Republican President-elect and disgruntled with the direction of the Federal government, the South Carolina General Assembly called delegates to meet in Columbia on the 17th of December to determine a course for the Palmetto State. A brief organizational meeting convened at the First Baptist Church, but adjourned to meet in Charleston on the 18th when an outbreak of smallpox threatened. The Citadel Cadets greeted the convention delegates in Charleston, honoring them with a parade on the Citadel Green.[5]

Gen. David F. Jamison of Barnwell presided over the reassembled convention, meeting first in Institute Hall before adjourning to the hall of the Saint Andrews Society. At the session on December 20th, Chancellor John A. Inglis read the proposed ordinance, a document written by Chancellor Francis H. Wardlaw. The Ordinance repealed the ratification of the United States Constitution and further declared that "...the Union now subsisting between South Carolina and other States, under the name of the 'United States of America' is dissolved." A unanimous voice vote of the 169 delegates followed.

That evening, the convention reassembled for the actual signing of the Secession Ordinance in Institute Hall.[6] The Reverend John Bachman of Charleston's St.

---

[4] *Charleston Mercury*, December 21, 22, 23, 1860; Crawford, 55. Samuel Wylie Crawford (1829-1892) was Surgeon of the 1st Regiment US Artillery and later rose to command of the Federal V Corps.

[5] Welch, 1; Crawford, 45-48; May, 9; Bond, 47. Stephen Elliott Welch (1843-1938) was Sergeant of the Charleston Zouave Cadets stationed as infantry support to the Citadel Cadets on Morris Island on January 9, 1861.

[6] May, 14-16; Crawford, 48-54. David Flavel Jamison (1810-1864) was a lawyer who, as a long-term member of the legislature, introduced the bill establishing the Arsenal and the Citadel. He

John's Lutheran Church opened the session with a prayer. Delegates signed the document, then, the formalities complete, Jamison announced South Carolina as "an Independent Commonwealth." The Republic of South Carolina had now officially declared itself separated from the United States. "THE UNION IS DISSOLVED" proclaimed the bold headlines of the *Charleston Mercury*.[7]

Almost immediately, the newly-independent commonwealth found itself compelled to assume the powers which had been formerly delegated to the Federal government. These powers were now assigned to the Executive Council, a group of state agencies headed by a cabinet subordinate to Governor Francis W. Pickens. As Secretary of State, Gov. Pickens appointed Andrew G. Magrath with David F. Jamison as Secretary of War, Christopher G. Memminger as Secretary of Treasury, Lt. Gov. William W. Harllee to be Postmaster General, and Albert C. Garlington as Secretary of Interior. This Executive Council, a national cabinet, met on virtually a daily basis from late December until after the Confederate government assumed the responsibilities later in 1861.[8]

---

served as a member of the Board of Visitors of the Academies from 1842 until his death. Two sons and his son-in-law attended the Citadel.

John Auchincloss Inglis (1813-1878), a lawyer, was chairman of the committee which drafted the Ordinance of Secession. He served as a lawyer and judge after the war.

Francis Hugh Wardlaw (1800-1861) was a long-time member of the legislature. Although not a member of the committee which prepared the Ordinance of Secession, he is credited with having prepared the original draft.

[7] Neuffer, 102; Cauthen, 139; Crawford, 54-55; *Charleston Courier*, December 22, 1860. Rev. John Bachman (1790-1874) was pastor of St. John's Lutheran Church in Charleston.

[8] Executive Council, x-xi. Francis Wilkinson Pickens (1805-1869) was the grandson of General Andrew Pickens. He was appointed by President Buchanan as Minister to Russia in 1858 and served as Governor of South Carolina from 1860-1862.

Andrew Gordon Magrath (1813-1893) was appointed Federal District Judge in 1856 by President Franklin Pierce. He was a member of the Secession Convention, having resigned his judgeship upon Lincoln's election. He was appointed a judge by the

An ecstatic celebration of the Secession Ordinance signing lasted throughout the night and the next day. As an outward symbol of the excitement, flags of quaint designs were flying throughout the city. One of Charleston's more eccentric citizens, Bill Trapier, had such a flag made for the Citadel, but instead of formally presenting the flag to the Corps of Cadets, he quietly slipped it into the Guard Room. During the night, the Guard ran it up the flag staff at the northern end of the parade ground. When Maj. Stevens spotted the strange flag in the morning, he immediately ordered it hauled down and returned to the Guard Room. Within a short time, however, it was again flying, this time from the roof, just above the sally port. Cadet C. Irvine Walker, the senior Adjutant from Charleston, then serving as Cadet Officer of the Day, again returned it to the Guard Room. However, within an hour, it was flying from the northeast bastion of the building. To avoid further trouble with the flag, Walker finally retired it to the Superintendent's office.[9]

Confederate government, serving until elected Governor in 1864. His son attended the Citadel.

Christopher Gustavus Memminger (1803-1888), a German immigrant, was a lawyer who served in the Secession Convention. In February 1861, he was appointed Secretary of the Treasury of the Confederate States, serving until July 1864. Postwar, he practiced law and became involved in business and educational matters.

William Wallace Harllee (1812-1897) was a member of the Secession Convention and served as Lieutenant Governor from 1860-1862. He raised a brigade, the Harllee Legion, of which he was Brigadier General. Postwar, he was active in politics and was president of the Wilmington and Florence Railroad. Two sons attended the Citadel.

Albert Creswell Garlington (1822-1885) was an attorney in Georgia and Newberry who served in the General Assembly. He was Major in the Holcombe Legion and later, Adjutant and Inspector General of SC Militia.

[9] Walker, 9. Cornelius Irvine Walker (1842-1927) (Citadel honor graduate '61) was a native of Charleston. In May 1861, he joined the 10th South Carolina, rising to Lt. Colonel in June 1864, being wounded twice. Postwar, he was active in veterans affairs and served as head of Walker, Evans & Cogswell, bookdealers and printers.

Out in the middle of Charleston harbor, Federal Maj. Robert Anderson was concerned about the results of the convention. Stationed at Ft. Moultrie on Sullivan's Island less than a month, Anderson was sent to avert war in Charleston. A Kentuckian who was married to a Georgia woman, he was thought to be sympathetic with the South, having himself owned property and slaves in Georgia.[10]

Anderson commanded a 73-man garrison of two skeleton companies of the 1st Regiment, U. S. Artillery. Ft. Moultrie was a small Revolutionary War era fort built as a sea-battery four miles from the city of Charleston. Meager forces also manned two other installations in the harbor, Castle Pinckney and Ft. Sumter. Castle Pinckney was a small fort located about a mile from the city of Charleston. However, it was so small and so near the city that it was worthless for the defense of the harbor. In December 1860, it was manned by an officer, an ordnance sergeant, and several laborers. Later it would serve as a Confederate prison. Out in the harbor and dominating it was Ft. Sumter, a large, incomplete fort located three and a half miles from the city on a man-made island. These fortifications were supplied from a Federal arsenal located in the western part of the city of Charleston proper.

Ft. Moultrie could provide effective defense against an attack from the sea. Against a land attack, however, the fort was untenable. With so much outcry to eject Federal troops from the harbor, Anderson decided to seek a more protected position. During the night of December 26, he abandoned Moultrie, spiking its guns and burning the carriages. After cutting down the flag

---

[10] Moore, 61, 65. Robert Anderson (1805-1871) (West Point '25) was promoted to Brig. Gen. after the surrender of Ft. Sumter. He served in the Depts. of Kentucky and Cumberland before retiring on disability in October 1863. He was brevetted Maj. Gen. in 1865. Before going north after the fall of Sumter, he left instructions with his factor to sell his slaves.

staff, Anderson with his small force and their families moved a mile across the harbor to Ft. Sumter.[11]

Soon after word of Anderson's transfer to Ft. Sumter reached the authorities in Charleston, Gov. Pickens dispatched two aides to Anderson to demand his return to Moultrie. Anderson refused this demand and was then informed of an unwritten agreement between former Gov. William Gist and lame-duck U.S. President Buchanan that no reinforcements would be sent to Sumter. Anderson replied that he was unaware of such an agreement and argued that he had not reinforced the fort but had merely transferred his command from one fort to another.[12]

Upon being informed that Anderson refused to return to Moultrie, Pickens ordered out the troops in the area. The local military organization then consisted of the Rifle Regiment under Col. J. Johnston Pettigrew, and the 17th Regiment under Col. John Cunningham, supported by four light batteries—the Washington, Marion, Lafayette, and German Artilleries—and two troops of cavalry, the Charleston Light Dragoons and German Hussars.[13] The Charleston Zouave Cadets,

---

[11] B&L, I, 40, 44-45, 51; Crawford, 4, 62, 107; Johnson, 16-21; Doubleday, 69; Sams, First, 2. Fort Moultrie was built in 1811 on the site of a palmetto log fort used during the Revolutionary War. The fort was "filled in with sand, presenting a battery of three sides on the sea-front," with a brick magazine and barracks.

[12] Doubleday, 79-80; Bond, 49; Crawford, 108-111. William Henry Gist (1807-1874), as Governor of South Carolina from 1858-1860, was instrumental in calling the Secession convention.

James Buchanan (1791-1868), fifteenth President of the United States from 1857-1861, tried to maintain the peace and failed to take action on South Carolina's secession.

[13] Welch, 2; Bond, 49. James Johnston Pettigrew (1828-1863) was a lawyer and state legislator who was active in the militia, rising to Colonel of the 1st Regiment of Rifles. He occupied Castle Pinckney and fortified Morris Island after Anderson occupied Sumter. He rose to Brigadier General and was mortally wounded in a rear guard action during Lee's retreat from Gettysburg, PA, and died at Bunker Hill, VA, in 1863.

John Cunningham (1818-1893) was a Georgia-born lawyer who served several terms in the SC General Assembly. In 1861, he was Colonel, 17th SC Militia. He later served as Major, Cunningham's

German Riflemen, and the Vigilant Rifles, a local fire company, along with the Citadel Cadets, completed the organization.[14]

Gov. Pickens immediately ordered State troops to occupy the abandoned Ft. Moultrie as well as the harbor island, Castle Pinckney. In the early evening of the 27th of December, the two forts were garrisoned. Soon thereafter, Col. Cunningham was sent to take possession of the Federal Arsenal to prevent "any destruction of public property that may occur in the present excited state of the public mind". Thus, with the notable exception of Ft. Sumter, South Carolina troops now held all Federal property in Charleston and the surrounding harbor.

In Ft. Sumter, Maj. Anderson immediately began strengthening his position while awaiting orders from Washington. Guns were mounted, hand grenades prepared, surplus embrasures closed off, and debris removed. The troops and their families settled in, expecting reinforcement momentarily. During the time he remained at Sumter, Anderson was not permitted by the authorities to receive large quantities of provisions. Each morning, though, the city boat brought local laborers along with the mail and fresh meat and vegetables.

The State authorities prepared for a collision of forces, believing that an attempt would be made shortly to reinforce Anderson. The city's workshops soon constructed gun carriages to replace those burned at Moultrie. The guns were remounted and new batteries constructed on Sullivan's, Morris, and James Islands. Several field pieces from the Citadel were mounted on Sullivan's Island.[15] A laboratory for the manufacture of ordnance was established at the Citadel. The east wing of the Citadel building was set aside for the manufac-

---

Bn., SC Reserves. Postwar, he was editor of the *Charleston Evening News*.

[14] Thomas, 114.

[15] Crawford, 92-105, 117, 127-128, 203; Johnson, 23; Fletcher, 10; Papers, 21; Doubleday, 78-79, 83-84; CV, VI, 66. The Federal Arsenal was occupied by South Carolina troops on December 30, 1860, and over 22,000 pieces of ordnance were captured. *OR*, I, 6.

ture of ammunition under the guidance of Capt. John
P. Thomas (Citadel '51), Professor of Belle Lettres and
Ethics.[16]

On the night of December 31, Lt. Col. John L.
Branch (Citadel '46) of the 1st Regiment of Rifles, SC
Militia, received orders to proceed to Morris Island with
three of his companies. Arriving on the afternoon of the
following day, Branch assumed command of the forces
on Morris Island until Col. Pettigrew arrived several
weeks later.[17]

Maj. Gen. John Schneirle of the State Forces was directed by Gov. Pickens to select a site on Morris Island
to command the channel, beyond the range of Sumter's
guns. Because of their military training, the Citadel
Cadets were recalled from their Christmas vacation
and directed to construct and man the battery located
near the northern end of the island.[18]

On the 1st of January, Maj. Peter F. Stevens
(Citadel '49), accompanied by a detachment of roughly
fifty Cadets and four twenty-four pounder siege guns
from the Academy proceeded by steamer to Morris
Island.[19] Lt. Nathaniel W. Armstrong (Citadel '51),

---

[16] Thomas, 106; Bond, 52; *Charleston Tri-Weekly Courier*, March
26, 1861. John Peyre Thomas-See Appendix B.
   One young Charlestonian, James Francis Redding, attempted
to join the Army, but due to his youth, then being thirteen, he was
assigned to make cartridges at the Citadel. CMH, 809.
[17] Thomas, 107. John Luther Branch (1825-1894) (Citadel '46) was
promoted to the colonelcy of the 1st Regiment Rifles, then
volunteered to provide engineering service at Fort Wagner and
Augusta. He engaged in civil engineering after the war in AL.
[18] Journal, 37. John Schneirle (1808-1869) was Maj. Gen., 2nd
Division, SC Militia, in immediate command of Charleston harbor.
He was President of the Charleston Gas Light Company and
former Mayor of Charleston.
[19] Thomas, 107; CV, IX, 404; Welch, 4; Sams, First, 2; R.O. Sams,
1; Charleston Yearbook, 1892, 208; UDC, XXXVI, 62; Smith, 15;
Manning, V, 110; *Charleston Mercury*, January 10, 1861. No
listing exists of the Cadets who composed the expedition. The
January 10, 1861, issue of the *Charleston Mercury* places the
number at 40; also, Edmund Ruffin. Joel D. Charles, J.A. Craig,
and the January 12, 1861, issue of the *Mercury* state the number
at 50. Charles, January 16, 1861; UDC, XXXVI, 62. Crawford

Professor of Mathematics and Military Engineering, selected the site and laid out the ground. The Cadets, in their "neat and jaunty uniforms," assisted by the Charleston Zouave Cadets, set about digging the gun emplacements and filling sandbags in the rain. Within a few days, plank platforms were set level with the sand bottom to support the four heavy guns. Each gun was mounted en barbette behind the dunes which had been strengthened with sandbags.

The sand fortification complete, the Cadets settled down to a week of guard duty in the rainy outdoors, the tedium broken on several occasions when they responded to the "long roll." They were housed in three tiny rooms of an old abandoned hospital. Stored in one of the rooms were thirty coffins, a grim reminder of the hard tasks ahead. Blankets were spread on top of straw which covered the floor. Sand was a constant dietary supplement since the ocean winds constantly blew the abundant grit into the frying pans, gravy, coffee, and any other exposed food.[20] Over in Ft. Sumter, Capt. Abner Doubleday eyed the Cadets working in the rain. He was to admit years later that he questioned whether they would endure the hardships and trials of the approaching conflict. During the next four years, the Cadets would show Doubleday and his comrades

---

states that there were 40 Cadets and two 24-pounders supplemented later by another 24-pounder. Crawford, 123-125.

[20] Sams, First, 2-3; *News and Courier*, December 18, 1898; Charles, January 16, 1861, 2; Burke, 2. Nathaniel Walker Armstrong - See Appendix B.

En barbette refers to the position of the gun on a platform to fire over a parapet without an embrasure.

Joel David Charles (1843-1898) (ex-'63) left the Citadel in the summer of 1861 and was appointed Lieutenant in Co. G (Marshall Riflemen), Orr's Rifle Regiment. He later was a merchant at Woodside and secretary/treasurer of the Reedy River Manufacturing Company.

Joseph F. Burke (1845-?) was 2nd Corporal of Chichester's Company (Zouave Cadets), 1st Regiment Rifles (Branch's Rifle Regiment), SC Militia. Later, he was in business in Augusta and Atlanta.

that they could, indeed, suffer the hardships of a military conflict.[21]

While the largest detachment of Cadets was on Morris Island manning the battery, others were equally busy. Seven were drilling recruits on Sullivan's Island and another nine were drilling the new volunteer companies in the city. The remainder of the Cadets, approximately 70, remained at the Citadel drilling twice daily while awaiting any orders.[22] Maj. Stevens had also detailed four Cadets, including C. Irvine Walker, to drill the troops of the 1st (Gregg's) Regiment situated on Sullivan's Island. Walker's assignment included instructing a battery of light artillery. Though unfamiliar with friction primers, Walker managed to acquire some hasty instruction overnight to impart to the new artillerymen.[23] Not all the Cadets were content to be drilling troops. William Gilmore Simms, the noted novelist, wrote that his son and namesake had been recalled early from the Christmas holidays to drill the new Arsenal Cadets. The younger Simms pleaded with his father for permission to proceed to Charleston where he could volunteer in the effort to take Ft. Sumter. "Not seventeen. I cannot," wrote the elder Simms. "He is the last hope of the family."[24]

The small garrison at Sumter, while not posing a serious physical threat, nevertheless, was an embarassment to the Carolinians. While the State troops were ready to remove the Federal forces from their territory, Anderson, with his small garrison, was not desirous of igniting the potentially explosive situation. On January

---

[21] Doubleday, 94. Abner Doubleday (1819-1893) was senior captain of the 1st Regiment US Artillery. Later he was promoted to Brig. Gen. and commanded a division at the battles of Sharpsburg, Fredericksburg, and Gettysburg. He is credited by some as the originator of the game of baseball.
[22] *Charleston Mercury*, January 12, 1861; UDC, XXXVI, 62.
[23] Walker, 14. The 1st (Gregg's) Regiment was organized in early 1861 under command of Col. Maxcy Gregg and served in Virginia throughout the war.
[24] Manning, V, 110. William Gilmore Simms, Sr. (1806-1870) was a poet, historian, and novelist who was appointed to the Board of Visitors of the Military Academy in 1864.
William Gilmore Simms, Jr.-See Appendix A.

5th, Anderson reported to Washington that he was secure at Sumter but requested additional troops at the leisure of the government. Gen. Winfield Scott, General-in-Chief of the Federal Army, wrote Anderson, "...should a fire likely to prove injurious be opened upon any vessel bringing reinforcements or supplies, or upon her boats, from any battery in the harbour, the guns of Fort Sumter may be employed to silence such fire, and the same in case of fire upon Fort Sumter." Anderson never received the letter and, unaware of these instructions, deemed it appropriate to maintain his position as quietly as possible.[25]

To protect the city against an anticipated invasion and to prevent reinforcements or supplies reaching Ft. Sumter, on January 5th, the Executive Council provided for increased vigilance. Two steamers, the *General Clinch* and the *Aid*, were ordered to nightly patrol between the bar and Cummings Point from 7:00 p.m. until daylight to intercept any vessel attempting to land troops or reinforce Sumter.[26]

In the meantime, President Buchanan had determined to reinforce Anderson without creating a furor. Believing that a merchant vessel would not draw fire, he authorized reinforcements to be sent on the *Star of the West*, an unarmed steamer under contract to the War Department. Late in the afternoon of January 5th, the ship, commanded by Capt. John McGowan, departed from Lower Manhattan to Governor's Island in New York Harbor where powder, shells, and a three months' supply of food were loaded. Later that evening, near Staten Island, the small steamship *Lockwood* tied up to the *Star of the West* and, under dim lights, 200 men and officers of the Ninth U.S. Infantry boarded with their arms and equipment. At 9:00 p.m., the

---

[25]OR, I, 120-132; Crawford, 175-176; Oliphant, 314. Gen. Winfield Scott (1786-1866) was General-in-Chief of the Federal Army until succeeded in 1861 by Gen. McClellan.

[26] Executive Council, 6; Crawford, 138. The *General Clinch* was named, ironically, for Major Anderson's father-in-law, Duncan Lamont Clinch, who was brevetted Brig. Gen. for his conspicuous service in the Seminole War and later served as a Congressman from GA. Moore, 65.

steamer crossed the bar and headed south. Only then were the men on board informed of their destination, the officers having been briefed just prior to the launch.[27]

Gen. Scott learned of the existence of the Morris Island battery on January 5th and, fearing that the *Star of the West* could not get past it, he telegraphed New York to detain the ship but she had already sailed. Since the *Star* couldn't be recalled, orders were issued for the *U.S.S. Brooklyn* at Fortress Monroe, Virginia, to intercept and escort the *Star of the West*. Should the landing then prove unsuccessful, the *Star of the West* was to return immediately to Fortress Monroe to discharge her troops.

Despite precautions to keep the expedition a secret, rumors quickly spread through Washington. Jacob Thompson of Mississippi, serving as Buchanan's Secretary of Interior, learned of the expedition and angrily resigned, feeling betrayed after assuring Southern friends that no additional troops would be sent to Sumter. Soon the news spread to the authorities in South Carolina confirming the sailing of the *Star of the West*. On the morning of the 7th, Lt. Ellison Capers (Citadel '57), Mathematics Instructor, ordered the Sergeant of the Guard at the Citadel, Cadet Amory Coffin, to turn out the guard. A field piece was run out in front of the sally port and fired three blank cartridges to alert the troops in the city.[28]

---

[27] OR, I, 9, 132; Crawford, 169-176. The *Star of the West* was later captured by the Confederates and sunk in the Tallahatchie River, Mississippi to block the Federal Yazoo Pass expedition, one of U.S. Grant's abortive attempts to assault Vicksburg.

[28] Crawford, 176-180; OR, I, 134; Woodward, 33; Coffin, 1. Mary Boykin Chesnut (1823-1886) was the wife of a former United States Senator who served as an aide to Jefferson Davis and Brig. Gen. Her diary chronicles persons and events throughout the Confederacy.

Ellison Capers (1837-1908) was appointed an instructor at the Citadel after graduation. After a year teaching at Mount Zion, he was then appointed Assistant Professor at the Citadel, serving until 1861. He was commissioned in Confederate service, rising to Brig. Gen., spending two years on the coast before being

The only person who appeared to be totally unaware of the impending reinforcement effort was Anderson. On January 8th, the supply boat from Charleston made its daily landing at Sumter, discharging employees of the Engineer Department. The workmen had a copy of a Charleston newspaper which carried an article about a relief steamer now en route and expected to arrive that night. Anderson, however, discounted the article, believing that reinforcements would surely come aboard a man-of-war rather than a merchant vessel.[29]

The *Star of the West* ran ahead of schedule on the run from New York and anchored off the coast at Georgetown, South Carolina. The troops whiled away the free time fishing and swimming. Before the ship got underway again, arms and ammunition were distributed to the troops in the event that the expedition was contested.

The *Star of the West* arrived off the darkened-Charleston harbor about midnight and apparently remained undetected. The coast lights had earlier been extinguished, and the outer channel buoy removed. Near daylight, the steamer caught sight of the light on Ft. Sumter. As the *Star of the West* proceeded into the main channel, she discovered the steamer *General Clinch* lying off the main channel. The crew of the *General Clinch* exhibited one blue light and two red lights, the signal requesting identification. Receiving no reply from the strange vessel, the *General Clinch* steamed up the main channel ahead of the alien ship, firing rockets to alert the troops on the surrounding islands.[30]

In the early morning fog, Cadet William Stewart Simkins, a First Classman from Beaufort, was walking his guard post along the beach. Suddenly, he noticed the *General Clinch* proceeding up the channel firing

---

transferred to the western theater. He later served as Episcopal Bishop of SC. CMH, 383-385.
   Amory Coffin - See Appendix B.
[29] Crawford, 133, 185; Doubleday, 101.
[30] *Charleston Courier*, January 15, 1861; OR, I, 9-10; Executive Council, 12; Crawford, 183; CV, XXI, 235.

flares. Close behind, just visible through the fog, loomed the expected intruder.. Immediately, Simkins yelled a report to the Sergeant of the Guard, Samuel Porcher Smith, a Second Classman from Charleston District.

Maj. Stevens was quickly notified, and the long roll summoned the Cadets to their stations in the battery. As the Cadets ran to their guns, two local volunteer companies, the Zouave Cadets and German Riflemen, took up position in their rear as infantry support.[31] Simkins, relieved of his sentinel post, was stationed on gun no. 1 where he was joined by Theodore Adolphus Quattlebaum, James Thurston, Paul Hamilton, William Mason Smith, Moses Benbow Humphrey, Robert O. Sams and George Haynsworth, with Cadet Capt. John Marshall Whilden acting as gun commander.[32] Other Cadets who supported the battery,

---

[31] Simkins, 1; Welch, 5; Sams, First, 3; Smith, 15. William Stewart Simkins (1842-1929) (Citadel '61) Beaufort. Enlisted in the Hampton Legion after graduation, then transferred to serve as Lt. of the 1st Regiment SC Artillery, He became a lawyer in FL and TX, before becoming a respected law professor at the University of Texas.

[32] Thomas, 443; Simkins, 1; CV, XXI, 234-236; Thurston, 1; News & Courier, March 4, 1929. Theodore Adolphus Quattlebaum (1842-1865) (ex-'64) Lexington District. He left the Citadel in Dec. 1861 to enlist in the 20th SC Volunteers, rising to the rank of Sgt. Maj. He then served as Lt. in the 1st (Butler's) Regiment and was commanding his company when mortally wounded at Averysboro, NC. SCHGM, XLVIII, 170.

James Thurston (1840-1904) (Citadel '61) Charleston. He served briefly as Corp. in the Boykin Rangers, then was a Lt. in the Confederate States Marine Corps. Following the war, he was a sawmill operator, farmer, and businessman.

Paul Hamilton (1842-1862) (ex-'63) Beaufort. Served as Asst. Adj. Gen. on Brig. Gen. Stephen D. Lee's staff and was killed in the Battle at Chickasaw Bayou near Vicksburg, Mississippi. SCHGM, XXXII, 224-225.

William Mason Smith (1843-1864) (Citadel '63) Charleston. He was 1st Lt. and Adjutant of the 27th SC Regiment and was mortally wounded at Cold Harbor.

Moses Benbow Humphrey - See Appendix A.

Robert Oswald Sams - See Appendix B.

George Edward Haynsworth (1841-1887) (Citadel '61) Sumter. Served as Lt. in the 1st Regiment SC Artillery. After the

shortly to fire the first hostile shot of the coming war, were Randell Croft, Daniel P. Campbell, John Rufus Mew, John Dozier Lee, Samuel Porcher Smith, Thomas B. Ferguson, Samuel Bonneau Pickens, Louis Raoul Stark, Samuel Cordes Boyleston, Robert Chisolm, and Charles Edward Watson.[33]

---

war, he served as a schoolmaster, lawyer, and judge. He was killed in his courtroom when he intervened in an altercation.

John Marshall Whilden (1839-1862) (Citadel '61) Charleston. Served as private and drillmaster in the 5th SC Regiment, before being appointed Capt., then Maj., of the 23rd SC Regiment. He was mortally wounded at Second Manassas.

[33] Smith, 70; *Sunny South*, May 26, 1896; Sams, 1-4; CMH, 526; UDC, XXV, 29; UDC, XXX, 28; Thomas Scrapbook; *News & Courier*, March 17, 1929; Campbell, 67; Two Great Carolinians, May 26, 1896.

Randell Croft (1842-1862) (Citadel '61) Greenville. He served with the Hampton Legion Cavalry, then was appointed Lt. in the 1st SC Artillery. He died while stationed at Ft. Sumter.

Daniel Porteous Campbell (1840-1862) (ex-'62) Charleston. He enlisted as a private in Co. I (Colleton Rifles), 11th SC Infantry and was killed in action at Pocotaligo in October 1862.

John Rufus Mew (1840-1916) (Citadel '62) Beaufort. He served in the Beaufort Volunteer Artillery. Postwar, he was a planter near Ridgeland.

John Dozier Lee (1840-1862) (Citadel '61) Sumter. Served as 2nd Lt., Adjutant, of the 9th SC Infantry and 1st Lt. of Palmetto Sharpshooters. KIA Frazier's Farm June 30, 1862. He was brother of G.W. Lee and 1st cousin of the Doziers.

Thomas B. Ferguson (1841-1922) (Citadel '61) served as Maj. in command of the artillery of Walker's Division of Johnston's army at Jackson, MS, in 1863, where he was shot in the lungs. He recovered to command the First Military District by the end of the war. Postwar, he was a scientist and U.S. diplomat. Dictionary, VI, 332-333.

Samuel Bonneau Pickens (1839-1892) (Citadel '62) Anderson District. After graduation, he rose rapidly in rank from 1st Lt. and Adjutant of the 12th AL Regiment to Col. by September 1862. Postwar, he was general freight agent for the South Carolina Railroad in Charleston.

Louis Raoul Stark (1841-1909) (Citadel '62) Richland. Was 2nd Lt., Chestnut Light Artillery, then 1st Lt. and Adjutant, 10th SC Infantry. Physician in LA and AR, then professor of gynecology at Little Rock Medical School.

Samuel Cordes Boyleston (1842-1913) (Citadel '61) Charleston. Was Adjutant of the 1st Regular SC Artillery. Railroad service in Charleston and Jacksonville.

Maj. Stevens personally sighted the four guns of the battery and then, satisfied that all was ready, awaited the ship's approach and his own brief moment in history. Overhead, a red palmetto flag flapped in the wind. The ladies of the Vincent family, owners of much of Morris Island, had presented this flag to the Cadets when they first arrived on the island.[34] To his dying days almost seventy years later, Cadet Sams would remember "instructions were issued to the cadets to fire across the pathway of the vessel, and then if she did not turn and change her course, to fire into the ship again and again until she was stopped." As the ship approached, one soldier noted, "...the day was beautiful, the sun just peeping over the horizon."[35]

On no. 1 gun, George Edward "Tuck" Haynsworth, a First Classman from Sumter, attached the firing lanyard which Maj. Stevens had rewound the night before and assumed the firing position. Stevens, mounted on the parapet, hesitated as the ship hove into range, apparently taking in the significance of the moment. Possibly he remembered Rev. John Bachman's admonishing sermon to the Cadets some two months before:

"Young men, let me offer you a few words of fatherly advice. We are linked together for peace or war; for plenty or want; for glory or shame. I have not a shadow of doubt of your courage; I would place my life in your hands in the midst of a host of enemies. But any act of rashness on our part would place us in the wrong. Act not without authority.

Robert Chisolm (1843-1910) (Citadel '63) Beaufort. Served with both the 5th and 20th SC Infantry. Attorney in Charleston and Birmingham.

Charles Edward Watson (1842-1909) (ex-'63) Abbeville. Was wounded at Gaines' Mill and Sharpsburg as a Lt. with Orr's Rifles. Railway service in Greenville.

[34] Hayes, 41; Smythe, 9; Burke, 2; CV, IX, 404. South Carolina had not adopted national colors after the secession so flags of many different colors and designs appeared before the General Assembly adopted the navy blue color in late January 1861.

[35] Sams, 1; Sams, First, 4; Unpublished account, Citadel Archives.

Remember courage consists in obedience
and prudence, as well as loyalty and firm-
ness. Above all act only in the fear and love
of God."[36]

Then, quietly, Stevens gave the order: "Commence
firing." Cadet Capt. Whilden passed it on: "Number one
fire" and "Tuck" Haynsworth yanked the lanyard
sending the first shot of the Civil War on its way.

United States Steamship "Star of the West". Fort Sumter at right.
(Reproduced from Harper's Weekly January 19, 1861)

Harmlessly, this shot passed over the bow of the
steamer, splashing into the ocean beyond. However, as
the steamer continued up the channel, number two
gun, its lanyard pulled by Cadet Samuel B. Pickens, a
First Classman who within less than two years would
command a regiment under General Robert E. Lee,
fired. This second shot struck the oncoming steamer,
inflicting slight damage. The third shot, fired from
Morris Island by Thomas B. Ferguson, fell astern of the
ship.

---

[36] Welch, 5; Simkins, 1; Sams, 1, 4; CV, XXI, 235-236; Bachman,
361-363; Neuffer, 102.

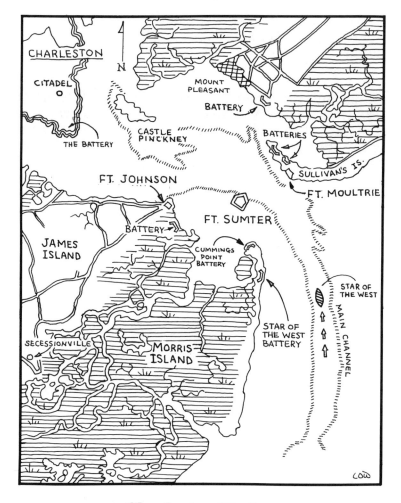

Charleston Harbor

At Ft. Moultrie, sentinels had spotted the signal from the *General Clinch*, and, immediately, the men ran to their posts. Lt. Col. Roswell S. Ripley, binoculars in hand, spotted the shots from the Cadet Battery and gave the command for the fort to join in stopping the steamer. Firing then became general as batteries on both Morris Island and Sullivan's Island joined in. Cadet C. Irvine Walker, assigned as a drillmaster on

Sullivan's Island, later recalled that all the troops there hurried out and lined the beach to get a close-up view of the action. The fact that they were literally under the guns of Ft. Sumter did not seem to occur to anyone.[37]

The *Star of the West* flew an American ensign on its flagstaff. But, after the warning shot was fired, Capt. McGowan raised a full-sized garrison flag. Below decks, the soldiers were posted with their loaded muskets, awaiting the orders of their officers. As the *Star* continued toward Ft. Sumter, most of the shots passed over the ship or did minor damage. One shot just missed the machinery while another struck just a few feet from the rudder, and a ricochet struck the forechains.

"Booh," scoffed Capt. McGowan as the firing continued, "you must give us bigger guns than that, boys, or you cannot hurt us." The shot which struck the forechains hit about two feet above the water, badly frightening a seaman who was holding the lead to take soundings. He was scrambling away when McGowan reassured him there was no danger of another ball striking so near that he resumed his position and dropped the lead again. The next shot struck elsewhere on the ship but was too far spent to go through.

Having no cannon to defend himself and receiving no support from Ft. Sumter, McGowan decided to turn back to sea rather than face capture or destruction. This avenue of retreat was then threatened, however, by the cutter *Aiken* which was being towed down the channel by a steamer. Giving the order, "Helm out of

---

[37] Welch, 5; R.O. Sams, 2; Sams, 4; Simkins, 1; CV, IX, 156, 404; CV, XXI, 235-236; The First Gun; *Harper's Weekly*, January 26, 1861; Crawford, 183-184; Walker, 14.

James Thurston credits James Moultrie Horlbeck (1844-1867) (ex-'62), rather than S.B. Pickens, with firing the second shot. CV, IX, 404.

Col. Henry Dickson Capers (ex-'56) recalled a more reluctant Stevens commanding, "Boys, it almost breaks my heart, but— Number One! Fire!" CV, III, 330.

Roswell Sabine Ripley (1823-1887) commanded the batteries on Sullivan's Island during the bombardment of Ft. Sumter and later commanded the Department of South Carolina, serving briefly in Virginia.

port" McGowan warped his ship around to retrace his route. As the *Star of the West* ran back out of the channel, a steady fire was maintained on the ship as it scraped the bottom several times.[38] Joseph Burke of Chichester's Cadets recalled that the *Star of the West*, as it turned and was struck by a ball, lowered the U.S. flag at the stern and did not raise it again while remaining in sight.[39]

The *Star of the West* succeeded in recrossing the bar and steamed back to New York, arriving there on the 12th. McGowan stated in his official report: "When we arrived about two miles from Fort Moultrie—Fort Sumter being about the same distance—a masked battery on Morris Island, where there was a red Palmetto flag flying, opening fire upon us, distance, about five-eighths of a mile."

In Ft. Sumter, Maj. Anderson had summoned his troops to their battle stations when the *Star of the West* was observed. A battery of two 42-pounders bearing on Ft. Moultrie was prepared, and the only guns on the Morris Island side of the fort readied. Loads of grapeshot were replaced with solid shot. One porthole facing the Cadet Battery was opened and the gun run out, forcing the supporting Cadets and troops to lie down between the sand dunes. Fortunately for the Cadets, the gun was never fired. Inside the fort, Anderson, ignorant of the earlier directive from Gen. Scott, withheld support for the *Star of the West*. One lieutenant remonstrated against any order to fire on Ft. Moultrie while, at the same time, the wife of a private had to be physically restrained as she attempted to fire one of the guns. Before any action could be decided, however, the *Star of the West* turned. Anderson directed his command: "Hold on. Do not fire. I will wait."

Anderson was provoked that South Carolina forces had fired on a ship of the United States and immediately dispatched a message to Gov. Pickens under a flag of truce. He protested the firing and implored

---

[38] *Harper's Weekly*, January 26, 1861; Crawford, 184; Doubleday, 102.
[39] Burke, 3.

Pickens to disavow the attack. If Pickens did not disclaim the act, Anderson threatened to fire on any vessels passing within range of the fort's guns.

In response, Gov. Pickens returned a letter which admonished Anderson for not being aware of the true political and military status of his position. Recalling the agreement with President Buchanan against any reinforcements being sent to Charleston, Pickens reasserted that the occupation of Ft. Sumter was "...the first act of positive hostility committed by the troops of the United States within the limits of this State..." The Governor then apprised Anderson that "....Special agents, therefore, have been off the bar to warn all approaching vessels, if armed or unarmed, and having troops to reenforce the forts on board, not to enter the harbor of Charleston, and special orders have been given to the commanders of all forts and batteries not to fire at such vessels until a shot across their bows would warn them of the prohibition of the State. Under these circumstances, the *Star of the West*, it is understood, this morning attempted to enter this harbor, with troops on board, and having been notified that she could not enter, was fired into. The act is perfectly justified by me." Pickens then warned Anderson, "...in regard to your threat in regard to vessels in the harbor, it is only necessary to say that you must judge of your own responsibilities. Your position in this harbor has been tolerated by the authorities of the State."[40]

In its January 10th issue, the *Charleston Courier* printed a dispatch from a citizen of Savannah, Georgia, which proclaimed: "Hurrah for the Citadel! The attempt will probably be made to land troops tonight. If so, give them a good warm welcome. Georgia will stand by you to the last man."[41] But a more somber Sue McDowell of Camden, a visitor to Charleston, noted in her journal on the excitement in the city, "...hundreds of the flower of our youth, on constant parade, in most exuberant spirits, and willing to endure every hard-

---

[40] OR, I, 10, 134-136; Crawford, 184-190; B&L, I, 61; Doubleday, 103-105; *Harper's Weekly*, January 26, 1861.
[41] *Charleston Courier*, January 10, 1861.

ship, probably to prepare themselves to feed the greedy cannon. The crisis has arrived with the *Star of the West*..."[42]

Northern newspapers soon reported on the attack. *Frank Leslie's Illustrated* reported in the January 26th issue that "thirteen shots were fired at her, of which three took effect, fortunately without wounding any of the persons on board."[43] The *New York Evening Post* reported that "The military men on board (the *Star of the West*) highly complimented the South Carolinians on their shooting in this first attempt. They say it was well done; that all that was needed was better range, which they probably could have obtained in a few minutes. Their line was perfect; and the opinion is expressed that some one had charge of the guns who knew his business...they were well manned. They were fired rapidly and with will."[44]

Sometime after the ship returned to New York, the recently-relieved superintendent of West Point, Brevet Maj. Pierre Gustave Toutant Beauregard, passed through on his way south and stopped to view the damage. He afterwards reported where several shot had taken effect. Though not severe, the damage was an indication that South Carolina meant serious business.[45]

On a boat crossing the harbor back to Charleston in mid-January with Maj. Stevens and the other Citadel officers was the ardent secessionist, Edmund Ruffin. Ruffin, given three cheers after a Cadet parade the pre-

---

[42] McDowell, January 9, 1861. Sue McDowell was a resident of Camden who kept a journal of her thoughts and events during 1861.

[43] *Frank Leslie's Illustrated*, January 26, 1861. W.A. Harris places the number of shots at 12; R.O. Sams puts the number at 1. Harris, 24; R.O. Sams, 1.

[44] Bond, 50.

[45] Roman, I, 15-16; Sams, 1. Pierre Gustave Toutant Beauregard (1818-1893) was a graduate of West Point ('38) who served as Superintendent there for five days in January 1861. He was appointed Brig. Gen. in the Confederate service and sent to Charleston and commanded the bombardment of Ft. Sumter. Subsequently, he commanded the Southern forces at First Manassas and Shiloh.

ceding November, noted the battery in a visit soon after
the firing:

> "This little battery is so small and incon-
> spicuous, that it is not distinguishable from
> the water side, unless by observing the
> muzzles of the three cannon—and I walked
> across the area, in the rear, and might not
> have known that I had been over a battery,
> if not noticing the cannon and the plank
> platform on which they stood on the
> carriages, and which is level with the sand
> bottom. There is no bank, except towards
> the sea."[46]

Fearing further attempts to reinforce Anderson, the
Executive Council stationed additional troops both in
Charleston and on the surrounding islands. Since most
of these "troops" needed instruction in the fundamentals
of military drill, for the next few months, Citadel Cadets
were utilized to provide this training.[47] The authorities
kept the Cadets briefly on duty on Morris Island
throwing up fortifications during the nights until
February 4th when they returned to their routine
academic studies. Sometime prior to their departure,
some Cadets had been supplied with a two gallon
demijohn of spirits which they artfully concealed in the
straw covering the floor of their rooms. Walker related:

> "When the order came, unexpectedly to re-
> turn to the city, it was about half full. What
> to do with it was the question. We and our
> friends had to drink it, with the most hilari-
> ous results. I had to be summoned to the
> Officer in charge and directed to preserve
> order in my room, where I was the only

---

[46] Scarborough, 499, 532. Edmund Ruffin (1794-1865) was a native
of Virginia. He is credited with firing the first shot from the
Stevens Battery on Cummings Point at Ft. Sumter.
[47] *Charleston Mercury*, January 12, 1861; Thurston, 1.

Cadet officer. On the way to the boat, the march of many of us was rather unsteady."[48]

Seventeen year old Joel D. Charles of Greenville, a Third Classman and member of the *Star of the West* detachment, wrote his sister soon after his return to the Citadel:

"I have got back to the city after six weeks hard service, and after all I am sorry we came back, for we are at our books and in the present state of affairs, it is hard to keep my mind on books. But expect we will be ordered out again soon."

Charles' attitude was shared by many at the two academies who found it difficult to keep their minds on their studies while preparations for war were taking place all around them. Many would soon find military life too inviting and leave before the excitement of the war could pass them by. By the end of the summer, Charles himself would resign from the Citadel to join Co. G of Orr's Regiment of Rifles.[49]

William Gilmore Simms wrote an acquaintance that his son and namesake, a classmate of Charles, was engaged in "...making cartridges and cannons, percussion caps, and mounting cannon, and drilling daily..."[50] The east wing of the Citadel was soon set aside for the manufacturing of ammunition under the supervision of Capt. Thomas.[51]

While the Cadets were still stationed on Morris Island, on January 28th, 1861, the General Assembly passed an act amending the original ones establishing the two schools:

---

[48] *Charleston Mercury*, February 5, 1861; Charles, January 16, 1861; Walker, 14.
[49] Charles, February 10, 1861; Bell, 67.
[50] Oliphant, IV (1858-1866), 326.
[51] *Charleston Tri-Weekly Courier*, March 26, 1861.

I.   That the Arsenal Academy and the Citadel Academy shall retain the same distinctive titles, but they shall together constitute and be entitled, "The South Carolina Military Academy."

II.   That the officers and students thereof, organized as "a Public Guard," into one or more companies at each Academy, shall constitute a military corps, entitled "the Battalion of State Cadets." That said battalion shall be part of the military organization of the State, under the separate and immediate control of the Board of Visitors, and shall not be subject to the command of the militia officers, except when specially ordered for parade, review, or service by the commander-in-chief; that the officers of said battalion shall be commissioned by the Governor, with such rank and titles (the highest not exceeding that of Major) as the Board of Visitors may determine; provided nevertheless, that the officers of said battalion may be removed by the Board of Visitors and their commissions thereby vacated, in like manner as is now provided for in the second Section of the said Act, for the removal of professors of the Academy; that the said battalion of State Cadets, while habitually maneuvering as infantry, may yet maneuver in any arm of the service, and shall take the right of all troops of the same arm in which it may at any time parade.

III.   That all graduates of the South Carolina Military Academy, in consideration of their four years service at the said Academy, shall be eligible to any commissioned office, not above the grade of colonel, in the military organization of the State.

In addition to combining the Cadets of the two academies into a unified corps to respond to any calls to the field as a public guard, the law gave the combined group the place of honor, on the right, at any parade. The designations "Battalion of State Cadets" and the "South Carolina Military Academy" were applied for the first time to the two academies, which, though separate and distinct, would be able to operate as one organization in an emergency.[52]

Gov. Pickens would remark, later in the year, in his annual message to the General Assembly:

> "The Cadets of the Citadel Academy in Charleston, under immediate command of the scientific officer then at the head of that institution, were the first corps I directed to occupy a new battery on the channel with positive orders to open the fire. At this battery they nobly did their duty, in conjunction with the Vigilant Rifles, German Riflemen, and Zouave Cadets. On the 9th January last, they drew the lanyard of the very first cannon that was ever fired into a vessel bearing the flag of the old Union, and triumphantly drove her back, filled, as she was, with armed men to invade our soil, and sailing under special orders from the Lieutenant General of the United States, marked by special circumstances of treachery and duplicity. It was this cannon which opened upon the 'Star of the West' that called a half million of freemen to arms in this our second war of independence."[53]

On February 18th, the Cadets participated in a parade to honor the Washington Light Infantry which was returning from duty on Morris Island. On their way to the wharf, the Cadets paid a congratulatory visit to Gov. Pickens at the Charleston Hotel. Capt. Thomas, in command of the Cadets due to Maj. Stevens' absence, addressed the Chief Executive in florid terms:

---

[52] Reports and Resolutions, 1861, 870-871; Thomas, 108-109.
[53] Thomas, 114.

"Sir: The battalion of State Cadets appears this morning to pay its respects to the Governor and Commander-in-Chief. In the absence of its Major, it devolves upon me to extend to your Excellency the assurance of our high respect and consideration. We trust that in the future as in the past, the Chief Magistrate of the State may find himself sustained by a brave and loyal soldiery, ready to attempt in arms what may be decreed in council.

As to the young men now before you, give me leave to say that they are waiting orders. Though engaged now in the peaceful pursuits of the Academy, they are ready, at a moment's notice, to exchange these for the hazards of the field. If the State be forced to resort to the arbitrament of the sword, they hope to show that they are not unworthy countrymen of those gallant Carolinians who in times past have thrown so much luster upon Southern arms. They feel that as students of a Military Academy, it is their mission, as far as in them lies, to make the radiant star "flame in the van" in arts as well as in arms."

The Governor answered Thomas' remarks by congratulating the Cadets on the laurels they had already won and commending them on their military training as well as the courage, zeal and valor which has always distinguished soldiers of the State. He further promised to promptly avail himself of calling upon the Cadets should the occasion arise. After the Governor's remarks, the Cadets proceeded on to escort the Washington Light Infantry back from the rigors of duty on Morris Island.[54]

As the occupation of Ft. Sumter continued to plague the South Carolina authorities, existing batteries were

---

[54] *Charleston Mercury*, February 19, 1861.

strengthened and new batteries constructed around the harbor, all bearing on Sumter and the channel. Huge Drummond lights were obtained to illuminate the harbor while additional ships were placed in the channel to keep out deep-draft war vessels.[55] Although rumors were rampant of attempts to take Sumter, the Cadets remained occupied with their schooling and drilling. Edmund Ruffin was a frequent spectator at their weekly parades during the early spring.[56]

Pierre Gustave Toutant Beauregard, now a Confederate Brig. Gen., arrived in South Carolina in early March to coordinate preparations for the coming encounter with Maj. Anderson. On March 22nd, Gen. Beauregard along with Col. Maxcy Gregg and the Board of Visitors reviewed the Corps of Cadets on the Citadel Green. The Cadets, lauded by a newspaper as the "...pride of the state...," were put through the various maneuvers of the line, including forming square to repel cavalry and firing by rank, before passing in review. In addition to the dignitaries, some three thousand spectators were present and, according to a reporter, in the buildings around Marion Square, "not an available window was there that did not exhibit a pair of rosy cheeks and laughing eyes...."[57]

New units rushed to offer their services for the capture of Ft. Sumter and, by early March, ten regiments, comprising some 8,836 troops, had been accepted into State service. Due to their knowledge of military duties and discipline, the Citadel Cadets were increasingly called upon to drill and train these new recruits as they

---

[55] OR, I, 282, 300; Crawford, 209-211, 272, 278-279; Doubleday, 109, 111, 116-117.

[56] Marszalek, 19; Scarborough, 561-562, 579. Emma Holmes (1838-1910) was a member of a distinguished Charleston family. She maintained a diary from 1861-1866, recording events from Charleston and, subsequently, Camden, after the family home burned in the December 1861 fire.

[57] *Charleston Tri-Weekly Courier*, March 26, 1861; Roman, I, 37-38; Reports and Resolutions, 1900, 9.

Maxcy Gregg (1814-1862) was a member of the Secession Convention who rose to Brig. Gen. and was mortally wounded at Fredericksburg, VA, while leading his brigade of South Carolinians.

arrived in Charleston and the surrounding area.[58] One of them, Amory Coffin, a Second Classman from Barnwell, was detailed to drill a company of Coast Guards. Every Friday afternoon, he caught the ferry to Mount Pleasant to spend that evening and the next day drilling the company. By Saturday evening, he had returned to his studies at the Citadel.[59]

In beleaguered Ft. Sumter, matters were growing critical. Through the courtesy of the State, soldiers' families were evacuated on February 3, providing for their protection and giving relief to Anderson's dwindling commissary. In early April, however, Beauregard stopped the thrice-weekly provision of fresh beef, cabbages, and potatoes. Supplies remained for just a few days. At the same time, South Carolina authorities became aware of an impending attempt to reinforce Anderson. Immediately, they placed troops on alert while plans were perfected to quickly occupy the fort.[60]

Throughout the State and the country, war fever was building. The fire-eaters demanded quick action while cooler heads called for restraint. On April 8th, that prominent fire-eater Edmund Ruffin again visited Charleston. Anticipating an imminent move on Sumter, he proceeded to the Citadel where he obtained a light musket from Maj. Stevens along with accoutrements and ammunition. Thus equipped, Ruffin travelled to Morris Island where he was initiated into the Palmetto Guards and remained with them throughout the coming week.[61] In Columbia, Lt. John B. Patrick, Professor of Math at the Arsenal, observed: "Unwelcome news from Charleston, to all lovers of peace. Volunteers are ordered to Charleston. We fire a signal of nine guns at the Arsenal to let the volunteers who live in the country

---

[58] CMH, 12; Bond, 51.
[59] Coffin, 2-3.
[60] Crawford, 206-207, 397-400; Doubleday, 117, 138-139.
[61] Scarborough, 581, 584-585.

know that their services are needed. I still cling to the
hope that no blood will be shed."[62]

Meanwhile, twenty-five seniors at the Citadel finished examinations and were awaiting commencement
on the 9th of April. Their graduation orations were presented on April 4th at Hibernian Hall. Next evening,
young ladies of the city were guests at the annual
Cadet Ball where Gen. Beauregard joined in the danc-
ing. At one point in the evening, the band played Dixie
which was just then "...all the rage..." and "...a lively
dance" ensued.[63]

The class Valedictorian, C. Irvine Walker, was
leaving his father's Charleston home on his way to the
Citadel to prepare his remarks for commencement
when he spied a classmate, John T. Morrison of
Beaufort, in civilian clothes. Morrison informed him
that the Board of Visitors had cancelled commencement
exercises due to the impending crisis. The Board, meeting on the 9th: "Resolved, That in consequence of the
imminent collision between the troops of the
Confederate States and the forces of the United States,
in the immediate vicinity of Charleston, the usual cer-
emonies of Commencement be dispensed with." The seniors were graduated, but without the presentation of
diplomas and the usual formalities. The ornate diplomas were not available since the South did not then
have facilities to lithograph them. When the diplomas
were subsequently lithographed, Walker was serving in
the Western army and could not apply for his. It would
be twenty-five years before Walker would receive a special diploma.[64]

The Cadets were generally granted a few days' leave
of absence after graduation. Some returned home, the
rest, with a fierce desire for action, remained to take

---

[62] Patrick, 4. John Bellinger Patrick - See Appendix B.
[63] Marszalek, 22-24.
[64] Walker, 15; Thomas, 109, 421; *Charleston Tri-Weekly Courier*,
April 9, 1861; Board of Visitors Minutes; R.O. Sams, 1. John
Timothy Morrison (1841-1907) (Citadel '61) Beaufort. Served as
Lt. with the 11th Regt. SC Infantry. Teacher and Baptist minister
in Lawtonville. Also served as school superintendent and 3 terms
in the legislature.

part in the anticipated confrontation at Sumter. Those that remained attached themselves to units in Charleston, some serving as aides to various officers.

On April 11th, Gen. Beauregard gave Maj. Anderson an ultimatum to evacuate Ft. Sumter or be attacked. When Anderson replied that, due to a shortage of supplies, he would be forced to evacuate on the 15th of April unless he was resupplied or received further instructions from Washington, Beauregard informed him that he would open fire on Sumter at 4:20 a.m. the morning of April 12th.

At 4:30 a.m., a shot was fired from a mortar at Ft. Johnson, signalling the start of a 34-hour bombardment. The Confederate troops directed over 3,000 shot and shell at Sumter, forcing the garrison to surrender on the 13th. Neither side sustained any killed and only four of the attackers were wounded. Then, while firing a 100 round salute to the flag just prior to evacuating the fort on the 14th, an accidental explosion killed one United States soldier and wounded five others, one mortally and another seriously.[65]

Second Classman S. Porcher Smith from Charleston, noted, "On the morning of April 14th, 1861, Fort Sumter was fired on and as soon as we got the news (the same day) we all returned to Charleston and reported at the Citadel and what few did report (the others not hearing the news as soon as we did) were ordered to White Point Battery to man some guns which had been placed there."[66] Miss Emma Holmes, a twenty-two year old Charlestonian and an admirer of the Cadets, noted in her journal of the 13th of April: "The Battery and every house, housetop, and spire, was crowded. On White Point Gardens were encamped about fifty cadets, having in charge, five, six, and twelve pounders on the extreme of the eastern promenade."[67]

---

[65] B&L, I, 76-81; Record, I, 77; Crawford, 422-448; Doubleday, 140-174.
[66] Smith, 15.
[67] Marszalek, 27; *Charleston Mercury*, April 12, 1861. The Battery encompasses the tip end of the Charleston peninsula where

The Cadets attached themselves to various units stationed around the harbor. Amory Coffin was drilling the Coast Guards when they were assigned to the earthwork battery at Haddrell's Point. After remaining all day within sight of the engagement, they were ordered at nightfall to Sullivan's Island. There, Coffin was given the temporary position of aide-de-camp to Col. John L. Branch, commander of the island. Coffin, utilizing Branch's field glasses, spent the day witnessing the bombardment from an observation tower.[68]

Little is actually known of the Cadets' involvement in the bombardment. In his memoirs of Ft. Sumter, then-Capt. Abner Doubleday credits South Carolina documents as indicating that the Cadets manned the Cummings Point Battery. Doubleday was apparently confused by the *Official Records* which reflect participation of three Citadel faculty officers in directing other units at the battery. Maj. Stevens, Lt. N.W. Armstrong, and Capt. John P. Thomas directed the batteries on Cummings Point although the guns were manned not by Cadets, but by members of the Palmetto Guards and other volunteers.[69]

Miss Holmes noted that, upon the news of the surrender of Ft. Sumter, the city's bells commenced ringing and the Cadet Battery fired salutes in honor of this bloodless victory. The next day she went to the still-crowded Battery and viewed the Cadets in a dress parade. The jubilant celebration was reminiscent of that following the signing of the Secession Ordinance. Steamers were anchored in the jammed harbor, displaying flags from every point.[70] In Columbia, bells were tolled and the seven cannon at the Arsenal fired

---

several batteries were erected during the war. White Point Gardens is a park located at the southern tip of the peninsula. Artillery positions which defended the city in colonial days earned the promenade its name.
[68] Coffin, 3-4. Haddrell's Point is located at Mt. Pleasant where Shem Creek flows into Charleston Harbor.
[69] Doubleday, 182; OR, I, 33-34, 45-46, 55; Thomas, 110. Nathaniel W. Armstrong & John P. Thomas - See Appendix B.
[70] Marszalek, 27-30.

to honor "the first victory against the northern fanaticism." Unfortunately, war was now inevitable.[71]

History would date the beginning of the conflict from the bombardment of Ft. Sumter, rather than the earlier firing three months before on the *Star of the West*. Thus, the Cadets were relieved of the burden of responsibility for the devastating conflict which was about to unfold.

On the 15th of April, the Board of Visitors met in Charleston to transact business, including action on six Cadets who had been suspended for creating a disturbance at the Citadel. Although the six were dismissed, the Board "highly commended the efficiency and soldierly bearing" of one of the suspended Cadets during the bombardment. Stating that they could not "endanger the discipline of the Academy by restoring him to his Cadetship," the Board showed they were unwilling to compromise the principles of the institution.[72]

The hero of the Ft. Sumter surrender, Gen. Beauregard, received the praise of the South Carolina legislature when, at its next session, the following resolution was passed:

> General Assembly, S.C.,
> November 28th, 1861

> Resolved, That the General Assembly of South Carolina, in grateful recognition of the distinguished services of General G.T. Beauregard in the cause of Southern independence, hereby tender to him the privilege of sending two pupils to be educated at the military schools of this State, etc.

Beauregard's younger son, Henri T. Beauregard, and his nephew, James T. Proctor, soon matriculated, to enjoy all the privileges of State cadets. They stayed a short while before leaving to join active military

---

[71] Patrick, 6.
[72] Bond, 52; Board of Visitors Minutes.

units. Gov. Pickens also presented a first lieutenant's commission in the 1st SC Battalion of Light Artillery to the General's older son, Rene T. Beauregard.[73]

After Anderson's surrender, most of the Cadets returned to the routine of academic life while war preparations continued around them. Some Cadets were, however, caught up in the war fever and soon left to enlist.

New companies and regiments, as they congregated in the Charleston area, were inducted into the mysteries of close order drill by the officers and Cadets. The drilling was not an easy task either for the young recruits or their even more youthful drill masters. As remembered by one veteran:

> "...for six hours daily the ears were greeted with 'hep-hep' to designate the 'left' foot 'down' while on the drill. It took great patience, determination, and toil to bring the men under military discipline. Fresh from the fields, shops, and schools they had been accustomed to the freedom of home life, and with all their patriotism, it took time to break into the harness of military restraint and discipline these lovers of personal freedom."

The units generally stayed in Charleston just long enough to learn the basics of military life and get fully outfitted, before receiving orders, primarily for Virginia, the expected site of the next encounter.[74]

---

[73] Reports and Resolutions, 1861, 55; Thomas, 113-114; Roman, I, 53-54. Henry (Henri) Toutant Beauregard (1844-1915) (ex-'65) spent two years at the Citadel, then left to join the 1st SC Regulars as Cadet. He also served as Acting Aide de Camp to his father, then was paroled as 2nd Lt. at Greensboro, NC, in April 1865.

James T. Proctor - See Appendix A.

Rene T. Beauregard (1843-1911) served as 1st Lt. in the 1st SC Light Artillery, then was promoted to Capt, then Maj., serving on his father's staff. Postwar, he was a judge in New Orleans.
[74] Dickert, 33-34; SCHGM, LXIII, 1.

In Columbia, the Arsenal Cadets performed much the same duty as their schoolmates in Charleston. The Cadets and officers were frequently called upon to drill new troops as they congregated in Columbia. Capt. James B. White, Superintendent of the Arsenal, along with a dozen Cadets, went, at the request of Col. Wade Hampton, to drill the Hampton Legion at their nearby camp for several days. As at the Citadel, the Cadet Corps was reduced as discharges were obtained to join military units headed for Virginia.[75] The remaining Arsenal Cadets were desirous of journeying as a body to Virginia to take their place in the Confederate force.

On June 23rd, Lt. Henry D. Kennedy (Citadel '48), Professor of Belles-Lettres and History at the Arsenal since 1856, died after a period of ill health. Second Lt. Alfred J. Norris (Citadel '59) was named by the Board of Visitors as his replacement.[76]

Normal academic routine, coupled with periods of drilling new units, occupied the Cadets at the two academies until late fall. In August, several Citadel Cadets were at Sandy Spring in Anderson District drilling the 1st South Carolina Rifles. Among them was Joel D. Charles who would afterward serve as a Lieutenant in G Company of this regiment which would be better known as Orr's Rifles. At the same time, another detail of Cadet drillmasters, William B. McKee, Louis R. Stark, Middleton S. Elliott, Aristippus Doty, John L. Taylor, and John C. Neil were at Camp Marion, White's Bridge, near Georgetown, helping to train the new 10th South Carolina Infantry.[77] In July, during

---

[75] Patrick, 9-13, 23, 25, 29, 32; Green, 364. James Benjamin White - See Appendix B.

Wade Hampton (1818-1902) was a wealthy SC planter who raised the Hampton Legion, taking it to First Manassas, where he was slightly wounded. He was active in the Virginia campaigns, rising to Lt. Gen. in command of the cavalry corps. He later served as Gov. and U.S. Senator.

[76] Patrick, 25; Thomas, 110-112; Board of Visitors Minutes. Henry D. Kennedy (1828-1861) (Citadel '48), a teacher in Darlington, was appointed Professor of Belles-Lettres and History in 1856, serving until his death.

Alfred Junius Norris - See Appendix B.

[77] Bond, 52; Walker, 73; Bell, 67; Adjutant General's Ledger.

summer vacation, Samuel Porcher Smith was assigned to the command of Capt. Stephen Elliott of the Beaufort Volunteer Artillery at Bay Point, Port Royal Harbor where he remained until October 1. Soon after the fall of Port Royal on November 7, Capt. White assigned Smith to Gen. Gonzales as Ordnance Officer.[78] Even at the "front" in Virginia, a detachment of Cadets was busy training the still raw Confederate regiments.[79]

William Bold McKee (1843-1911) (Citadel '62) Beaufort. He served as Lt. of Artillery in three different units. He worked for the Charleston and Savannah Railroad after the war.

Middleton Stuart Elliott (1841-1921) (Citadel '62) Beaufort. Private, Beaufort Volunteer Artillery and 2nd Lt. of Engineers. Postwar, a planter, cotton buyer, and deputy collector of customs in Beaufort.

Aristippus Doty (1842-1890) (Citadel '63) Charleston. He enl. 20th SC Infantry, then transferred to 19th Bn SC Cav. He was detached for service in the Signal Corps and wounded in a cavalry skirmish near Edisto Swamp in Feb. 1865. He later was a teacher and principal in Charleston.

John Lawton Taylor (1841-?) (Citadel '62) was drillmaster of the 22nd SC, and Private in the Stono Scouts.

John Calhoun Neil (1837-1862) (ex-'63) York District. He left the Citadel shortly after the rebellious Rangers and was killed at Second Manassas while on summer vacation. He gave his sister a cup made of forty silver dollars, which contained the inscription: "Presented to Lieut. John C. Neil, by the Georgetown Rifle Guards, now Company A, 10th Regiment, S.C.V.P., C.S.A., as a Mark of Esteem." Apparently, the cup was given to Neil in appreciation for his service as a drillmaster. Hartness, 69-70.

[78] Smith, 15-16.

Stephen Elliott (1832-1866), older brother of Middleton Stuart Elliott, organized the Beaufort Volunteer Artillery. He commanded Ft. Sumter for several months, then assumed command of the Holcombe Legion and was later promoted to Brig. Gen. Two of his regiments occupied the Crater. He was seriously wounded in its defense and died from the effects of his wound shortly after the end of the war. CMH, 390-391.

Ambrosio José Gonzales. (1818-1893) was a Cuban revolutionary who had been a fellow student with Gen. Beauregard in NY. He was Beauregard's Chief of Artillery and Inspector Gen. of the Dept. of SC, GA, and FL. Postwar, he was in business and a teacher in NY. SCHGM, LVI, 67-76.

[79] CMH, 905.

During this period, two Citadel officers, Maj. Stevens and Lt. Ellison Capers, tested an old twenty-four pounder cannon which had been rifled. The gun was mounted on a carriage and taken by rail to a point near Summerville where, on June 6th and 8th, it was fired about 100 times before bursting. Stevens and Capers recommended that bands be shrunk around the breech to provide additional support. The design, with some modifications, was subsequently adopted for use in the manufacture of Confederate ordnance.[80]

On August 6th, Gov. Pickens inspected and reviewed the Arsenal Cadets during recitation hours. Just two days later, aware that the scene of action had shifted to Virginia and that his services were no longer necessary to defend South Carolina, Maj. Stevens resigned as Superintendent of the Citadel to pursue a call to the ministry. At its August meeting, the Board of Visitors adopted the following resolution:

> Resolved, That the positive character of the resignation of Major P.F. Stevens, as Superintendent of the Citadel Academy, leaves the Board no alternative but to accept it; but they cannot sever the relation which has so long existed between them and Major Stevens, without bearing testimony to the marked ability and fidelity with which he has discharged all his duties while connected with the Institution; and, while parting from him with regret, they tender him their best wishes for his future welfare.

Later that year, with the coast of South Carolina threatened, Stevens set aside his ministry and proffered his services to Gov. Pickens. Stevens was authorized to raise a legion of infantry, cavalry, and artillery, the Holcombe Legion. Stevens served in the brigade of Gen. Nathan G. Evans and participated in the battles of 2nd Manassas, Rappahannock, Boonsboro Gap, and Sharpsburg where he received an arm wound. Seeing

---

[80] Bond, 52n.

that his services were not needed in the immediate defense of South Carolina, he resigned his commission and returned to his pastorate.[81]

To fill Stevens' place at the Citadel, Capt. James Benjamin White, Superintendent at the Arsenal, was promoted to Major and transferred to the Citadel. Capt. John Peyre Thomas was transferred from the Citadel to take charge of the Arsenal. Capt. Hugh S. Thompson, 1st Lt. Nathaniel W. Armstrong, 2nd Lt. W.H. Wright, Wm. Hume, Surgeon Henry Boylston, and 2nd Lt. A.H. Mazyck completed the organization at the Citadel. On the staff at the Arsenal was 1st Lt. John B. Patrick, 2nd Lt. Alfred J. Norris, 2nd Lt. John W. Jamison, and Surgeon A.W. Kennedy.[82]

William Gilmore Simms advised his namesake at the Citadel against carrying any unnecessary "impedimenta" while in service while counselling:

> "...You are to remember that you are to defend your mother country and your natural mother from a horde of mercenaries and plunderers and you will make your teeth meet in the flesh...Obey orders, do your duty faithfully and cheerfully and patiently and wait your time and watch your time and keep your head, so, that where your leader may falter you shall be able to keep him up, counsel him on and where he falls, take the lead yourself. A strong, with a brave heart, and clear head in the moment of danger, these constitute the elements of heroism. Let nothing at any time divert your mind from the immediate duty which is before you. This is FIRST and therefore OVER ALL. But I will not bore you with laws and maxims. Be

---

[81] Patrick, 38; Thomas, 111; CMH, 859-861; Board of Visitors Minutes.

[82] Thomas, 111-113. Hugh Smith Thompson - See Appendix B.

John Wilson Jamison (1839-1886) (ex-'62) was son of David F. Jamison, President of the Secession Convention.

W.H. Wright, William Hume, Henry Boylston, A.H. Mazyk, A.W. Kennedy, Nathaniel Walker Armstrong - See Appendix B.

a man, faithful and pure and put yourself in God's keeping. All that the love and confidence of parents can do for you will be done. Yourself, with God's aid, must do the rest. We are in His hands, all of us! Pray to him..."[83]

The seriousness of war did not keep the Cadets from their college pranks, constantly testing the patience of the faculty. Lt. Patrick reported an incident in which one or more Cadets amused themselves by extinguishing the gas lights at the Arsenal. Realizing the futility of ascertaining the offenders, Patrick made "... a few remarks to the corps which I am sure will stop that kind of amusement. There is an art in ruling boys."[84]

On November 2, the Arsenal Cadets were ordered out to escort 150 prisoners being sent from Richmond. The Cadets, along with local citizens surrounded the prisoners and escorted them from one of the railroad depots to the Columbia city jail. The escort was needed as much to ensure their confinement as to protect them from the taunts of some local citizens. "It certainly does not evince a noble and courageous spirit to wound the feelings of a man, when he is unarmed, and surrounded by soldiers, armed with bayonets and loaded muskets," observed Lt. Patrick.[85]

In his annual address to the legislature on November 5th, Gov. Pickens proposed that the Cadets of the Arsenal and the Citadel be united and stationed at Ft. Moultrie. His intent was to give the Cadets practical experience while saving the Confederacy the expense of maintaining the fort. His recommendation went unheeded and consequently, the two campuses remained physically separate throughout the war.[86]

Just two days later on November 7, a Federal combined army and naval expedition pounded Confederate Fts. Walker and Beauregard guarding the entrance to

---

[83] Simms.
[84] Patrick, 49.
[85] Patrick, 58.
[86] Thomas, 114-115.

Port Royal Harbor, some seventy-five miles south of
Charleston. About 9:30 a.m., the Federal fleet began
shelling both forts, routing the outgunned and out-
manned garrisons by midafternoon. Federal troops, under Brig. Gen. Thomas W. Sherman, landed in small
boats and occupied the two forts. Soon, Beaufort and
Hilton Head were occupied, establishing a base from
which to operate against the South Atlantic coast for
the remainder of the war. This, the first possession by
the enemy in South Carolina since their evacuation of
Ft. Sumter seven months earlier, alarmed South
Carolina authorities. They feared that the enemy would
immediately follow up their success with an expedition
further up the coast to capture Charleston. The Holy
City was accessible through the Stono River at the
southern tip of Folly Island where, by following the
Stono to Elliott's Cut at Wappoo Creek, the Ashley
River could be reached directly opposite the city. The
Citadel Cadets were ordered out to Wappoo Cut where
they supported a light battery of the Washington
Artillery protecting the James Island approach to
Charleston.[87]

Forty-two Arsenal Cadets, under Capt. Thomas, the
new Superintendent, were dispatched to Charleston on
November 9th to assist in the defense. Lt. Patrick, remaining at the Arsenal with eight Cadets, was ordered
by the Chairman of the Board of Ordnance in
Charleston to rush him all arms in his possession and
to prepare to receive forty thousand pounds of powder.
Patrick busied himself receiving and issuing arms and
munitions until the crisis was over.[88]

Soon it became apparent that the Federals were not
planning to follow up their earlier success with an immediate attack on Charleston, and the Cadets returned
to their studies, the Arsenal Cadets returning on the
22nd to Columbia. This ended their active service for

---

[87] CMH, 31-36, 905; B&L, I, 671-691; Johnson, 24-25. Thomas
West Sherman (1813-1879) (West Point '36) commanded Federal
troops in SC until 1862 when he was transferred to the western
theater. Boatner, 750.
[88] Patrick, 59-60.

the first year of the war. Lt. Patrick regretfully noted a spirit of disaffection among the Citadel Cadets as a result of their return to the academic routine. This feeling would haunt the academies throughout the war as the Cadets were called out frequently for brief periods of active service only to return to their studies after a few weeks. On November 26th, the Arsenal Cadets were paraded for the Board of Visitors who were in town for the annual examinations. The corps flawlessly displayed their drill and discipline, pleasing Lt. Patrick.

Two days later, the Board of Visitors requested Lt. Patrick to serve as their Secretary, a position he held throughout the remainder of the war. Patrick's duties further expanded while he briefly took charge of the Arsenal in early December when Capt. Thomas was ordered to assist in preparing fortifications for Charleston.[89]

On December 20, the Cadets held a ceremony commemorating the first anniversary of the signing of the Ordinance of Secession. Over the stage hung a lithographed copy of the Ordinance, the frame festooned with evergreens. Above, the date 20 Dec 1860 was worked in wreaths of evergreens. The Stars and Bars draped the wall behind while evergreens decorated each window. In this setting, the Ordinance was read by Cadet William B. McKee, followed by a "very fine and spirited oration" by Cadet Daniel P. Campbell. The hour-long oration was "...rapturously applauded throughout." Campbell, the youngest son of the elderly clerk of the Charleston City Council, would die on the battlefield at Pocotaligo in just ten months.[90]

In reply to a question posed in the *Charleson Mercury*, "Who fired the shot at the *Star of the West?*," Mrs. Edmund Lowdir of Philadelphia replied:

"Who fired the first shot at the *Star of the West?*"

---

[89] Patrick, 62-64.
[90] *Charleston Daily Courier*, December 21, 1861.

Let the name of a traitor be stamped on his
    breast,
Unworthy to dwell 'neath the shade of the
    tree
Our forefathers planted to shelter the free!

Oh! false to the Union all true men must
    love,
The scorn of all nations thy course must ap-
    prove!
No eagle high-soaring shall watch thy last
    sleep
When vultures and buzzards their vigil
    shall keep.

Carolina! thy star has gone out in the night,
No longer floats o'er thee our banner so
    bright,
Base traitors are luring thy footsteps
    astray;
While folly and madness thy counsellors
    sway.

Oh pause! for the blood thy forefathers have
    spilt
Calls out from the ground all amazed at thy
    guilt!
Repent thee and still as of yore be thy pride,
That bravely for freedom they suffered and
    died.

Alas! for the hopes of a down trodden world
When the "Stars and the Stripes" are no
    longer unfurled.
Alas! for the ears that shall hear the sad
    knell
When brethren no longer in unity dwell!

A member of the Secession Convention, William
Strother Lyles of Fairfield, answered Mrs. Lowdir's ca-
nard:

"Who fired the first shot at the *Star of the
    West*"?
No traitor with love of his country unblest,
But a brave Southern boy who still clings to
    the tree,
Our forefathers planted to shelter the free.

Still true to the cause all good men must
    love,
The brave of all nations that act will ap-
    prove.
While eagle high-soaring his vigil shall
    keep.
And angels watch o'er the grave where he'll
    sleep.

Carolina! thy star hath emerged from the
    cloud,
With which a nation of despots its bright-
    ness would shroud.
While Statesmen and heroes are guiding
    thee on,
To fields where freedom is again to be won.

Then haste! for the blood thy forefathers
    have shed,
Calls aloud from the depths of their moss-
    covered bed
To redeem by thy valor the best blood of thy
    veins,
The land which the Yankee would fetter
    with chains.

'Tis well for the hopes of a down-trodden
    world
That the flag of the South has at last been
    unfurled,
And now floats in its pride o'er the good and
    the great

In the bonds of a Union untarnished by
hate.[91]

---

[91] *The State*, October 11, 1892. William Strother Lyles (1813-1862)
was a large planter from Fairfield District. A member of the House
of Representatives for two terms, he signed the Ordinance of
Secession and was a member of the Secession Convention until his
death. Two of his sons attended the Citadel. May, 175.

1862

Meeting on February 19, 1862, the Executive Council of South Carolina passed a resolution instructing the commandants of the Citadel Academy and Arsenal Academy to hold their Cadets in readiness to act any night as a police guard.[92] Three days later, the Arsenal Cadets were used to guard Federal Prisoners at the Columbia city jail after local citizens became agitated at the escape of thirteen prisoners.[93]

Two weeks later, the Executive Council exempted from militia service or the Confederate draft the officers and men of the academies, but subjected them to perform patrol duty or other local service. However, in mid-April, the Confederate Congress passed a Conscription Act covering all white males between 18 and 35 with a few exemptions.[94]

Attendance at other colleges in the state had declined as the students entered military service. Young men considering college could attend the Academy and receive an education in the arts and sciences while also learning the art and science of war. Upon matriculation, they would immediately enter the military service, subject to the Governor's call. The Academy also afforded students a haven from conscription and the bloody battlefield to those unwilling or unable to endure the hardships of active service.[95]

---

[92] Executive Council, February 19, 1862.
[93] Patrick, 79. Federal prisoners were sent from the coast and kept in the Columbia city jail while awaiting transportation north to be exchanged.
[94] Executive Council, March 7, 1862, April 30, 1862.
[95] Bond, 54.

Since many of the Cadets were over the age of eighteen and thus subject to the Confederate draft, state authorities were concerned that the Cadets would not wait to be called into Confederate service but would leave immediately in order to join the particular units in which they desired to serve. Fearing that the Academy would be disbanded if great numbers of students departed, the Executive Council adopted a resolution which was forwarded to Secretary of War George W. Randolph by Colonel James Chesnut on April 30, 1862:

"...The students of the academy are always ready, being well officered, organized, armed, and equipped. We have always held them as a most efficient reserve, and if occasion should require they will be far more effective organized as they are than they could be if thrown out separately and absorbed in the various corps of the army. I earnestly hope that it may be consistent with your views of policy to issue very soon an order giving effect to the request of the Governor and Council in this particular..."[96]

Secretary Randolph responded two weeks later that the Confederate Congress had stipulated no discretion regarding such an exemption. Having received similar requests from other states, Randolph speculated that Congress would give the matter atten-

---

[96] Executive Council, April 30, 1862; OR, Series IV, I, 1106-1107. James Chesnut, Jr. (1815-1885) resigned his seat in the US Senate in November 1860. He served as aide-de-camp to Gen. Beauregard and President Davis, with the rank of Col. In 1864, he was appointed Brig. Gen. in charge of reserve forces in SC.

George Wythe Randolph (1818-1867) was a Virginian who served as a Confederate Peace Commissioner. He served briefly as Secretary of War from March-November 1862. Prior to and subsequent to this service, he was an active field officer, with rank of Brig. Gen.

tion at its next session.[97] It was not until March 1864 that then-Secretary of War James Seddon allowed the Cadets to remain, but requested that then-Gov. Milledge L. Bonham not appoint any men to the Academy who were already in the service.[98]

Later in the year, the Board of Visitors noted a large number of applicants to the Academy but lacking sufficient barracks space, rejected more than two hundred applicants. The Board recommended that unoccupied college space be provided to offer more students the opportunity of an education. The General Assembly did not heed the request so the Board was forced to reject a large number of applicants.[99] At the end of the semi-annual examinations on May 21st, the Arsenal Cadets were reviewed by Gen. James Jones at his residence.[100]

On June 1, 1862, enemy troops under Maj. Gen. David Hunter left Beaufort by ship, landing the next day on James and John's Islands. Lt. Col. Ellison Capers of the 24th South Carolina met them at Legare's Place, below Secessionville on James Island. Federal gunboats in the Stono River poured in a heavy 11-inch gunfire. This fire and an unprotected right flank forced Capers to withdraw across the causeway, leaving the enemy in control of that part of the island as well as the area around Legareville on John's Island.[101]

---

[97] OR, Series IV, I, 1121.

[98] OR, Series IV, III, 205. James A. Seddon (1815-1880) was a Virginian who had served in the US Congress and the Confederate Congress before being appointed Secretary of War, serving from November 1862 to February 1865.

Milledge Luke Bonham (1813-1890) was appointed a Brig. Gen., serving until his election to the Confederate Congress and then as Governor of SC from December 1862-December 1864. He then was reappointed to his old rank and served under Gen. Joseph Johnston until his surrender at Durham, NC.

[99] Thomas, 129; Bond, 55.

[100] Patrick, 98.

[101] Hagood 82-85; CMH, 82-83; OR, XIV, 27-31; Johnson, 25; B&L, IV, 21. David Hunter (1802-1886) commanded the Federal Dept. of the South from March-August 1862. He later led the

Maj. Gen. John C. Pemberton, commanding the Department of South Carolina, Georgia, and Florida, ordered Maj. White to move guns from the Citadel to emplacements on James Island west of Newton's Cut. A later order directed the move to the east of Newton's Cut, quickly countermanded by the third Special Order No. 67:

"The City of Charleston being at this time threatened, Maj. J.B. White, Superintendent of the State Military Academy, will proceed with as little delay as possible with the Corps of Cadets and the eight pieces at the Citadel belonging to the State of South Carolina to James Island and report to Brig. Gen. S.R. Gist, Provisional Army of the Confederate States, to occupy the west side of the line of entrenchments at Newton's Cut."[102]

Almost the entire Corps of Cadets participated in mounting the eight artillery pieces, apparently on the "old west lines," a five mile length of defensive works on James Island. After completing their fortifica-

---

Union forces in Virginia that burned the Virginia Military Institute (VMI) and presided over the Commission that tried the Lincoln assassination conspirators.

[102] OR, XIV, 536-538. John Clifford Pemberton (1814-1881) was a Pennsylvanian who refused a Federal colonelcy to go with his wife's native state, Virginia. He was in command of the Dept. of SC, GA, and FL. until October 1862, then was promoted to Lt. Gen. and transferred to the western theater. He is best known for surrendering Vicksburg to Gen. U.S. Grant in 1863.

States Rights Gist (1831-1864) was the adjutant and inspector general of SC in 1861. He served in Virginia, taking Gen. Barnard Bee's brigade upon his death, then returning to his post. He then was commissioned Brig. Gen., serving on the coast until ordered to Vicksburg to provide assistance to Gen. Pemberton. He was one of six generals killed at Franklin, TN, in November 1864. His younger brother, who died in service, had attended the Citadel.

tions, Pemberton retained the Cadets in the line as another attack seemed imminent.[103]

Gen. Hunter, having decided to postpone operations against Charleston, returned to Hilton Head, leaving Brig. Gen. Henry W. Benham in command with orders not to undertake any offensive movements. Benham, however, advanced with his troops at 4 a.m. on June 16th to perform a "reconnaissance" against Confederate Ft. Lamar near Secessionville. Although the Yankees almost surprised the fort's garrison, they lost their advantage and were repulsed when the troops were committed piecemeal. This allowed Southern reinforcements time to come up and turn the tide. Benham withdrew his troops to their encampment, and, several days later, they abandoned their foothold. Returning to Hilton Head, Benham was relieved of command by Gen. Hunter, who arrested him for disobedience of orders and sent him North to Washington where his appointment was revoked by Lincoln.[104]

The Cadets had been ordered out in accordance with Gen. Pemberton's order since Maj. White thought that the military emergency justified it. Thus, Gen. James Jones, Chairman of the Board of Visitors, was not immediately notified. As the Cadets remained on duty, Maj. White sent Capt. Hugh S. Thompson (Citadel '56), Professor of Belles-Lettres and Ethics, to Columbia to inform Gen. Jones that the Cadets appeared to be permanently required for Charleston's defense. Thompson reported:

> "General Jones heard me without remark
> or comment, and, after I had completed my

---

[103] Thomas, 209; Bond, 63; Marszalek, 173.

[104] OR, XIV, 42-45; CMH, 83-92; Johnson, 25; B&L, IV, 21. Henry Washington Benham (1813-1884) took part in the capture of Ft. Pulaski and James Island. For his disobedience to orders involving the engagement at Secessionville, he was relieved of command, arrested for disobedience to orders, and his appointment revoked. The revocation was cancelled in early 1863, and he returned to distinguished service. Boatner, 58-59.

statement of the reason which influenced Major White in the course he took, wrote a brief and peremptory order to him to remand the Corps of Cadets forthwith to the Academy and to report in person to him at Columbia.

"I immediately returned to James Island with the Order, which I delivered to Major White. He at once proceeded to Charleston and asked General Pemberton to relieve him, that he might obey the order of his immediate superior. This General Pemberton positively refused to do. Subsequently, however, by the advice of Lieutenant Col. T.M. Wagner, Chief Ordnance Officer, at whose suggestion the Cadets had been ordered to James Island, General Pemberton relieved them from further duty there."[105]

Gen. Jones' order was reinforced on June 17th when Attorney General Isaac W. Hayne offered a resolution in the Executive Council ordering the Cadets to return to the Citadel and hold themselves in readiness for active duty.[106]

Reflective of the feelings of many of the Cadets, thirty-six left the Academy when ordered to return to their studies rather than participate in the defense effort. The walkout was well-organized. The Cadets at-

---

[105] Thomas, 209; Bond, 63-64. James Jones (1805-1865) was a lawyer who raised a company to serve in the Seminole War. He then became Adjutant and Inspector General of SC. He was appointed Chairman of the Board of Visitors of the Military Academies in 1842, serving in that position until 1865. Thomas, 183-188.

Thomas Martin Wagner (1825-1862) was Lt. Col. of the First Regiment SC Artillery (Regular) who died in July 1862 when a gun burst at Ft. Moultrie. Johnson, 22.

[106] Executive Council, June 17, 1862. Isaac William Hayne (1809-1880) was Attorney General from 1848-1868. A signer of the Ordinance of Secession, he was a member of the Executive Council. Three of his sons attended the Citadel. May, 157-158.

tended their normal activities of recitations, drill, and dress parade. After supper, the "rebellious" Cadets gave their names to the Officer of the Day, Cadet Capt. John C. Neil, who shook the hand of each as they departed through the gate.[107] These cadets including five in the First and eleven in the Second Class along with twenty in the Third Class and several freshmen from the Arsenal were determined to form their own cavalry company. Organized under the name of the Cadet Rangers (also known as the Cadet Company), the new unit was commanded by Capt. Moses Benbow Humphrey with Anthony W. Dozier, 1st Lt., William J. Nettles, 2nd Lt., and Alfred Aldrich, 3rd Lt. It was officialy designated Company F of a new regiment, mustered into service as Col. Hugh K. Aiken's 1st Regiment South Carolina Partisan Rangers, but shortly retitled the 6th Regiment South Carolina Cavalry.[108] Another Cadet who walked out at the same time, 17 year old sophomore Jim Hagood decided to enlist in the 1st (Hagood's) Regiment SC Infantry, then serving in Jenkins' Brigade in VA. He would rise to the colonelcy of the regiment ten days before his 19th birthday.

---

[107] Thomas, 209-210; Bond, 64; Marszalek, 36-37; Patrick, 102; Citadel Magazine, April 1895, 36.

[108] Thomas, 210, 289; Bond, 66; Citadel Magazine, April 1895, 36. Hugh Kerr Aiken (1822-1865) was a farmer in Fairfield District before moving to Charleston in 1856 to become head of a cotton factor firm. In 1862, he organized the 6th SC Cavalry. At Trevilian Station, VA, he was severely wounded and later returned to command of Butler's Brigade. Aiken was killed in a skirmish in Darlington District, SC, on February 27, 1865.

Manning refers to the Cadet Company as the "Carolina Partisans," a name not used in other sources. Manning, V, 111.

Anthony W. Dozier, William J. Nettles, and Alfred Aldrich - See Appendix A.

James Robert Hagood (1844-1870) (ex-'64) was the younger brother of Brig. Gen. Johnson Hagood (Citadel '47). He rose from pvt. to Sgt. Maj., Adjutant, Company Commander, and Col. of the 1st (Hagood's) Regiment SC Infantry. Ironically, he survived the war without a wound only to be killed later in a railroad accident.

As Superintendent of the Citadel, Maj. White, meanwhile, believing that they were still associated with the Academy, merely suspended the absent Cadets. On June 14th, when Col. Aiken requested that the Executive Council allow him to enlist the suspended Cadets in his partisan corps, the Executive Council, believing that their suspension did not terminate their cadetships at the Citadel, refused him. Shortly thereafter, the suspended Cadets were expelled by the Board of Visitors.[109] Capt. Humphrey, on behalf of his fellow suspended Cadets, wrote a letter to the Editors of the *Charleston Tri-Weekly Courier* to set the record straight that they were not deserters as they had been branded, but instead were conscientious men intent on serving their country.[110] Not until August was a request approved allowing Confederate officers to muster the suspended Cadets into the service.[111]

Many of the remaining Cadets also expressed a desire to leave, a feeling recognized by Miss Holmes, "...It was very hard on them—at one time ordered to take to the field as men and soldiers, and the next moment treated as mere boys in a military academy..."[112] Lt. Patrick aborted a rebellion brewing among the Arsenal Cadets when he arrested the ring leaders. Suspensions were averted when the Cadets were assembled for a reading of the regulations followed by an address on their impropriety.[113] Wishing to assuage like spirits at the Citadel, Maj. White requested that Judge Andrew G. Magrath, whose son was a Fourth Classman, address the Corps. The future governor gave them an earnest and eloquent explanation of their duty to their State and the Cadets returned, however reluctantly, to their studies. These would be interrupted only intermittently over the next

---

[109] Executive Council, 204; Citadel Magazine, April 1895, 36; Board of Visitors Minutes; CV, II, 178.
[110] *Tri-Weekly Courier*, June 19, 1862.
[111] Executive Council, 242.
[112] Marszalek, 175.
[113] Patrick, 105.

two years by military necessity.[114] In July, a group of these remaining Cadets were detailed to Centerville, Virginia where they spent a month drilling Confederate troops.[115]

Gov. Pickens thought highly of the suspended Cadets. In a letter to the Secretary of War on August 2, he recommended their assignment in places of honor throughout the army.

> State of South Carolina
> Headquarters
> Columbia, August 2nd, 1862

To Honorable G.W. Randolph
Secretary of War

Dear Sir,
  There is a corps of very choice young men who have withdrawn from our Military Academy, and entered into service under Colonel Aiken. Every one of these young men is a well drilled and educated soldier of the highest order, and fit to command as first or second lieutenants in any branch of service, and it strikes me that you will do well to assign them as drill officers in such Regiments as require it, or appoint them throughout the Army to places of first and second lieutenant. Many of them are some of the best citizens and gentlemen....

Gov. Pickens[116]

Most of the youthful Rangers were indeed proficient in the duties of all military branches. Cadets from both institutions had been instructed in infantry and artillery drill, as well as bayonet and broad sword

---

[114] Thomas, 210; Bond, 64.
[115] UDC, IX, 205.
[116] CSR, 6th SC Cavalry.

exercises.[117] Other units of the newly-formed 6th South Carolina Cavalry were not nearly so well prepared or so well-manned. Thus, the "Cadet Rangers," now Company F, provided the drill cadre to instruct the other companies. The 6th was made up mainly of very young men or older men who were not subject to conscription. These extremes were aptly represented by Capt. J.J. Maguire's Company H, the "Yeadon Rangers," which included both a fifteen year old boy trooper as well as Maguire's own 62 year old father.[118]

Those boys under the conscription age of 18 were required to get their parents' consent before joining the army. Numerous stories exist of young men who either lied about their age or otherwise "obtained their parents' consent." One of several Cadet Rangers who encountered this problem was James T. Proctor, nephew of Gen. Beauregard and one of the Arsenal Cadets who joined the company. Beauregard assumed that the State institutions were like West Point where leaving without a discharge was desertion. When he heard of his 16 year old nephew's actions, he wrote Capt. Thomas to put Proctor in irons and send him to Ft. Sumter. If the boy remained unmanageable, Thomas was to shoot him.[119] Gen. Wilmot DeSaussure, Adjutant and Inspector-General of South Carolina, managed to prevail on Col. Aiken and other officers to return Proctor to the Arsenal where he remained only a short time before again leaving to join Gregg's 1st South Carolina Infantry. This time his uncle appears to have acquiesced in his choice. Proctor was promoted lieutenant for "valor and skill" at Fredericksburg, only to lose a leg the next

---

[117] Thomas, 101-102; Patrick, 2,19; Bond, 37. Col. Lewis M. Hatch (1816-1897), former Capt. of the Washington Light Infantry, provided a course in the use of the broad sword to about half of the corps in 1860. Two members of the corps subsequently thanked him for the instruction, one for the confidence instilled in battle and the other for having saved his life in a bayonet attack.
[118] CSR, 6th SC Cavalry.
[119] Marszalek, 195.

year at Chancellorsville. Subsequently, he served on his uncle's staff.[120]

For the next eighteen months, the Sixth South Carolina Cavalry was assigned to routine patrolling and picketing duty on the coast of their native state. The Cadet Rangers, initially stationed at Adams' Run some 25 miles southwest of Charleston, were part of the squadron commanded by Maj. John Jenkins, of the 3rd South Carolina Cavalry. Jenkins, older brother of Micah Jenkins (Citadel '54) who was then commanding a brigade in Virginia, was assigned to picket the area around John's Island, the back door to Charleston. In turn, he assigned Capt. Humphrey's company the task of covering the area near the Haulover Cut.[121] During this routine, often boring duty along the coast, the officers of the Cadet Rangers were repeatedly detailed by Col. Aiken to instruct the regiment's officers and non-commissioned officers in Hardee's tactics.[122]

This period, lasting from the fall of 1862 until early winter of 1864, was one of little real action for the Sixth. Days in camp seldom varied, consisting of policing the yards and cleaning out the stables by 9 every morning, then drill and saber exercises on foot, followed by drill on horseback. In the evening came dress parade, either on foot or horseback, with stable calls, watering calls, mess calls, and roll calls in between. A regimental parade was held every Tuesday while Fridays were spent in saber and rifle inspection. Once a month, the regiment stood a General Review and Inspection.[123] Many of the ex-Cadets who had joined up to fight and, at the same time, escape

---

[120] OR, XIV, 595; CSR, 6th SC Cavalry; Roman, I, 54. Wilmot DeSaussure was a Charleston lawyer who, as Lt. Col., commanded the artillery on Morris Island during the bombardment of Ft. Sumter.

[121] Sphinx, 1900, 91-97; *Sunday News*, August 15, 1895. Major John Jenkins (1834-1905) was Major of the 3rd SC Cavalry and a planter on Johns Island in civil life.

[122] Thomas, 214; Bond, 66.

[123] McDaniel, 62; UDC, IX, 61. James Michael Barr (1829-1864) was a private in Co. I, 5th SC Cavalry. Barr, 7-8.

the irksome routine of the Citadel or the Arsenal, must have been sorely disappointed.

While the Rangers were organizing, the Cadets at the Citadel and Arsenal continued their routine of drilling and studies. However, in November 1862, in lieu of Christmas holidays, the Arsenal Cadets were ordered to remain in Columbia prepared to respond to any emergency. The enemy had made an unsuccessful attack in the vicinity of Pocotaligo and, though they had been repulsed, Gen. Jones, commanding the Department, anticipated a renewal of the attack. Several weeks passed, however, and the Federals showed no inclination to attempt another advance. Once again, the Cadets returned to their books without getting a shot at the hated Yankees. During this period of alert, faculty officers Lt. Patrick and Lt. Norris had, at the request of the Governor, filled their spare time testing samples of locally manufactured gunpowder.[124]

---

[124] Patrick, 132, 134.

Throughout the war, the Cadets were called out to provide military honors at the funerals of officers killed in battle, among them Brig. Gen. Maxcy Gregg who had fallen in December 1862 at Fredericksburg. Early in the new year, the Cadets of the Arsenal provided the escort for the burial of Capt. Langdon Cheves McCord. McCord, an officer of the Columbia Zouaves, had died in late January 1863, succumbing to his severe wound received at Second Manassas the previous August. The Cadets were marched about a mile and a half to Elmwood Cemetery to fire the salute over his remains, proceeding along a street which had previously been sprinkled to keep the dust down. Apparently it had been overwatered for, as the Cadets, in their dress uniforms of gray wool with white duck trousers, marched along, thick wet sand stuck to their trousers. One of them, Alexander McQueen Salley from Orangeburg, lost the heel of his shoe in the sticky street. If he wasn't miserable enough, he was further chagrined when his rifle refused to fire during the salute.[125]

Typical of the patriotic spirit of the day, some young ladies of Charleston, Misses Annie Brewster, Carrie Desel, and Carrie Waties, made a flag which they presented to the Cadet Rangers in an elaborate

---

[125] *Tri-Weekly Southern Guardian*, Dec. 22, 1862; UDC, LXIII, 93-94.

Capt. Langdon Cheves McCord (1841-1863) who commanded the SC Zouaves, Hampton Legion (Co. H, Infantry Regiment, Hampton Legion), at Second Manassas recovered sufficiently to rejoin his unit, then died from the effects of the wound in January 1863. SCHGM, XXXIV, 190.

Alexander McQueen Salley - See Appendix B.

ceremony. The flag was later described in the Courier as: "a very beautiful one of red and white silk. On one side is written the name of our company 'Cadet Rangers,' and beneath it, on the white ground, 'Christmas 1862.' On the other side, above, on the red ground, is the inscription 'Pro aris focis que certare' (To fight for your altars and hearth), and under three stars of gold on the white." Capt. Thomas later added that the flag also contained a crescent embroidered in gold in the upper corner of each side.

On February 18, 1863, the banner was, with suitable ceremony and fiery oratory, presented to the Company. Escorted by Lt. Alfred Aldrich, the three young ladies arrived at the parade ground where the Rangers were formed, the regimental brass band lending a festive air. Lt. Aldrich, at the request of the donors, presented the flag to Capt. Humphrey. Humphrey clasped it and addressed the assemblage, recounting the events which brought the Cadets into active service. Then, acknowledging the influence of the fair sex, he charged:

And now that our course has been approved by the great, and has won the smiles of the fair, our duty is still go forward:
"For when woman points onward what coward will stand
And see shame and dishonor descend on his land?"

Humphrey closed his remarks, exhorting his subordinates:

While we who have been less fortunate are equally determined to emulate your virtues, that when we again sue at beauty's altar we may hope to gain a reward. It is with the confidence that each of you will do your duty that I receive this banner in behalf of the Cadet Rangers, and that I tell the fair donors to rest assured that,
"One stain of dishonor they never shall see

On the folds of that banner we swear to defend.
Till victory or death the struggle shall end."

Humphrey then handed the flag over to Corp. Gabriel M. Hodges, the company's first color bearer, bidding him:

And before high heaven, and in the presence of Heaven's God, I charge you never to allow its sacred folds to trail in the dust.
If you fall, sir, with your dying grasp preserve that banner still erect, and let it float proudly to heaven's breeze in the very face of the foe.

When Humphrey had finished his florid remarks, Hodges replied with another speech expressing, among other things, his own undying determination to uphold the banner with his life. As Hodges finished, Capt. Humphrey commanded, "To your colors—Present arms!"

The ceremony over, the Rangers were marched back to their company street by Orderly Sgt. E. Drayton Earle of Greenville. Before he dismissed the troop, he proposed "three cheers for our flag and the ladies who sent it."

Humphrey Boswell, apparently a nom de plume of a member of the Rangers, recorded the event in the *Courier* article, and later wrote a poem about the event:

OUR BANNER

Presented to the Cadet Rangers by
the Ladies of Charleston

Unfurl its bright folds to the free winds of Heaven
    To keep it free as the winds shall be our pride;

By Carolina's fair daughters this banner is
given
 Unto men who'll be free till the last one has
 died;
Our flag has been wrought by woman's fair fin-
gers—
 Her breath has perfumed it, her touch made
 it dear;
Around its fair folds her sweet prayer still lingers
 "Oh! God, prosper those who this banner
 shall bear."
  Then by all that is sacred and true, we
  swear
 Our standard in triumph to carry,
  For the bright eyes of those we hold
  most dear,
   "Pro aris et focis certare."
"Tis colored with red like the life blood which
freely
 Shall flow for its sake, and alone shall stain
 it;
And its spotless white but betokens how purely
 With liberty's spirit we will ever maintain
 it.
In the fierce din of arms when conflict is rag-
ing,
 Let your eye seek that flag floating proudly
 above;
And think as the foe in sharp strife you're engag-
ing,
 To see it dishonored is to lose woman's
 love.
  Then by all that is sacred and true,
  we swear
   Our standard in triumph to carry,
  For the bright eyes of those we hold
  most dear,
   "Pro aris et focis certare."

Then rally, my brothers, the hour approaches,
 The war cloud now is resting on our fair
 land;

The vandal at length on Carolina encroaches,
    And we 'neath this banner together must
    stand.
Remember who gave it, and never, oh! never,
    Let it for one moment descend from on
    high;
But living, defend it, forever and ever,
    And grasp it, and shield it—aye, e'en when
    you die.
        Then by all that is sacred and true, we
        swear
            Our standard in triumph to carry,
    For the bright eyes of those we hold
    most dear,
        "Pro aris et focis certare."

"Boswell" went on to describe the spirit and enthusiasm of the young soldiers as they received their own standard:

Young, brave and impetuous, with very few
who can yet boast a fair partner of his joys
and cares, our corps may be said to worship
at the shrine of woman, and let me hope
with equal ardor at that of liberty. Let the
ladies then, be assured that while the Cadet
Rangers exist as a corps, for while one of
their members still survives, there will ever
be found one to defend the beautiful flag
they have given us, to strike for their rights
and their liberties. "Pro aris focis que
certare."

There was little doubt that many Cadet Rangers were, with youthful ardor, ready to die under the folds of their cherished banner for their homeland.[126] However, the flag was to be under fire only briefly.

---

[126] Sphinx, 1900, 91-97; Citadel Magazine, April 1895, 37. Gabriel M. Hodges and Elias Drayton Earle - See Appendix A.
    "Boswell" was probably James Gadsden Holmes - See Appendix A.

Maj. John Jenkins feared that the prominent white
stripe might give the impression of a flag of truce.
Thus, Sgt. Hodges sent it to his home in Abbeville
where it remained until 1886 when he presented it to
the Association of Graduates.[127]

The seriousness of war business and camp routine
was again set aside for awhile in early February
when a race was run between a mare belonging to a
member of the Rebel Troop, Co. E, 3rd SC Cavalry,
and the eventual winner, a Cadet Ranger's quarter
horse.[128]

In early 1863, the Citadel Cadets were ordered to
man the battery established at the New Bridge connecting   Charleston   to   James   Island.   Gen.
Beauregard, who had been reassigned to Charleston
the previous September, proposed that the Cadets
could practice at the battery while continuing to live in
their barracks on Marion Square. On the 14th of
March, Beauregard reviewed the Cadets and
afterwards inspected the facilities. The library of the
Citadel was impressed for use as a military court.[129]
In anticipation of an enemy attack on Charleston,
Gen. Jones informed Lt. Patrick on March 16 to place
the Arsenal Cadets in readiness to move there, if
necessary, however, the Cadets were not called out.[130]

In early March, four cannon, two Parrotts and two
Wiards, captured in the recent battle at Murfreesboro,
Tennessee arrived in Charleston as a present from
the Army of Tennessee to the State of South Carolina.
Each piece was inscribed with the name of one of the
four officers from the 10th and 19th Regiments South
Carolina Infantry who had fallen in the bloody charge
which   wrenched   the   guns   from   Company   C,   1st

---

[127] Marszalek, 37-38. Hodges returned the flag of the Cadet
Rangers to Gen. Johnson Hagood, President of the Association
of Citadel Graduates, in 1886. The flag hung in the
Commandant's Office at least until 1895, but no record has
been discovered of its present location or disposition.
[128] SCHGM, LV, 76.
[129] OR, XIV, 835; *Charleston Tri-Weekly Courier*, March 14,
1863.
[130] Patrick, 150.

Illinois Light Artillery. The names inscribed were those of Col. Augustus J. Lythgoe and 2nd Lt. John T. Norris of the 19th and Capts. John Sanders Palmer and Joseph H. Nettles of the 10th. All four had previously attended the Citadel and all but Palmer were mortally wounded. Palmer recovered from his wound only to die the next year in the defense of Atlanta.[131]

Twelve Cadets graduated on the 15th of April.[132] Appointed to the new class entering the Arsenal was Arthur W. Thomson of Barnwell. A friend of Lt. Patrick's related the circumstances surrounding this appointment:

> "A Lt. of the 1st Reg. S.C.V. commanding a company (in the battle of Sharpsburg in September 1862), lost all his men but one killed, wounded, or missing. Standing behind this one, he waved his sword over his head exclaiming 'go it Thomson!', 'go it Thomson!', and while in this attitude he fell severely wounded. His man Thomson remained on the field alone until he too fell from the effects of a severe wound."

---

[131] *Charleston Daily Courier*, March 7, 1863. Col. Augustus Jackson Lythgoe (1830-1862) (ex-'47) was educated at the Citadel, leaving shortly before his class graduated. Prior to the war, he worked with the railroads and then engaged in the mercantile business. He enlisted in the 19th SC Volunteer Infantry, rising to the rank of Col. While leading his regiment in the capture of the four-gun battery at Murfreesboro, he received a mortal wound.

2nd Lt. John T. Norris (1842-1863) (ex-'61) was 2nd Lt. in Co. A, 19th SC Infantry and died Janury 9 or 10, 1863 at Foard Hospital, Chattanooga, TN.

Captain John Sanders Palmer (1836-1864) (ex-'54) commanded Co. K (Eutaw Volunteers), 10th SC Infantry and was seriously wounded on December 31, 1862, but recovered to be killed later in the Atlanta campaign.

Capt. Joseph Henry Nettles (1840-1863) (ex-'60) commanded Co. H (Liberty Volunteers), 10th SC Infantry. He was wounded on December 31, 1862, and died January 14, 1863 while a prisoner.

[132] Marszalek, 248.

For his service on that occasion, Gov. Bonham appointed Pvt. Thomson a State Cadet.[133]

On July 10th, academic studies were again suspended, and all Citadel and 52 Arsenal Cadets were ordered into service when the enemy captured the northern end of Morris Island, threatening Battery Wagner. Anticipating some real service, the Cadets were gathered on the wharf awaiting transportation when Gen. Roswell Ripley, commanding the Charleston Military District, directed them to return to the Academy. The commander of Morris Island had telegraphed Ripley that he needed no more troops to man the batteries he had.[134]

The plethora of troops in the Charleston area that summer, many hastily raised local defense forces with little or no training, forced the *Charleston Tri-Weekly Courier* to ask:

> "Will our friends of the Home Guards and citizen soldiery enrolled for home defense pardon us a hint. It is not proper or convenient to carry the musket with the bayonet fixed in all sorts of styles along the streets. Put the bayonet in the sheath or keep it up, and thus avoid danger or menace the eyes or flesh of friends."[135]

Cadets from both institutions remained on duty in the city guarding government stores. On the 21st of August, the Yankees began shelling the city, but the Cadets soon got used to the shrieking shells. Ten Arsenal Cadets were sent back to Columbia to guard the magazines. One of the returning Cadets, Julius L. Bartlette, expressed his dislike for guard duty but was even less anxious to return to his studies. The bore-

---

[133] Patrick, 160. Arthur W. Thomson - See Appendix B.
[134] Thomas, 210; Bond, 64; Patrick, 169; OR, XXVIII, 188, 193. Battery Wagner was a small sand fortification on Morris Island located close to the position of the Star of the West battery, approximately a mile and a half from Ft. Sumter.
[135] *Charleston Tri-Weekly Courier*, July 14, 1863.

dom was relieved briefly on the afternoon of August 24th when the Corps attended the funeral of Cadet William Ravenel who died from typhoid fever contracted while on guard duty. On September 3rd, the Arsenal Cadets returned to their books in Columbia while the Citadel Cadets were kept on duty in the city until later in the month. Lt. Patrick noted that the officers and Cadets were paid for their service in Charleston, apparently the only time they were so compensated.[136] When finally relieved on the 23rd, Gen. Beauregard formally thanked them for their promptness as well as their zeal and discipline while under his orders.[137]

Shortly afterward, however, twenty-one Arsenal Cadets were suspended after threatening to leave the Academy, with or without their parents' consent, to form a company. Their leader was Samuel Cosmo Lowry from York District. He had previously served in the army but had been discharged at his father's request because of his age. Lowry determined to raise a company from the Arsenal and take it into the army. Many pledged to join, but Capt. Thomas found out about the plan before Lowry and his friends could leave and placed the entire company under arrest. Any boy who "...did not expect to stick to the Academy" was ordered to step out of ranks. Almost the entire company stepped out. Lowry was expelled and the others suspended. Lowry rejoined his old regiment, the 17th South Carolina Infantry, was elected a 2nd Lt. and fell at the Crater at Petersburg the following year.[138]

Lt. Patrick noted some resistance to the extended period of service:

---

[136] Patrick, 169, 181, 186; Thomas, 210-211; Bond, 64; Bartlette, July 20 and August 22, 1863. William Ravenel, Jr. (1845-1863) (ex-'66).

[137] OR, XXVIII, pt. 2, 383.

[138] Patrick, 182; Lowry, 18; UDC, LXIII, 95-96. Samuel Cosmo (Catawba) Lowry (1846-1864) was a Fourth Classman at the Arsenal from York District. He joined Co. F, 17th SC Volunteers, rising to 2nd Lt. by the time he was killed at the Battle of the Crater in VA.

"...parents will not consent for their sons to serve the Confederacy for an indefinite period while they are paying the State to educate them. If they have to remain in service, their parents will withdraw them from the Academy and let them serve in an organization that will not require pay of them."

The two months of active duty time kept the Cadets from their books, consequently, they were poorly prepared for their final examinations in November.[139]

Early Christmas morning, Lt. Col. Delaware Kemper's Battalion of Light Artillery, supported by the Cadet Rangers, opened fire on the U.S. gunboat *Marblehead* anchored in Edisto inlet. The *Marblehead* sustained some damage, but was soon joined by the *Pawnee* and a mortar schooner. Together, the Yankee ships drove away the Confederate forces, capturing two 8-inch howitzers. A few weeks later, the Cadet Company supported Maj. Jenkins' artillery in an abortive attempt to sink the *Pawnee* in Stono River.[140]

---

[139] Patrick, 181, 195; Meet, 65.
[140] Thomas, 214; Bond, 66; Ripley, 101-102; Manning, V, 111. Delaware Kemper (1833-1899) was Lt. Col. of a Bn. of Lt. Artillery on the coast. Postwar, he was a professor at the Citadel and at Hampden-Sydney College and US Consul in Shanghai.

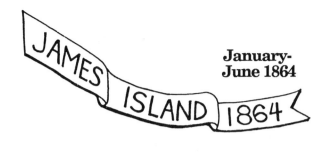

This final full-year of the war was a busy one for the Cadets and the Rangers. They would both see arduous duty, and, by the end of the year, both would "see the elephant."

Throughout the war, young men continued to matriculate at the Academy. By late 1861, 125 young men were enrolled at the two institutions. In spite of conscription, the thrill of wartime service, and the tight financial situation, enrollment had increased to 175 in mid-1864. Before the end of the year, the enrollment would skyrocket to 325. Additional recruits would even join the Arsenal Cadets in the field in April of 1865, even as the Confederacy was crumbling.[141]

However, by 1864, inflation had become a big factor in the Confederacy. Prices of virtually everything had increased considerably during four years of war. Tuition was no exception. In early 1861, pay Cadets had been charged $200 annually for board, uniforms, and tuition. By December 1862, the fee was $400 with the Cadets having to provide certain items. This rate had doubled to $800 by the following December with Cadets having to "furnish their own underclothing, including shirts, drawers, and socks; also their shoes, combs, and brushes." During 1864, the Board of Visitors increased the fee to $1,200.[142] A letter to the *Charleston Courier* signed "Parent" complained:

"The amount to be paid during the coming year is unwise and impolitic, and

[141] Thomas, 113, 177, 247.
[142] Thomas, 113, 128, 148, 175; Board of Visitors Minutes.

will seriously injure the school, inas-
much as none but the sons of the wealthy
can afford to pay the expenses demanded.
To have our young men educated as soldiers at this particular time no one can
doubt, and if the sons of the rich are to be
allowed the privilege the school must fall
through. Did the Board of Visitors recol-
lect that the incomes of a large majority
of our planters, merchants, mechanics,
and others, who once enjoyed a large in-
come, are now greatly reduced in means,
and unable to do more than support their
families in a plain way?"[143]

Despite the plea, however, no Board action was taken
so the inflated tuition charge remained in effect.

The academic program was structured with new
students entering the Fourth Class at the Arsenal in
Columbia. Students who successfully completed this
freshman year were transferred to the Citadel for
their final three years of schooling. However, new
students were permitted to enter the Citadel directly if
they successfully passed an examination on the
Fourth Class studies. The examination encompassed
algebra, United States history, and French.[144]

Among the sixteen young men who took the examination in January 1864 were Joseph W. Barnwell and
William Henry Heyward from Beaufort, and John
Kershaw from Kershaw District. Kershaw had served
as a courier to his father, Gen. Joseph Brevard
Kershaw. Heyward had been a Fourth Classman at
the Arsenal when he left to join the Cadet Rangers in
1862 but, lacking his parents' consent, he was soon
discharged. All three applicants were admitted, and,

---

[143] *Charleston Courier*, January 1864. The plea was reminiscent of the class distinction which was recognized in society
and was reflected in the makeup of the Citadel Corps. The un-
pleasant mixture of the social classes had resulted some years
earlier in discontinuation of the annual Graduating Ball.
Walker, 7.
[144] Bond, 25; Barnwell, 156.

with a Charlestonian named John Dougherty, roomed together.

New recruit Lee Hagood was the envy of the Cadets when he entered in his ragged Confederate uniform, having served on Gen. Micah Jenkins' staff.

Although no physical hazing was allowed, the older Cadets made the new recruits the butt of their jokes. As new recruits were entering the mess hall for the first time after having just completed the entrance examination, a Second Classman from Charleston, Frank Murdoch, announced the names of several older Cadets who would examine them on the regulations. Barnwell was busily committing to memory regulations governing the number of Cadets admitted from each county and the details of the uniform when a friendly upperclassman informed him and his roommates of the joke.[145] Meanwhile, Kershaw had been invited into the room of an older Cadet where he was introduced to several other Cadets, with others coming in. All were smoking and soon, a thick blue haze permeated the room. As the upperclassmen tried their best to nauseate the newcomer, young Kershaw pulled his pipe from his pocket and lit up, thus foiling the attempt.

Shortly thereafter, the new Cadets were seated in their room when a gorgeously attired officer accompanied by several privates entered. Ignorant of the regulations, the new Cadets did not stand up and salute. They were given copies of the book of regulations and ordered to report the next morning for an examination on it. Naturally, they failed miserably and were ordered to pack their trunks and leave in disgrace. Before they departed, however, they were given a "reprieve" and further time to study. Upper classmen also attempted to sneak into their rooms at night and blacken their faces.[146]

---

[145] Barnwell, 157-158, 160. Joseph W. Barnwell, John Kershaw, John Dougherty, Frank Murdoch, and Lee Hagood - See Appendix B.

William Henry Heyward - See Appendix A.

[146] Kershaw, 146-147.

All, however, was not fun and games. Cadet Joseph Barnwell reflected on the poor fare at the Citadel:

> "The material was inferior and the cooking worse. Hominy with the husks left in and rice badly boiled, coffee with brown sugar and no milk, tough beef for dinner and hash for breakfast made up the usual course, but on Sunday we were given poultry for dinner. At supper we had corn-bread mostly. Yet our appetites were good, and I recall very little sickness among us."[147]

In a letter written to his mother from the Arsenal on January 10th, Henry Norwood Obear of Fairfield, who had turned 17 just six days before, described the daily life of a Cadet:

> "At 6 o'clock the drum beats and we all go down to answer to our names; this is Reveille. We are then allowed 30 minutes to dress and fix our rooms. After this an officer comes round and sees that all is right. Then comes prayer call, and the roll is called again and we all march to prayers which are read by Captain Thomas. After that I have a recitation till breakfast. We have either beefsteak or bacon, baker's bread, and hominy, with wheat coffee and sugar. After breakfast are recreation hours, and then study hours till twelve. Then comes drill, and after that dinner of baked beef or fried bacon, boiled rice, and potatoes or corn bread. Then recreation, then study till four, then drill, then supper of wheat, and corn bread, and molasses, then

---

[147] Barnwell, 160.

recreation, then study, then tattoo, then
bed, and so on the next day."[148]

Cadets were issued only a jacket and pantaloons of
Confederate gray. In the summer, two suits of striped
cotton cloth, called russian, were also provided. White
gloves were now so scarce that they were forbidden.

As the new Cadets learned the vagaries of military
life, the routine of academics and drill began. Every
Friday afternoon, a dress parade was held on the
Citadel Green. The young ladies of the city gathered
on the galleries to watch as, at the conclusion of the
parade, the week's offenses were read out, embar-
rassing the offenders. Those Cadets whose conduct
was unblemished, or at least, whose ingenuity in
evading detection or framing excuses was finely
tuned, were allowed to go on leave on Saturday and
Sunday.[149] Discipline was strictly observed. Once,
while acting as Corporal of the Guard, Cadet Salley
fell asleep in the guard room and failed to turn out the
guard when a fire alarm was sounded. For this indis-
cretion, he was ordered to serve 42 extra hours of
duty.[150] Another Cadet, a one-armed veteran, was
suspended for violating Academy regulations less
than twenty-four hours after the Arsenal faculty had
determined to retain him there in spite of his handicap and his academic deficiencies.[151]

Not far down the coast, a Federal expedition under
Brig. Gen. Alexander Schimmelfennig left Folly
Island on February 7, 1864, with orders to destroy the

---

[148] Obear, January 10, 1864.
[149] Barnwell, 163; Kershaw, 147-148.
[150] UDC, LXIII, 93.
[151] Thomas, 82-84; Patrick, 208. The Academy began admitting
handicapped veterans soon after the Mexican War. Allen H.
Little (1831-1854) (Citadel '52), a sixteen year old boy in the
Palmetto Regiment, lost an arm in one of the battles of that
war. He was awarded a scholarship to attend the Academy, but
due to inadequate preparation, it took him two years to complete
the course at the Arsenal. Little perservered so that he graduated at the top of his class in 1852. Several instances are on
record of handicapped veterans being admitted during the
Civil War period.

Charleston and Savannah Railroad and threaten
Charleston. This movement was a feint to draw attention away from Maj. Gen. Truman Seymour's ill-
fated expedition to Florida. The Federal troops traversed Kiawah and Seabrook Islands during the
evening of the 8th and early morning hours of the 9th.
A small picket post at the bridge to John's Island,
composed of several Cadet Rangers, was captured
and a Federal position established there.[152]

Within ten minutes after Capt. Humphrey received word of the loss of his picket post at the bridge,
the Rangers were in the saddle galloping to regain it.
When the company reached 'White Gate,' Humphrey
found the bluecoats in possession of the embankment
in rear of the picket post, their line now extending
from Bohicket Creek to Haulover Creek. Quickly,
Humphrey dismounted his thirty-five men between
the road and Bohicket Creek and advanced across the
open field, their movement covered by a dense fog.

When the Rangers were within 200 yards of the
Federal line, Humphrey ordered his men to kneel and
fire. Sighting some Federals, probably couriers,
crouching and running to the rear, Humphrey mistakenly assumed the enemy was wavering and
ordered his small force to charge. Rushing forward
with loud cheers, the Rangers stormed the embankment and drove the Federals from their immediate
front. Within a few feet of the embankment, Sgt. John
S. Dutart, struck simultaneously by three bullets, was
killed instantly, while his cousin, Corp. George A.
McDowell, received a mortal head wound.[153]

---

[152] Johnson, 199-200; CMH, 299-300; Boatner, 725-726; OR,
XXXV, pt. 1, 30-31, 106-107, 144; Barlow, 158; Hyde, 63-65;
Sunday News, Aug. 15, 1895. Alexander Schimmelfennig
(1824-1865) was transferred to the Department of the South after
some rather inglorious service with the Army of the Potomac.
During the Battle of Gettysburg, he was wounded on the first
day and remained hidden in a barn the next two days. He was
also subject to criticism for his role in the rout of the 11th Corps
at Chancellorsville in early May.
[153] Sunday News, Aug. 15, 1895; Thomas, 215. John S. Dutart &
George Archibald McDowell - See Appendix A.

The *Charleston Mercury* described the action at
this point:

"In a few minutes the enemy's line broke
under our vigorous fire, and scattered in
the utmost confusion and in every direction. Three of the terrified Yankees ran
straightway into Capt. Humphrey's encampment and, with a fourth, who had
struggled into a neighboring field, were
made prisoners."[154]

Just before daybreak, a courier from Humphrey
had informed Maj. John Jenkins at Adam's Run that
Federal troops, advancing in force, had taken the
picket post by surprise. Riding forward, Jenkins met
a portion of the routed pickets at the 'White Gate,'
some six or seven hundred yards in rear of their
picket post. In the meantime, Lt. T. Waring Mikell relayed a message that Capt. Humphrey had advanced
with his company to feel the enemy and ascertain his
strength. Because of the dense fog, the pickets had
been unable to ascertain the exact size of the Federal
force, but estimated it to be about four hundred. Capt.
Jennett, commanding Company C of the 59th
Virginia Infantry, was ordered by Jenkins to advance
and support Humphrey's troopers, while Lt. Mikell
remained at the 'White Gate' to forward other companies as they came up.
Moving forward with what few troops he could
muster immediately, Maj. Jenkins advanced about a
hundred yards forward of the 'White Gate' as Capt.
Jennett's company came up on Humphrey's left.
Suddenly, a light wind dissipated the fog, revealing
the relatively small Confederate force to the bluecoats
who opened a heavy musket fire on them. Jennett and
his Virginians fell back, leaving one man killed and

---

[154] *Charleston Mercury*, February 12, 1864.

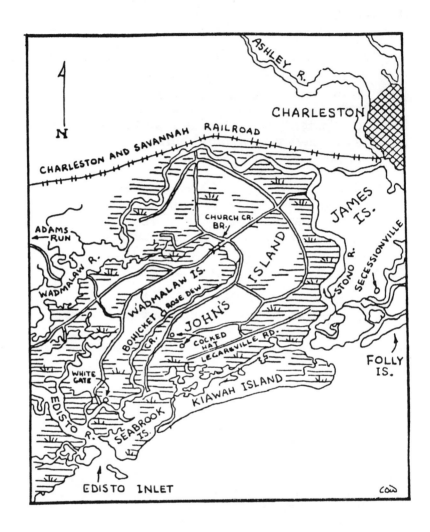

John's Island

three wounded. With no support, Humphrey ordered
the Rangers to retreat. As they began to withdraw, the
Federals reoccupied the embankment, pouring fire
into the men retreating across the open field. The
Federals rushed over the embankment and into the
field to exploit the Southerners' retreat. Jenkins ral-
lied his small force and returned a volley. This fire di-
verted attention from Humphrey's troops for a time,
giving them an opportunity to reach cover. Still
mounted, Capt. Humphrey made a conspicuous and
attractive target. Suddenly, two bullets struck his leg
and a third perforated his clothing, and three more
hit his mount. Dismounting, the youthful captain
turned his horse loose to die while Orderly Sgt.
William Gilmore Simms, who had reached the
Federal position when the company was recalled,
rode up and assisted Humphrey off the field.
Benjamin Martin, a private in a flanking company
which had already reached safety, rode back and assisted Humphrey to mount, the three escaping the oncoming Yankees in a hail of bullets.[155]

Jenkins and his men stubbornly contested each
foot of ground as they fell back. Retreating nearly two
miles, they met reinforcements, turned, and, after
repeated charges, drove the Federals back nearly the
whole distance. That evening, a battalion of the 59th
Virginia along with a section of the Marion Artillery
arrived to reinforce the meager defensive force. The
next morning, five companies of the 26th Virginia
Volunteers came on the field. These, along with two
and a half regiments ordered up by Beauregard from
Gen. Colquitt's Georgia Brigade, increased the Rebel

---

[155] *Sunday News*, Aug. 15, 1895; Thomas, 215; Manning, V,
111. Townsend Waring Mikell (1837-1893) commanded Co. I
(Rebel Troop), 3rd SC Cavalry and was later a clerk and accountant in Charleston.

James Jennett was Captain, Co. K (South of Dan Rebels),
59th Virginia Infantry.

William Gilmore Simms, Jr. - See Appendix A.

Benjamin Martin was Private, Co. I (Rebel Troop), 3rd SC
Cavalry.

strength to about 1,000 men. Also, now on the field and in command was Brig. Gen. Henry A. Wise.

On the afternoon of the 10th, the Federals advanced up the Bohicket and Mullet Hall Roads to the Cocked Hat. As the bluecoats appeared, the Marion Battery opened fire, forcing them back to the woods. An artillery duel ensued until about 5 p.m. when the enemy troops withdrew. For a number of reasons, Gen. Wise, commanding the Charleston area, did not pursue the withdrawing enemy. He did, however, send his available cavalry, including the Cadet Rangers, to maintain contact and report on their movements. Additionally, two Napoleons of Kanapaux's Lafayette Artillery were sent over Church Bridge to Rose Dew on Wadmalaw Island to enfilade the Federal reserve and rear.

Early on the morning of the 12th, Federal gunboats began heavy shelling to cover the withdrawal of their troops. As the Confederates advanced, they found that the Yankees had withdrawn, leaving their dead along the way and obstructing the road. The enemy had also burned several houses and the bridge at the Haulover Cut.

Gen. Wise reported his total effective strength on the 11th as 1,850 infantry, two batteries of artillery, and about 100 cavalry. He estimated the Federal strength at 2,000 with a reserve of 300 at the Haulover. Major Jenkins had lost 13 out of a total Confederate loss of 17 against Federal losses of 34. In addition to Dutart's death and the mortally wounded McDowell, Humphrey had been wounded. Lt. Dozier and Pvts. Franklin B. Appleby and William H. "Willis" Brannon were wounded, and along with Howell F. Horton, William H. Long, Peter Mellett, and Henry A. Spann, were captured.[156]

---

[156] *Sunday News*, Aug. 15, 1895; OR, XXXV, pt. 1, 144-145; Thomas, 215; *Charleston Mercury*, February 13, 1864; *Charleston Courier*, February 15, 1864. Lt. Anthony White Dozier, Jr., Franklin B. Appleby, Willis Brannon, Howell F. Horton, William H. Long, Peter Mellett, Henry Asbury Spann - See Appendix A.

Maj. Jenkins, in his report, recommended that Simms, Schipman, and Martin be considered for commissions. Pvt. Berent M. Schipman, while loading and firing repeatedly during the retreat on the 9th, had tried in vain to rally his comrades to return the fire, and thus earned the notice of his superiors.[157] Maj. Jenkins and Capt. Humphrey were both commended by Gen. Wise for their gallant service. Wise reported, "He (Humphrey) was devotedly daring and dashed upon ten times his number; was first in the fight and last out of it." Gen. Beauregard added his endorsement to that of Gen. Wise, calling special attention to "...Major Jenkins and Captain Humphrey who are fully entitled to promotion by their resolute gallantry."[158]

For the Cadet Rangers, however, this engagement has a tragic sequel involving Lt. Anthony White Dozier of Williamsburg. In the advance of February 9th, Lt. Dozier had impetuously galloped forward on his charger "Shark" and, with his saber, cut his way through the Federal ranks on the embankment. Suddenly finding himself in the enemy rear alone and cut off from the rest of his company just as the Confederates were retreating, he decided to try to get back on foot. Riding into a nearby thick copse of woods, he dismounted and hitched his horse to a tree. As he emerged from the trees, however, a company of bluecoats spotted and pursued him. After an extended race, his pursuers gradually dropped out one by one until only a single man remained. Seeing this, Dozier stopped, and both adversaries, now breathless and exhausted, emptied their weapons at one another. Dozier's shots went wild while one of his opponent's shots cut a piece out of his chin. The Yankee, incensed that he had not killed Dozier, dropped his head and rushed at him like a bull. The two men met hand-to-hand in the middle of a small stream. As they grappled, Dozier managed to pull a knife from his belt

---

[157] *Sunday News*, August 15, 1895. Berent M. Schipman - See Appendix A.
[158] OR, XXXV, pt. 1, 147, 149; Courage of Citadel Cadets.

and plunge it into the bluecoat. Realizing the man was dead, Dozier appropriated his bulging haversack and then made his way into the canebrake at the edge of the island. Now, desperately hungry, he opened the haversack to discover it contained not rations, but only an extra blue flannel shirt.

After nightfall, Dozier started back toward friendly lines but found his way blocked by a Federal picket post. That night and the next day he hid in the canebrake. Ravenous by the second night, he realized that he must get back to his lines or starve. Attempting to pass through the enemy outposts just beyond the spot where he had encountered pickets the previous night, he suddenly found himself surrounded by the enemy waiting in ambush. One shot caught him in the shoulder just as a charging bluecoat struck him with his rifle butt. Too weak to resist, Dozier was immediately overwhelmed.

Once at Federal headquarters on John's Island, Dozier asked about his fine horse, and was informed by the commanding general "...that we found him and he is the finest horse I ever rode." Dozier pleaded for him to be returned to his brother Edward, also a member of the Cadet Rangers, for which the general would receive the finest horse there in exchange. "No sir," replied the general, "that is the horse I have been looking for ever since the war commenced, and he will be my saddle horse to the end of the war."

Dozier was sent to Hilton Head where his problems worsened. Having been captured within the Federal lines though in uniform, he was charged with being a spy. At a court martial, though, enemy witnesses testified regarding his combat status, and he was acquitted of the trumped-up charges. Soon after, he was sent to Washington and again tried on the same spy charges, this time without the testimony of any first hand witnesses. Even though this second trial was more difficult, he was again acquitted and was transferred to the Federal prison at Fort Delaware.

Soon after his arrival at Fort Delaware, Dozier read a copy of a Philadelphia newspaper which contained an account of the lone charge and capture of the gallant color bearer of the 23rd Regiment SC Volunteers at Cold Harbor. The account mentioned the color bearer as Dozier's brother, Peter "Cuttino," and related how he had wrapped the colors around his neck to stem the flow of blood from his mortal wound. Depressed about the death of his brother, Dozier was stunned several weeks later, when walking across the parade ground, he felt a hand on his shoulder and heard a familiar voice, "Hello, Anthony, what are you doing here?" His supposedly-dead brother was alive and well. The two related their tales and rejoiced in being together during their confinement. Cuttino related how, when a bullet plowed into his neck, he wrapped the colors around the wound but continued to press forward until he was captured. The newspaper correspondent who had seen the action assumed the wound was mortal and, typically, had embellished his story.

Soon after, Dozier encountered more problems. Four enemy officers arrested in Richmond had confessed to being spies and, subsequently, were sentenced to death. When news of the sentence reached Washington, Federal authorities ordered that four Confederate officers would likewise be executed in retaliation. Anthony Dozier was one of the four selected and was put in chains under close confinement to await the noose.

Unwilling to see four innocent lives sacrificed, President Jefferson Davis offered to change the sentences to life imprisonment if the Federal authorities would do the same for the four Confederates. President Abraham Lincoln accepted the proposition but still kept the four Confederate officers in chains and close confinement. When Davis was informed of this unfair treatment, he proposed to reduce the sentence for the Federal spies to fifteen years. Lincoln also accepted this second proposal but still ordered no change in the medieval conditions in which Dozier and his three fellow prisoners were held.

Sometime later, the authorities at Ft. Delaware ordered that the four prisoners be released from their cells for brief periods and be put to work with the other prisoners hauling dirt and rock. When the order was relayed to the four prisoners, Dozier, acting as spokesman for the group, replied: "Though entitled to treatment due to prisoners of war, captured in battle, we have been confined in dark, unventilated cells without just cause, until our health is broken and life made not worth living; and now they want to heap insult upon injury for the purpose of humiliating us. We will not submit, and we refuse to obey the order." When this ultimatum was given, the Federal officer voiced his astonishment: "Why men, this is an order from the commandant of the fort, and don't you know that if you refuse to obey you will be shot?" "Yes," replied Dozier, "we know that, but we prefer death to humiliation." This answer was relayed to the commandant, a former U.S. Navy officer, who ordered the men brought to his office. They were brought in fully expecting a sentence of death. There, the commandant looked at Dozier and asked: "Is your name Dozier?" "Yes, sir, it is," he said. "Did you have a brother in the Navy?" Dozier replied, "Yes, sir, I had," referring to his older brother, William Gaillard Dozier, now a Confederate Naval Lieutenant. "Well, he was a good friend of mine. You men go back to your cells."

Spared the death sentence, the prisoners were permitted to make a written statement to President Davis concerning their confinement. Upon receipt of the communication, Davis offered Lincoln an exchange of the four spies in Richmond for the four Confederates. Lincoln accepted this deal and, by prearrangement, the eight officers met in Washington, D.C. on their way home and dined together, the two groups relating the contrasting treatment each had received. This was in February 1865 and, after his exchange, Dozier, feeling the effects of his harsh confinement, went home for a period of recuperation. Because of his health, he was never able to rejoin his regiment. He joined the local Reserve forces as they attempted to resist Sherman's march through the Carolinas. Dozier's poor health, including tuberculosis contracted during his close confinement, caused his early death on October 31, 1874, in California.[159]

As Dozier was enduring his harsh captivity, Confederate generals around Charleston were preparing for additional enemy attacks. On March 3rd, Maj. White offered the services of the Cadet Battalion, leading the *Charleston Courier* to applaud the eagerness of the Cadets, calling them "...the gallant scions of our noble nursery of soldiers, whose predecessors opened the war..."[160] Impressed with their enthusiasm, Beauregard reviewed the Cadets on the Citadel Green on the 14th of March.[161]

Early 1864 found the Cadets again on duty, being called out on several occasions to guard commissary stores and picket the wharves around the city.[162] The Cadet Rangers remained on John's Island, supporting Walter's Battery, the Washington Artillery, in an artillery battle in early March.[163]

Later that month, the 4th, 5th, and 6th South Carolina Cavalry Regiments were ordered to Virginia as part of Brig. Gen. Matthew C. Butler's Brigade. Although these three regiments were sorely needed on the coast of South Carolina, Gen. Robert E. Lee needed them even more to replenish his weakened cavalry arm.[164] Butler had previously planned to take

---

[159] Dozier, 37-40; Thomas, 215; OR, Series II, VII, 419, 422, 807, 1191, 1264 & VIII, 87. Peter "Cuttino" Dozier (1835-1877), an ex-Cadet) was Ensign of the 21st SC Volunteers when the unit charged at Cold Harbor, VA on June 3, 1864. Dozier, 9.

William Gaillard Dozier (1833-1908) graduated from the US Naval Academy in 1856 and served in the Navy until SC's secession. He spent most of the war running the blockade. Dozier, 2-5.

[160] *Charleston Courier*, March 3, 1864.

[161] *Charleston Mercury*, March 14, 1864.

[162] Kershaw, 148; UDC, LXIII, 96.

[163] Thomas, 214.

[164] Brooks, 350; Wells, 29. Matthew Calbraith Butler (1836-1909) resigned from the legislature to serve as Capt. of cavalry in Hampton's Legion, serving in the major battles of the Army of Northern Virginia. He lost his right foot during the cavalry battle at Brandy Station, VA, and was promoted to Brig. Gen. in September 1863 and Maj. Gen. a year later. After the war,

the 3rd, 4th, and 5th Regiments until he met Brig. Gen. Johnson Hagood (Citadel '47) in Charleston. Hagood had offered to substitute the 6th for the 3rd Regiment. When Butler replied that the 6th had a reputation in Virginia for being "a set of wild Arabs," Hagood answered, "What they formerly were, they are not now. For the last four or five months, Miller (Lt. Col. Lovick P.) has been in command and he has made them a regiment of soldiers."[165]

Butler's Brigade was well-mounted, each officer and soldier providing his own horse. Most of the brigade had revolvers, and all were armed with sabers. The brigade had sometime earlier been issued Enfield rifles. Though bigger and bulkier than the normal cavalry carbine, the Enfield provided stronger and more accurate firepower at a greater distance. Loading was slow, however, and it became increasingly more difficult to operate as it became fouled from repeated discharges. In addition, unlike breechloading carbines, the muzzleloading Enfield could not be easily loaded by a man either lying down behind cover or mounted on his horse, and the paper cartridges were susceptible to damage by dampness or rain.[166]

When, in April 1864, the three regiments concentrated in Columbia ready to move north, the townspeople greeted them with open arms. A huge feast was served by the ladies on the grounds of the Insane Asylum, followed by a stirring speech and review by their new division commander, Maj. Gen. Wade

---

he served in the US Senate and later was Maj. Gen. of Volunteers in the Spanish-American War.

[165] Brooks, 347. Johnson Hagood (1829-1898) (Citadel '47) commanded the First Regiment (Hagood's) at First Manassas, then returned to serve on the coast of South Carolina until May 1864. He was transferred to Petersburg and was sent to Fort Fisher in December to participate in the North Carolina campaign. He was elected Comptroller-General twice, then became Governor in 1880. Capers, 401-403.

Lovick Pierce Miller (1832-1921) was Lt. Col. of the 6th SC Cavalry. He was a teacher in Newberry before the war and later served as a legislator before moving to FL.

[166] Wells, 29-30, 33-34; Brooks, 350.

Hampton. The Arsenal Cadets attended the festivities, acting as an escort of honor to the departing units. After the celebration, the regiments set about making final preparations for their move, with the men being given brief furloughs, half allowed to be absent at a time. Then, when all was ready, half of the men drove the command's horses across the countryside while the remainder proceeded to Richmond in box cars.[167]

The Cadet Rangers left Columbia for Richmond on May 17. The pace of the movement was rather slow and, in a letter to Maj. Thomas B. Ferguson of the 6th South Carolina Cavalry written on the 23rd of May, Col. Aiken prodded him:

> "...We are much needed here—will go into service at once. We are very much censured for the delay. General Butler has issued orders to the colonels to report what has become of the respective regiments each day since the order was received. Prepare a report accounting for each day as I have written upon the back....
> ...Be careful not to let men ride horses with sore backs.
> Come on in good order and be on the lookout all the way. Instruct your advance guard to keep near the wagon trains...."[168]

Upon their arrival with Lee's Army of Northern Virginia, the cavalrymen, with their long Enfields, new butternut uniforms, and fresh horses, were a sharp contrast to the veterans of Stuart's Cavalry. Stuart's veterans were worn down from hard service and fighting, their dress was haphazard and they were equipped to meet basic military and personal needs. Their mounts were worn down from their poor diet and hard use. Stuart's veterans taunted the fresh

---

[167] Patrick, 216; Wells, 32; Brooks, 547.
[168] Brooks, 216; Manning, V, 111.

troopers with their long muzzle-loaders, "I say, Parson, let me have your long-shooter and I'll bite off the end."[169] Only Gen. Thomas L. Rosser's Virginia Brigade was thoroughly armed with revolvers and improved carbines.[170]

Recently-arrived Gen. Ulysses S. Grant commanded the Federal troops. In early May, he opened an offensive drive on Richmond, engaging Lee at the Wilderness and Spotsylvania Court House. Though sustaining significant losses, Grant continued to press Lee's flank to reach Richmond.

Butler's Brigade reached Richmond in time for the 5th and part of the 4th Regiments to participate in a battle on the 28th of May, when Federal Brig. Gen. David McM. Gregg's Cavalry Division encountered Confederate cavalry brigades of Brig. Gens. Williams C. Wickham and T.L. Rosser about a mile from Haw's Shop. Butler's Brigade, less the 6th and half of the 4th which had not yet arrived, reinforced the Confederate line, and helped repulse Gregg's repeated attacks in a seven hour engagement. Throughout, the bluecoats assumed their foes had been reinforced by a brigade of infantry, having been fooled by the Enfield rifles of Butler's Brigade. The Confederates held their positions until Brig. Gen. George A. Custer's Michigan Cavalry Brigade reinforced Gregg, and with one final assault, managed to flank the Southern line. Casualties were heavy on both sides, but the newly arrived Carolinians had shown that they could and would fight. The remainder of Butler's Brigade arrived later that evening, completing the organization.[171]

---

[169] Wells, 29-30, 33-34, 38.
[170] Myers, 295. Thomas L. Rosser (1836-1910) (West Point ex-'61) was a good friend and classmate of George A. Custer. Rosser was named a Lt. of Artillery and rose to command a cavalry brigade and division. Postwar, he was a railroad construction engineer, farmer, and Brig. Gen. during the Spanish-American War.
[171] Brooks, 209-210, 548; Hampton, 155-168; Wells, 38-44. Ulysses S. Grant (1822-1885) (West Point '43) newly-promoted Lt. Gen. had been appointed General in Chief of the Armies of

Two days later, Butler led his brigade on a reconnaissance to determine where Grant was moving near Matadoquin and Totopomoi Creeks. He found a strong cavalry force which he vigorously attacked, the engagement lasting for several hours. Butler quickly realized that the Federals were converging on Cold Harbor where several roads leading from different crossings of the Chickahominy River converged. At day's end, Butler withdrew toward Cold Harbor, bivouacking there for the night. By the next morning, Gen. Jubal Early's Division of infantry was on hand to contest Grant's flank movement. The 3rd of June brought the second battle of Cold Harbor where Federal losses in an eight minute advance were seven thousand men against a Confederate loss of less than fifteen hundred. "In that little period more men fell bleeding as they advanced than in any other like period of time throughout the war."[172]

As Grant continued his relentless clockwise movement to capture Richmond, he moved his army south of the James River, trying to pin Lee to the Richmond defenses. As the seat of the Confederate

---

the United States on Mar. 12, 1864. He went on to serve two terms as US President.

David McMurtrie Gregg (1833-1916) (West Point '55) rose from Col. to Brig. Gen. of cavalry and saw distinguished service at Gettysburg. Six months after being promoted to Maj. Gen. in 1864, he abruptly resigned from the army.

Williams Carter Wickham (1820-1888) was a lawyer, judge, and planter. He served in both houses of the VA legislature and rose from Capt. at First Manassas to Brig. Gen. in 1863. He participated in nearly every major battle or cavalry engagement in the Eastern theater, was twice wounded, captured and exchanged and served in the Confederate Congress in 1864.

George Armstrong Custer (1839-1876) (West Point '61) rose quickly to Maj. Gen. of cavalry. He remained in the army after the war and died in the ambush known as Custer's Last Stand.

[172] Brooks, 224-226; Hampton, 171-175; Wells, 49-57; B&L, IV, 217. Jubal Anderson Early (1816-1894) (West Point '37) was commissioned a Col. in his native VA. He went on to brigade, division, and corps command. After the war, he practiced law and was quite active in historical and veterans affairs.

government, the city was being given prime defensive consideration by Davis and Lee. Grant's advance was hampered by natural obstacles along the Chickahominy, the thick timber, underbrush, and troublesome swamps. With Lee operating on interior lines from which he could cover the various roads to Richmond with his infantry, his cavalry contested Grant's advance. Finally, in an attempt to draw off the Confederate cavalry and open the way to Richmond, Grant sent his cavalry in a massive raid toward Charlottesville to break up the Virginia Central Railroad. Besides occupying Lee's cavalry, this raid would also damage both his lines of supply and communications and speed the fall of the Confederate capital.[173]

Lee, having received word on June 8th from his scouts that Maj. General Philip H. Sheridan had left the enemy lines with about 8,000 troopers heading west toward the Shenandoah Valley, ordered Wade Hampton to pursue with his own cavalry division as well as that of Gen. Fitzhugh Lee. Hampton's orders were to protect the railroad and to prevent Sheridan from reinforcing Union forces in the Valley.[174]

Sheridan's force included 125 wagons and four artillery batteries while each of his bluecoated troopers carried three days' rations and two days' grain for the horses, along with forty rounds of ammunition. One medical wagon and eight ambulances were included in the column along with enough canvas-covered boats to construct a small pontoon bridge. Hampton's

---

[173] Grant, II, 281-282; Sheridan, I, 416; Sherfessee, 5.

[174] Hampton, 187-188; Wells, 60-61. Philip H. Sheridan (1831-1888) (West Point '53) rose from a commissary Capt. to head the Cavalry Corps of the Army of the Potomac. He later commanded the Shenandoah Valley district where he defeated Early. He rejoined Grant around Petersburg and achieved success during the Appomattox Campaign. After the war, he rose to General in Chief of the Federal Army.

Fitzhugh Lee (1835-1905) (West Point '56) was a nephew of Gen. Robert E. Lee who rose to command of the cavalry corps of the Army of Northern Virginia. Postwar, he was a farmer and politician before re-entering the Federal Army during the Spanish-American War.

force numbered about 4,700 with three batteries of horse artillery of four guns each.[175]

The mortal wounding of Gen. J.E.B. "Jeb" Stuart at Yellow Tavern less than a month before had left open the question of who would succeed him in command of the Cavalry Corps. Of the two possible successors, Wade Hampton, without formal military training, had proven himself at Gettysburg, Brandy Station, and elsewhere while the other, thirty year old Fitzhugh Lee, was both a professional soldier and the nephew of the commanding general. Since both officers were equal in seniority as Maj. Gens., it presented a difficult choice for Gen. Robert E. Lee. In the end, however, when word arrived at headquarters of Sheridan's movement, Lee gave Hampton temporary command of the cavalry.[176]

Hampton's philosophy of command differed significantly from that of his dashing predecessor. Previously, the cavalry had performed reconnaissance and outpost duties, acted as couriers, and, when necessary, fought on horseback with pistols and sabers. Hampton, however, realized that the horse best provided tactical mobility, enabling his troops to move swiftly to points of danger and then dismount to fight as infantry. The difference between Hampton's fighting style and Stuart's was succinctly summed up by one veteran officer. "...while Stuart would attempt his work with whatever force he had at hand, and often seemed to try to accomplish a given result with the smallest possible number of men, Gen. Hampton always endeavored to carry every available man to his point of operation, and the larger the force, the better he liked it...."[177]

---

[175] OR, XXXVI, 1095; B&L, IV, 233, 239; Calhoun, 124; Sherfessee, 1; UDC, XXIII, 192; Hampton, 189; Wells, 61-62; Kidd, 342.

[176] Wells, 35; Hampton, 132-135; Freeman, III, 436. James Ewell Brown Stuart (1833-1864) (West Point '54) was an aide to Robert E. Lee at Harpers Ferry during the capture of John Brown. He was Lt. Col. of infantry before being commissioned Capt. of cavalry and rising to command of the Cavalry Corps.

[177] Wells, 29; Hampton, 148-151; Myers, 291.

Another cavalry officer, writing to his wife on June 10th, indicated,

> "...If he (General Sheridan) had real merit he would have cut all our railroads supplying the army at Richmond on both sides of the James River and, with our crippled resources, it would be very difficult for us to repair. He has a very large force, equipped with the finest and most improved repeating rifles and good horses, and with every possible supply known to the cavalry service. On our side our horses are worn down, and there is no source where we can recruit. We have only pistols, sabres, and old-fashioned rifles, worn-out saddles, and none of the equipment in the way of portable furnaces, horse shoes, and transportation requisite for efficient cavalry work; and above all, we have not enough food to keep the horses up..."[178]

Butler's troops were ordered to prepare three days' rations for men and horses and to be ready to move out at a moment's notice. One of Hampton's troopers remembered the scarcity of food during the summer campaigns:

> "The regular rations intended for each man daily were a half pound of bacon, or salt pork, and a pint of corn meal, or flour, but frequently this was from necessity reduced to one half, and even this often could not be had for days together. This was all; no tea, coffee, sugar, or any stimulant. No foraging was allowed. Now and then 'bull beef' would be issued instead of bacon; and, in winter quarters,

---

[178] Blackford, 253. Charles Minor Blackford (1833-1903) was Capt. of the 2nd Virginia Cavalry.

but not until then, infinitesimally small
doses of sugar and coffee were doled
out."[179]

The weakest point in the Confederate cavalry organization was probably the horse supply. Each man
had to supply his own mount. If his horse was killed,
he received its valuation in depreciated currency.
More often, however, horses were disabled or simply
broke down from hard service and, once the owner
was dismounted, he had to either provide another
horse or be transferred to another branch of service.
General Rosser explained his way of replacing
mounts: "I often went into battle or on a raid with one-
third of my men dismounted, and generally succeeded in mounting them from captures." Despite
these problems, however, the cavalry corps under
Hampton was about to give a superb account of itself
in action.[180]

Starting out on June 8th in hot, unusually dry
weather, the troops were soon unrecognizable to
friends as the red clay in the road became a very fine
pulverized dust. Hampton led his two divisions west
by the most direct route, trying to intercept the enemy
before they could do real damage. Sheridan, forced to
take a more circuitous route, learned from prisoners
that Confederate cavalry had left its position and was
moving toward Gordonsville, a vital railroad junction
northwest of Richmond. By the next evening,
Sheridan had reached Clayton's Store, three miles
northeast of Trevilian Station on the Virginia Central
Railroad, unaware that Hampton was close behind.
During the day, a portion of his command had been
fired upon by some of Hampton's scouts. Thinking,
however, that this was some local defense force,
Sheridan paid little attention to the incident. Only
years later, in his *Memoirs*, was he able to deduce
that "from the boldness of the scouting parties, the
main enemy force was nearby." For now, the brash

---

[179] Reconstruction, 45; Hampton, 83; Calhoun, 123.
[180] Hampton, 97, 99; Brooks, 162.

little Irishman was about to pay dearly for his over-
confidence.[181]

That evening, Hampton was located with his own
division at Green Spring Valley, three miles beyond
Trevilian Station, while Rosser's Laurel Brigade was
situated on the left, a short distance down the
Gordonsville Road from Matthew Butler's Brigade at
the station with Col. Gilbert J. Wright's Cobb Legion
between them. Fitz Lee was camped near Louisa
Court House, about four miles behind. Long into the
evening, Hampton, Butler, and Rosser pored over
maps and questioned their scouts about the surrounding terrain.[182]

Hampton's troops were roused before dawn on the
11th and quietly prepared for the expected encounter.
No bugles sounded, the troops having been instructed
to maintain their silence. Soon the entire force was in
the saddle, awaiting orders. The Cadet Rangers were
halted near a corn field and were ordered to dismount
to partake of the crop. Pvt. Jacob V. Baxley was sitting
by the roadside after refreshing himself and his horse
when:

> "...a fine looking old Virginia gentleman
> rode up and accosted us. He inquired
> who was in command of our troops and
> knowing that he was angry because we
> had been in his corn field, I replied in
> this way: 'That is a fine horse you are
> riding. I would like to make a trade.' The
> old man said, 'I asked you who com-
> manded these troops?' Whereupon I
> replied, 'Why the famous General
> Hampton is in command.' His next ques-
> tion was: 'Where can I find the general?
> You boys have been damaging my corn.'

---

[181] Hampton, 190-193; Calhoun, 124; Sheridan, I, 418-419.
[182] Hampton, 193; Girls, 12-13; Brooks, 238; B&L, IV, 237.
Gilbert Jefferson Wright (1825-1892) was Col. of Cobb's Legion
Cavalry and the 9th GA Cavalry. He was a lawyer, judge, and
Mayor of Albany, GA.

I glibly answered that the general was over the hill breakfasting with a Virginia family, the direction in which I pointed him being the opposite direction to what the General had taken when he left us. About that time I heard something go ZIP and looking around saw that the old man had been struck by a bullet in the thigh. I asked him what was the matter and he said that he had been shot. I replied, we have tasted corn and you have tasted bullet."

The gentleman's attention turned from the corn and Gen. Hampton to a surgeon, who was subsequently sent to tend him. The troops got a supply of corn and proceeded on their way.[183]

At sunrise, when Gen. Rosser rode down to Gen. Butler's bivouac to inquire about the plans, he found that both were equally uninformed. Proceeding to Hampton's headquarters at Netherland's House to get their orders, the two youthful generals found Hampton lying on a bench in an oak grove. After greeting them, he unfolded his battle plan: Fitz Lee's Division was to attack up the road leading from Louisa Court House at the same time that Butler's Brigade attacked along the road from Trevilian Station to Clayton's Store. Rosser's Brigade would initially be held in reserve. Hampton's objective was for his two divisions to, after driving in the Federal vanguard, unite at Clayton's Store and drive the Yankees back across Hickory Creek, hopefully shattering them against the North Anna River.[184]

While Gen. Rosser rejoined his command, Hampton and Butler proceeded up the road to Clayton's Store to reconnoiter the road. There, they met Capt. A.B. Mulligan's squadron of the 5th South Carolina Cavalry which had just been driven in from their picket posts. Realizing that speed was now criti-

---

[183] UDC, I, 166-167.
[184] Brooks, 239-240, 565; B&L, IV, 237.

cal, Hampton ordered an immediate attack. He told Butler that they should soon hear Fitz Lee's guns on the right as he moved up from Louisa Court House. In the meantime, Capt. Samuel J. Snowden's squadron of the 4th South Carolina was ordered forward to charge whatever he met and develop the force in front. Federal pickets were soon engaged and driven back on their supports.

The Yankees had been roused that morning by their usual bugle calls along with the noise of a camp awakening. Their advance guards moved out early toward Trevilian Station to begin the job of tearing up the railroad. The main Union force was still preparing breakfast when their advance guards collided with the 4th South Carolina Cavalry. As the unexpected and unwelcome sound of gunfire filtered back from the direction of the station, bluecoated troopers quickly filled canteens with coffee and either dumped the contents of their frying pans on the ground or shoved half-cooked bacon into their haversacks as "boots and saddles" was sounded.[185]

Meanwhile, as he advanced onto what he realized was a large force in his front, Butler decided the thickly-wooded terrain was unsuitable for mounted operations. Dismounting his entire brigade except for Capt. John C. Calhoun's Squadron of the 4th South Carolina, Butler deployed the 4th on the left of the road, facing northward, and the 6th on the right side while he held the 5th in reserve. Rosser took up a reserve position on the left at the Gordonsville Road. Butler sent forward a thin line of skirmishers. Pvt. Baxley, with two other troopers, was on picket duty when the enemy was discovered so close by that he had to jerk up the bush to which his horse was hitched in order to escape. Putting spurs to his horse,

---

[185] Hampton, 194; Bowen, 184; B&L, IV, 237. A.B. Mulligan organized Co. B (Dixie Rangers), 5th SC Cavalry and participated in that unit's battles in VA until wounded at Burgess' Mill.

Samuel John Snowden (1838-1902) was Captain of Co. I (Williamsburg Light Dragoons), 4th SC Cavalry and Capt. Steele's Co. in 1865. Farmer.

Baxley reported the enemy regiment proceeding down
the road. Having been informed by Hampton that
P.M.B. Young's Brigade would reinforce his line if
necessary, Butler now advanced his line until the
Federals had enveloped his left flank. Baxley mounted
and lit out, but mistook a Yankee regiment for
friendly troops who asked for his surrender. To
Baxley's reply that he was no Damned Yankee, he
was informed, "Yes, but we are." He was taken prisoner, and his horse appropriated by an enemy officer.[186]

During this advance, Col. Hugh Aiken led his 6th
South Carolina Cavalry, including the Cadet
Rangers, through thick woods, toward a rail fence
which he intended to use as breastworks. Federals
were on the other side of the fence, approaching with
the same intent. As Aiken stooped to go under a chin-
quepin bush in his way, a minie ball from over the
fence struck him in the collarbone, knocking him over
as it tore down through his chest and exited under his
shoulder blade. This wound would keep him out of action for several months. His wife journeyed to
Virginia to nurse him. His men, however, now drove
the bluecoats from the fence and out of the woods.[187]

In the Federal lines, high-spirited Brig. Gen.
George A. Custer was following a country road leading from the Buck Chiles' farm to the main highway
east of Trevilian when he learned that it intersected

---

[186] Brooks, 240-241, 565; B&L, IV, 237; UDC, I, 167-168. John
Caldwell Calhoun (1843-1918) was the grandson of his namesake statesman. Calhoun served with the Hampton Legion,
then commanded a company in the Adams Battalion. When
the battalion was merged into the 4th SC Cavalry, he commanded a squadron and led several charges at Trevilian.
Postwar, he was active in cotton planting, railroads, and other
business ventures.
   Pierce Manning Butler Young (1836-1896) (West Point ex-
'61) was commissioned in the Confederate artillery, then rose
to command of the Cobb Legion Cavalry, then later Hampton's
Division. Later, he was sent to GA and SC to defend against
Sherman. Postwar, he was a planter, Congressman, and
diplomat.
[187] Aiken, 12; McMaster, 3.

with the Gordonsville Road a mile and a quarter from
the station. Following the road westward, Custer soon
found himself near Hampton's wagon park in sight of
about 800 of Butler's led horses. Realizing his good
fortune, he charged, capturing some 250 wagons,
three caissons of ammunition, about a thousand
horses, and approximately 350 prisoners.[188]

When he received word of Custer's appearance in
his rear, Hampton quickly ordered a withdrawal.
This necessitated the remounting of Butler's Brigade,
however, due to heavy pressure from Sheridan in
front and on his flank and Custer in his rear, Butler
replied to Hampton's courier, "Say to General
Hampton it is hell to hold on and hell to let go."
Instead, he could only disengage carefully by mounting a regiment at a time on such horses as could be
reached. This took time and Hampton, in the meantime, ordered Rosser in from the west with part of
Butler's command, to attempt to recapture the horses
and trains.[189]

Confederate troops filed in behind Custer and cut
his force in two, leaving him with two regiments and
part of a third, as well as his artillery and wagon
train. Rosser held the crossroads to the west, part of
Butler's Brigade pushed down from Trevilian Station,
and Lee's Division advanced from Louisa Court
House along the road and through the woods.
Custer's rash advance and capture of the Confederate
trains had suddenly become an ironically ominous
trap.

Two of Custer's guns were ordered up, one placed
on the road and the other behind a tall board fence. As
the guns were emplaced and loaded with canister,
one of the gunners prepared to knock the fence boards
down to enable one gun to enfilade a Confederate battery. Their first discharge was to signal a charge.
However, before the boards could be dismantled, a line
of dismounted Confederate cavalry was spotted cross-

---

[188] OR, XXXVI, 807-808, 830; B&L, IV, 233; Bowen, 188.
[189] B&L, IV, 237-238; Brooks, 245; Calhoun, 126.

ing a rail fence about a hundred yards away. Hastily,
Custer ordered his men "to get out of there."

As Custer's Michigan troops scrambled to get out
of the trap their impetuous young general had led
them into, Hampton's attacking division began to

close in, killing some of the Yankee gunners and artillery horses as Fitz Lee's men pressed in from the
east, capturing Custer's trains and liberating the
Confederate wagons. One enemy conveyance captured
was Custer's own headquarters wagon along with his
cook Eliza, a devoted black woman, who was riding in
an antique family carriage captured on an earlier
raid.[190]

---

[190] B&L, IV, 233-234, 237-238; Brooks, 243-246, 565; Sherfessee,
3.

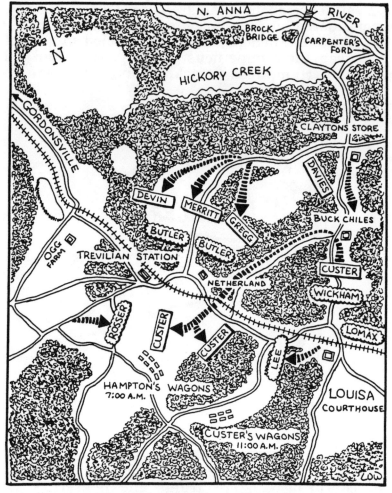

Trevilian Station—First Day

As the seesaw battle raged and confusion reigned, the Charleston-raised horse artillery battery of Capt. James F. Hart (Citadel '57) was charged by a Federal cavalry column. Seeing the danger his guns were in, Gen. Hampton dashed to the right of the 6th South Carolina Cavalry and ordered Maj. Tom B. Ferguson to mount his men and charge to save the battery. The only company at hand and ready was the Cadet

Rangers who were quickly aligned by Lts. Alfred Aldrich and William J. Nettles. When they were ready, Hampton rode to their front and personally led them in a fierce charge, the shock of which broke the oncoming Federal line and saved Hart's guns.[191]

Typically, Hampton himself charged headlong into the fray. At one point, the General found himself within ten feet of a lieutenant of the 7th Michigan Cavalry. Hampton and the Yankee emptied their pistols at each other, and, although each was a good shot, neither hit the other. Both men and their horses were obviously in too high a state of excitement.[192] Hampton, still on his charger "Butler," reloaded and killed two enemy troopers with well-placed shots. Many years later, when one of his former troopers was interviewing him for a book, he asked Hampton the number of Yankees he had personally slain. When the author felt Hampton had understated the number, he reminded him of the two at Trevilian, at which the old General scoffed: "Oh! I did not count them. They were running." Lt. John Bauskett of Company B of the 6th South Carolina Cavalry dispatched a Federal trooper who had drawn a bead on William Gilmore Simms, Jr. of the Cadet Rangers.[193]

Years later, Federal Gen. James H. Wilson, wrote of Custer's predicament: "According to unofficial reports the rest of Sheridan's corps had a very lively time in endeavoring to get Custer out of trouble, while Custer, with his usual energy, was endeavoring to assist those out of trouble who had been sent to assist

---

[191] Brooks, 195, 245, 548; Thomas, 216; Sherfessee, 1; Manning, V, 111; Kennedy, 55. James F. Hart (1837-1905) (Citadel '57) joined the Washington Artillery after Ft. Sumter as Lt., then in November 1861, assumed command of Hart's Battery. His right leg was amputated from wounds received in October 1864. Postwar, he was a lawyer and state senator. Cyclopedia, 224-225.

[192] Isham, 57; Kennedy, 55.

[193] Brooks, 195, 548; Manning, V, 111.

John Bauskett, Jr. (1841-?) was 3rd Lt., Co. B, 6th SC Cavalry. Later, he was a lawyer in Columbia.

him."[194] For now, Custer managed to escape from the trap into which his own rashness had led him. Twelve years later, on a hot afternoon in Montana, again attacking without adequate reconnaissance, he would not.

Meanwhile, Gen. Butler, in an attempt to buy time to remove his ambulances and led horses, ordered Lieut. Long of the Sixth to attack with his small thirty man provost detachment. Long's mounted charge occupied the enemy for a few minutes though at a cost of many empty saddles. Using this time, Butler evacuated his ambulances and horses and formed a new line on the crest of a small hill perpendicular to his earlier position and adjacent to Rosser.

Thus deployed, both sides continued the contest until nightfall, a total of eleven hours. Finally, the opposing forces broke contact, Hampton returning to his previous night's bivouac at Green Spring Valley. Water there was abundant at the Confederate camp site, but the exhausted troopers got no food. They had had nothing to eat since early Friday, almost two days before. The command's horses fared little better, feeding on bearded wheat. The troops, exhausted and hungry, fell asleep on their arms as a light rain settled the stifling dust.[195] Butler would later praise his troops for bearing the brunt of the day's disastrous fight, "...but for their stubborn and invincible courage (we) must have been annihilated."

During the afternoon while the Yankees were moving their prisoners, a Confederate unit charged, sending many of the prisoners scrambling for safety. Pvt. Baxley, who had been captured in the morning, grabbed a horse being ridden by a big German who begged for his life when told to dismount. Baxley

---

[194] Wilson, 57. James H. Wilson (1837-1925) (West Point '60) rose to command of a cavalry division. His troops captured Jefferson Davis in May 1865. He remained on duty until he left to enter the railroad business then returned to the army during the Spanish-American War.

[195] Brooks, 246-247; B&L, IV, 238; UDC, II, 65; Myers, 303. Henry A. Long (1841-1864), a farmer from Bennettsville, was 2nd Lt., Co. E, 4th SC Cavalry.

escorted his prisoner to the rear, then, failing to reach the Rangers, Baxley settled down with other Confederates to feast on the German's country ham.[196]

The fighting during the day had been fierce and often confused. The correspondent for the *Charleston Daily Courier* reported, "the combat...was mostly at close quarters, and the wounds in consequence were generally severe."[197] While the wounded were cared for and the dead buried, Wade Hampton was planning for the next day. Unbeknown to him, Sheridan was reluctant to renew the battle because, as he would later claim, that day "...had reduced my supply of ammunition to a very small amount—not more than enough for one more respectable engagement...." His objective, the Virginia Central Railroad, had hardly been damaged.[198]

On the morning of the 12th, Hampton placed Butler in command of his division in order to devote full energy to command of the corps. Butler's Brigade was in turn commanded by Col. Benjamin H. Rutledge of the 4th South Carolina, Col. Aiken having been seriously wounded the day before. The division was moved forward and deployed around Mallory's Crossroads on the crest of a hill about a mile above Trevilian Station. Butler's Brigade was posted on the left along a railroad embankment. The 4th and 5th South Carolina regiments occupied the left of the division line while to their right, the lines of the Sixth, following the terrain, formed a right angle where a wagon road intersected the railroad. The Cadet Rangers were positioned in this angle with half of the company facing the wagon road and the other half facing the railroad. Two Napoleon guns of Thompson's Virginia Battery were posted near the right center of the brigade with the remaining two guns and Hart's Battery along the remainder of the brigade line.

---

[196] UDC, I, 168.
[197] *Charleston Daily Courier*, June 17, 1864.
[198] Sheridan, 423.

The 6th faced onto a large open field, the far side of which, about 200 yards across, was bordered by woods and skirted by a rail fence. A two story house occupied by the Ogg family sat in an oak grove about 100 yards in front of the regiment. To the left, the 5th South Carolina partially occupied the railroad cut, which was later to be enfiladed completely by artillery and sharpshooters. Another part of the line at the fence corner was enfiladed by sharpshooter fire from the woods and the Ogg house. P.M.B. Young's brigade of Georgians held the center of the defense line to the right and at right angles to Rutledge while Rosser held the extreme right. About noon, Fitz Lee, after marching all night in a wide flanking movement, joined Hampton. Breastworks, hastily constructed of fence rails and whatever else was at hand, were thrown up, providing some protection for the dismounted troops.[199]

Throughout the morning, both sides deployed, their maneuvers interrupted only by some desultory skirmishing. Federal troops spent several hours destroying as much railroad as they controlled, from Louisa Court House to a point one mile west of Trevilian Station, a total of about four miles. They had brought special tools along to ruin tracks and succeeded in burning the depot and several box cars on a nearby siding as well as the water station.[200]

About 3 p.m., Col. Rutledge was sitting on a pile of wood near the railroad track when a sharpshooter's rifle was heard in the distance, shortly followed by a bullet striking one of the logs. Gen. Butler, standing nearby, remarked, "That is the opening of the ball."[201] He was quickly proven correct as Sheridan's skir-

---

[199] B&L, IV, 238; Brooks, 247-248, 565-566; Thomas, 217; Sherfessee, 3; Calhoun, 126; UDC, I, 168; Kennedy, 55. Benjamin Huger Rutledge (1829-1893) was a signer of the Secession Ordinance. He commanded the Charleston Light Dragoons at the beginning of the war and rose to the rank of Col. in command of the 4th SC Cavalry. Lawyer and politician.
[200] OR, XXXVI, Pt. 1, 1097.
[201] Wells, 66.

mishers advanced from the woods firing briskly. Confederate troopers returned the heavy fire from behind their hastily constructed breastworks. The two Napoleons of Thompson's Battery opened on the enemy but this drew such concentrated return fire that, with several gunners down, Butler ordered Maj. Preston Chew, commanding the horse artillery, to withdraw the guns. The other guns of the battery, positioned to the rear of the line in an open field just right of the angle, were similarly exposed and had to be withdrawn.

On Gen. Butler's orders, Capt. Humphrey moved his squadron, consisting of his own company and B Company, across the railroad with instructions to fall back as soon as he was attacked. Accordingly, as they pulled back, Lt. Bauskett halted the men in the railroad cut. At the same time, Yankee sharpshooters occupied the Ogg house up the railroad and, able to enfilade the Sixth's line from the second story windows, began to pick off men. Despite their precarious position, Gen. Butler sent a message to hold on, prompting Lt. Bauskett to reply back: "Send us ammunition, General, and we will hold it." Belton Orchard, a young trooper standing nearby when Bauskett gave his answer, piped up with his own personal message: "Tell General Butler that we will hold it until hell freezes over." The squadron held on in the cut until an enemy charge forced them to retreat back to the angle.[202] Pvt. Baxley was wounded while retiring but managed to drag himself back to the unit's line and continued fighting. He was picked up early the next morning by an ambulance and carried to a field hospital where he was nursed by a beautiful Virginia girl. At this point, Gen. Butler ordered Capt. Hart to open with his guns on the Ogg house and set it afire.

---

[202] Brooks, 248; B&L, IV, 238. Roger Preston Chew (1843-1921) raised an artillery company and served with Turner Ashby and Stonewall Jackson. Hampton considered him to be the best commander of horse artillery. CV, XXX, 151.

Frank Belton Orchard (1842-1920) was a member of Co. B, 6th SC Cavalry.

Although Mr. Ogg and his family had taken refuge in the cellar when the fighting started, they managed to escape uninjured as the house caught fire.[203]

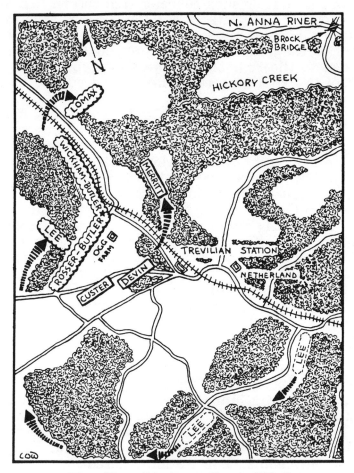

Trevilian Station—Second Day

Seven times that afternoon, Federal forces charged the Confederate line only to be repulsed each time. As the bluecoats prepared for their third assault, the

---

[203] UDC, I, 168; Wells, 66; Brooks, 249-250; Sherfessee, 4.

Cadet Rangers could see and even hear the officers,
swords in hand, exhorting their troops to a special effort to carry the lines. When the assault resumed,
these officers led the way. Capt. Humphrey restlessly
paced the line, joshing his men, "Don't be afraid,
boys; you can't get killed; your sweethearts are at
church praying for you." On a more practical note, he
added, "Now, boys, you will have a chance to show
your training; I want you to fire fast and aim straight,
but wait for the command to commence firing." The
Rangers followed his instructions and held their fire,
awaiting the order. As the Federals moved to within
seventy-five yards, their officers fell back from their
places in front of their troops, passing through the
ranks to take position in the rear. One Ranger, Pvt.
"Benny" Schipman of Charleston, seeing them melt
into the background, suddenly yelled out, "Stay in
front if you want to get those Yankees here!" Rebel
yells mixed with laughter rippled along the line of the
Sixth as the enemy began another unsuccessful assault.[204]

As the enemy was forming for the seventh and
what would prove to be their final charge, Confederate
officers were worried that they were extremely low on
ammunition and made desperate efforts to replenish
the supply. While some prepared to repulse the next
charge with rocks, Sgt. Neely Grant of the 4th South
Carolina galloped along the rear of the lines, driving
his now bullet-riddled wagon and pitching cases of rifle cartridges to the desperate cavalrymen.[205] Gen.
Butler ordered Hart's Battery up to support the brigade, regardless of the risk, with canister. With the
sun beginning to set, he further ordered Maj. Chew to
cooperate with Capt. Hart by bringing another battery
to bear on the Yankee artillery.

---

[204] Brooks, 248-250, 566; Calhoun, 127; *Sunny South*, May 26,
1896; Thomas, 217; Kennedy, 55. Neely Marion Grant (1826-
1907) was a private in Co. B, 4th SC Cavalry. Farmer and
sawmill operator.
[205] Brooks, 250; Calhoun, 127.

Hearing the Federal bugles assemble their troops for their final assault, Gen. Butler surmised that they would charge over the rail fence at the woods and ordered Maj. Chew to double shot his guns with canister to open on the advancing troops when they came into the open. As the Yankee attack emerged from the woods and passed over the fence to begin ascending the small ridge at the front, Butler calmly sat on his horse in the rear of Hart's Battery with his right leg cast over his saddle pommel. Intently watching the batteries of Hart and Chew duel with the Federal artillery, he nervously drummed a neatly cut switch on the cork foot which had replaced his own, shattered at Brandy Station the year before.

As the Yankees closed in on Butler's line, canister and musketry halted their attack, and they fell back to the protection of the woods, their retreat covered by their artillery. These guns fell silent when, as the remnants of the Yankee's final effort began to fade toward the woods, a shot from Hart's Battery struck and exploded a Federal caisson. Suddenly, as if by prearranged signal, the whole Confederate line jumped to its feet, leaped over their breastworks, and ran down the embankment, sweeping the bluecoats off the field. This ended the two-day engagement. As Sheridan withdrew during the night, he crossed the river at Carpenter's Ford, moving east along the north bank. With his pontoon train, Sheridan could still recross the river at almost any point. To counter this threat, Hampton followed on the south bank, staying between him and Grant's army.[206]

The Yankees took with them 370 prisoners as well as 377 of their own wounded, leaving some 90 more wounded and some prisoners too badly injured to move. Federal losses totalled 1,007 soldiers of whom 102 were killed, 470 wounded, and 435 captured or missing. Hampton reported 612 casualties in his division including 59 killed, and 258 wounded, with the balance captured or missing. The Sixth lost 175 of less than 500 carried into the action. While no official re-

---

[206] Brooks, 250-251; 264-265; B&L, IV, 238-239.

port of Fitz Lee's losses survives, they were relatively light since he was only slightly engaged in the two day affair.[207]

A Yankee prisoner captured during the retreat noted in his diary, "Saturday, June 11, fight at Trevilian Station, captured and killed six hundred Rebs. Sunday, June 12, fought on same ground, got whipped like the devil, lost more than the Rebs did the day previous."[208]

In their exposed position, the Cadet Rangers had suffered severely, although only two, Pvts. John Milling and William A. Sarratt, had been killed. Capt. Humphrey was wounded in the right leg; Lt. Aldrich in the right thigh, left arm, and right shoulder; and Sgt. Simms had a finger on his left hand shot off. Other wounded included Corp. Gabriel M. Hodges in the chest; Pvt. Hugh Y. Gladney in the right leg; and Pvt. Junius A. Hodge in the left arm. Pvts. Jacob V. Baxley and James F. Cloud were also wounded. Lt. Aldrich had commanded the left wing of the company where all of the wounded, except for Humphrey, had fought within twenty feet of each other. Simms spent several weeks in a Charlottesville hospital, then was furloughed and served with Alfred Rhett's artillery on Sullivan's Island and later at Ft. Sumter.[209] Six Rangers were missing after the two day engagement, Corp. John W. Jordan, and Pvts. Hiram Appleby, E.A. Morgan, Sherod H. Owens, John E. Saulesbury, and Iverson G. Sarratt.[210] Appleby and Saulesbury turned up, wounded, within a few days, but the other four had been captured and imprisoned at Ft.

---

[207] OR, XXXVI, 186-187, 1096; B&L, IV, 234; Hampton, 206; Calhoun, 128.
[208] UDC, XXIII, 193.
[209] Thomas, 217-218; UDC, I, 168; Manning, V, 112; *Charleston Mercury*, June 23, 1864; Kennedy, 55. John Milling, William A. Sarratt, Hugh Y. Gladney, Junius A. Hodge, and James F. Cloud - See Appendix A.
[210] CSR, 6th SC Cavalry; *Charleston Mercury*, June 23, 1864. John Walker Jordan, R.H. Appleby, E.A. Morgan, Sherod H. Owens, J.E. Saulesbury, and Iverson G. Sarratt - See Appendix A.

Delaware. Jordan, a 21 year old Corp. from Fairfield District, would later die in prison camp. Another of the dead was James Oscar Sheppard of Edgefield who had recently been promoted to Regimental Sgt. Maj. Sheppard, presaging his end, looked up his friend, Edwin Calhoun of C Co., the night previous and requested that his horse be returned to his father as he expected to be killed. Pvt. "Benny" Schipman of the Rangers was appointed to fill the vacancy created by his death.[211]

Hampton dogged the enemy's tracks as Sheridan retreated toward their base at White House Landing, arriving there on June 20th. After he was back in his own lines, Sheridan supposedly remarked: "I have met Butler and his cavalry, and I hope to God I will never meet them again." His desire came true as he never again faced Butler.[212] Later in the summer, Sheridan questioned a captured Rebel colonel whether he knew Butler. Receiving an affirmative response, Sheridan observed, "That damned man has caused me more trouble than all the rest of the Rebel Cavalry put together."[213] One of Sheridan's subordinates, Gen. A.T.A. Torbert explained their recent failure by the fact that Hampton had been reinforced on the 12th by "one or two regiments of infantry from Gordonsville." The "infantry" was, of course, Butler's Brigade with their Enfield rifles.[214]

Sheridan's biographer, who also commanded a brigade at Trevilian, would write some 30 years later:

> "Much of the very stubborn resistance ex-
> hibited in this action was due to the pres-
> ence in the field of the troops from South
> Carolina referred to. This brigade, raised

---

[211] CV, XXII, 408; UDC, XXIII, 195; Sease, 11; *Charleston Mercury*, September 28, 1864. Edwin Calhoun (1839-?) was pvt. in Co. C, 6th SC Cavalry. He was wounded on June 12, 1864.
[212] Brooks, 142, 211.
[213] Brooks, 213.
[214] Hampton, 166. Alfred T.A. Torbert (1833-1880) (West Point '55) commanded the 1st Division, Cavalry Corps of the Army of the Potomac at Trevilian.

in South Carolina at the beginning of the
war, had never before left that State nor
had seen any active service, and when,
with full ranks, and weapons and uniforms all fresh and untarnished by war
or service, they joined the veterans who
had been for three years exposed to the
losses and trials of active duty in the
field, their reception was not of the
warmest, and it was not thought that
much would be expected of them. The existence of this prejudice and their own
desire to show themselves at least the
equals of their comrades, caused them to
exhibit a desperate courage in this, their
first engagement; and as was said by veterans on both sides, they were too inexpe-
rienced to know when they had suffered
defeat, and continued to resist long after
it was apparent that the position they
held was turned and efforts to maintain
it were hopeless."[215]

Although preferring to believe that he had gained a
great victory, Sheridan submitted a report which,
though a masterpiece of dissembling, contained an
apology to his superiors for "...my inability to carry
out your instructions."[216]

Hampton himself, while not claiming a great victory, certainly did not consider the engagement a defeat. He had turned Sheridan back from uniting with
Hunter in the Valley and protected the vital Virginia
Central Railroad from all but minimal damage.[217]

As Hampton had pursued Sheridan from the
Trevilian battlefield, there was constant skirmishing
until the enemy reached the protection of their gun-

---

[215] Hampton, 212. Henry E. Davies (1836-1894) was Brig. Gen.
in command of the 1st Brigade, 2nd Division in the Army of
the Potomac Cavalry Corps.
[216] OR, XXXVI, pt. 1, 785.
[217] Sherfessee, 5; OR, XXXVI, pt. 1, 1097.

boats at White House Landing. At one point, Butler's Brigade surprised a reserve picket post at the White House and captured every man without firing a shot. The 5th South Carolina Cavalry was then formed to charge the garrison, but at the last minute instructions came from Hampton not to take such aggressive action. Butler then withdrew to await further instructions, all the while enduring fifteen-inch shells fired from Federal gunboats in the nearby Pamunkey River. During a minor engagement at Nance's Shop on June 22nd, Pvts. John W. Humphrey, older brother of his Capt., and R.T. Yarborough were slightly wounded, each having a finger amputated.[218]

After three day's rest, part of Sheridan's Cavalry Corps moved out to escort 800 wagons transferring supplies from White House to the James River camp where Grant had moved his base of operation. Hampton immediately moved to intercept the train, engaging Gen. David McM. Gregg on the 24th of June at St. Mary's (or Sumeria) Church. Although he executed a successful flanking movement, forcing Gregg to withdraw, Hampton was unable to follow up his advantage due to the exhausted condition of his men and their mounts. Sheridan's wagons escaped unharmed.

While Hampton was occupied with Sheridan at Trevilian Station, Grant determined to turn Lee's right and cut his lines of communication. Accordingly, on June 21, Brig. Gen. James H. Wilson with about 6,700 sabers of his own and Brig. Gen. August V. Kautz's divisions set out to destroy the Southside and Danville Railroads near Burkeville Junction. In planning the raid, Wilson had written to Headquarters prior to starting: "If Sheridan will look after Hampton, I apprehend no difficulty." Unaware

---

[218] OR, XXXVI, pt. 1, 1097; Hampton, 224-225; *Charleston Mercury*, July 15, 1864; Calhoun, 132-133. Grant suffered severe losses in attempting to turn Lee's south flank to capture Richmond. In mid-June 1864, he transferred his operations toward Petersburg which he planned to capture and then move upriver to Richmond.

that his chief had failed to destroy or even contain
Hampton for any length of time, Wilson set about his
task, destroying the station buildings at Ream's
Station and tearing up track for a short distance on either side. He then attempted to destroy the Staunton
River Bridge, but was foiled by local militia holding a
good position. Wilson turned back to regain his lines,
but on June 28th encountered Hampton near Sappony
Church.

Portions of Butler's and Rosser's Brigades hit
Wilson's left flank while Chambliss attacked in front.
This joint attack drove Wilson from his entrenchments, pushing him back toward Ream's Station. Fitz
Lee's division met Wilson there, inflicting heavy casualties, capturing all twelve of Wilson's field guns,
and burning his wagons and ambulances. Wilson retreated back toward the Nottoway River near Jarratt's
Station in a long detour, finally reaching the Federal
lines in an exhausted and disorganized state. Kautz,
meanwhile, had become separated from Wilson and
led his division directly into an ambush set by
Hampton near Ream's Station. Hampton captured all
but 300 of Kautz's troopers as they charged and broke
through. Kautz himself was one of the few who were
fortunate enough to escape.

When Hampton returned to Stony Creek Depot to
rest his men, he positioned his corps to be able to react
quickly to intercept the retreating Federals wherever
they might try to cross the railroad, either at Ream's
Station, further south at Jarratt's Station, or at
Hicksford. On the early morning of the 30th, Hampton
received a note from Fitz Lee that Wilson was expected to cross at Jarratt's Station. However, by the
time Hampton arrived, the Federals had withdrawn
into their lines.[219]

---

[219] Brooks, 267-269; Hampton, 230-242; Calhoun, 133-134;
Kennedy, 56. August V. Kautz (1828-1895) (West Point '52)
commanded the Federal Cavalry Division, VA and NC. Later,
he was a member of the military commission trying the
Lincoln assassination conspirators.

Hampton wrote of his activities beginning with Trevilian:

> "The pursuit of the enemy, which ended near Peter's Bridge, closed the active operations which commenced on the 8th of June when the movement against Sheridan began. During that time, a period of twenty-three days, the command had no rest, was badly supplied with rations and forage, marched upwards of 400 miles, fought the greater part of six days and one entire night, captured upwards of 2,000 prisoners, many guns, small arms, wagons, horses, and other material of war, and was completely successful in defeating two of the most formidable and well organized expeditions of the enemy. This was accomplished at a cost in my division of 719 killed, wounded, and missing, including twenty-one casualties in Chew's battalion not mentioned in my previous report."[220]

Gen. Robert E. Lee, in reporting the engagement, stated:

> At every step, indeed, the peril thickened, for Hampton, who had crossed the James, now came to W.H.F. Lee's help with a strong body of horse, and attacking the enemy on Tuesday evening (June 28th), at Sappony Church, drove him until dark, harassed him the livelong night, turned his left in the morning, and sent him helter-skelter before his horsemen.[221]

---

[220] SHSP, IX, 171.
[221] SHSP, XI, 275; Lee's Official Dispatch, June 29, 1864.

One grayclad trooper summed up recent events as having "...not a square meal...little water to drink and none to wash our faces."[222]

By early July 1864, the hard campaigning of June had begun to tell on the men and their mounts. Nearly 1,600 in Butler's Brigade were now dismounted as a result of dead or disabled horses. Those horses of Butler's Brigade which could travel but were unfit for service were sent to the recruiting camp near Dover's Mill, about 20 miles above Richmond. While waiting for their mounts to recuperate, some 300-500 men of Butler's Brigade were ordered to Stony Creek, 10 miles south of Petersburg. Here, James G. Holmes of Charleston, a Private in the Cadet Rangers, organized what was termed the "mob" into an infantry unit. Formally named the "Dismounted Battalion, Butler's Cavalry Brigade," it was derisively called "the Stud Horse Battalion" by the fortunate mounted troopers. Pvt. B. Miller of the Cadet Rangers was assigned as "acting captain" of the 4th Regiment's dismounted troopers while Joseph F. Hook held the same position for the troopers of the 6th Regiment. The organized "battalion" deployed later in the summer at Gravelly Run and served well as dismounted cavalry.[223]

On May 23rd, while the Rangers were beginning to experience their first hard service in Virginia, Maj. James B. White was posted with 45 Cadets on James Island at the battery at the head of Grimball's Causeway. The Cadets advanced as skirmishers to re-establish picket lines, found no enemy, and the next day were ordered back to the causeway. There, they formed the reserve, being detailed out for picket duty along the Stono River.[224] An enemy soldier of the 54th Massachussetts, a black regiment, noted that: "On James Island there was not a single infantry regiment; and for some time the Citadel Cadets, com-

---

[222] Calhoun, 124. Charles Moseley Calhoun (1838-1921) was a private in the 5th SC Cavalry from Greenwood.
[223] Brooks, 301, 380-381; CV, II, 178. James G. Holmes, B. Miller, and Joseph F. Hook - See Appendix A.
[224] Ripley, 163, 167-168; Kershaw, 148.

posed of youths, and some companies of city firemen, armed for the duty, served at that point." The only troops available for reinforcement were the reserves, all other available troops having been ordered to other threatened areas.[225]

During this period of active service, the Cadets subsisted on bacon and hardtack and considered themselves fortunate to have tents. By the time they returned to Charleston, their uniforms were so worn in places that their underclothing showed through, an embarassing sight tactfully described as "blossoming" by blushing young ladies of Charleston, who on seeing the Cadets' underwear poking through their normally neat clothing, were reminded of cotton blossoms.[226]

In mid-May, the Arsenal Cadets had formed a guard of honor for the remains of Brig. Gen. Micah Jenkins, (Citadel '54), who had been killed on May 6th at the Wilderness. Other graduates, Col. James Drayton Nance (Citadel '56) of the 3rd South Carolina and Pvt. Oliver Johnston Youmans (Citadel '59) of the 2nd South Carolina, had also fallen on the same day as Gen. Jenkins, while on May 12th at Spotsylvania, Lt. Col. Washington Pinckney Shooter (Citadel '59) of Gregg's 1st South Carolina had died. In late July, the Arsenal Corps attended the funeral of Maj. William C. Preston who had fallen near Atlanta. These casualties led Lt. Patrick to lament in his journal: "Alas! that so many of our young men should be called to fill an early grave."[227]

---

[225] Emilio, 194; OR, XXX, pt. 2, 489, 493-495, 532, 534, 538. Luis Emilio (1844-?) was a member of the 54th Massachusetts Infantry, a black unit.

[226] Barnwell, 167-168.

[227] Patrick, 219, 229; Thomas, 158-164, 263, 266, 268. Micah Jenkins (1835-1864) (Citadel '54) founded the King's Mountain Military School after graduation. He commanded the 5th SC, and later the Palmetto Sharpshooters. In 1862, he was promoted to Brig. Gen., commanding a brigade at Fredericksburg, Chickmauga, Knoxville, and the Wilderness. He was fatally shot in the same volley which wounded Gen. Longstreet.

The Citadel, 1865

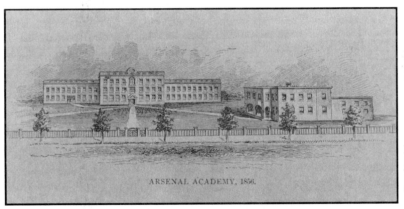

ARSENAL ACADEMY, 1856.

The Arsenal

The Citadel taken from the tower of the Charleston Orphan House

The Citadel Cadets firing on the Star of the West, January 9, 1861
—by David Humphreys Miller

The Citadel

Those who manned the Star of the West Battery

Peter Fayssoux Stevens
Class of 1849
Superintendent of the
Citadel, 1859-1861

Nathaniel Walker
Armstrong
Class of 1851
Professor of Mathematics
& Mechanical Philosophy

George Edward
Haynsworth
Class of 1861
Gunner on Gun No. 1

Robert Chisolm
Class of 1863

Those who manned the Star of the West Battery

The Citadel

Thomas B. Ferguson
Class of 1861

Thomas Waring

William Stewart Simkins
Class of 1861

from Mason Smith Family Letters
by D.E. Huger Smith

William Mason Smith
Class of 1862

A. Gordon Quattlebaum

Theodore Adolphus
Quattlebaum
Cadet, 1860-1861

John Dozier Lee, III

John Dozier Lee
Class of 1861

The Citadel

John Marshall Whilden
Class of 1861

Prof. Lou Towles

Samuel Porcher Smith
Class of 1862

Flag of the Citadel Corps of Cadets—
presented by the Washington Light Artillery, 1857

Reverse side of the Cadet flag

Four comrades who fired on the Star of the West

John Rufus Mew, William Wayne Gregg, William Fordham McKewn, and George Archibald McDowell

Mew, McKewn, and McDowell, 2nd Classmen, graduated in the Class of 1862; Gregg, a 3rd Classman, left that spring. Gregg was killed at Gaines' Mill, McKewn fell at Fredericksburg, and McDowell in a cavalry battle on John's Island. Only Mew survived the war, living into the 20th century.

Officers of the South Carolina Military Academy

James Benjamin White
Class of 1849
Superintendent of the
Citadel, 1861-1865

John Peyre Thomas
Class of 1851
Superintendent of the
Arsenal, 1861-1865

Robert Oswald Sams
Class of 1862
Assistant Professor of
Mathematics & French

Hugh Smith Thompson
Class of 1856
Professor of Belles Lettres
& Ethics
(in postwar militia
uniform)

Moses Benbow Humphrey
Cadet 1859-1862
Captain, Cadet Rangers

The Citadel

The charge of the Cadet Rangers at Louisa Court House, June 11, 1864
—by David Humphreys Miller

The Citadel

The charge of the Citadel Cadets at Tulifinny, December 7, 1864
—by David Humphreys Miller

Cadets at the close of the war

Edward Thomas
Class of 1865

William Peebles Baskin
Class of 1865

John Elias Boinest
Cadet 1862-1865

Moses Sanders Haynsworth
Cadet 1862-1865

The Citadel

Unidentified Cadets in undress uniform

The Citadel

The Citadel

Joseph Valentine Morrison
Class of 1864

Aristippus Doty
Class of 1863

S.C. Historical Society

the Dutart Family

Charles Petigru Allston
Cadet 1865

John Steel Dutart
Cadet 1865

Cornelius Irvine Walker
Class of 1861

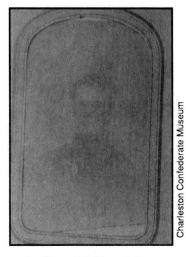

Andrew Moffett Adger
Cadet 1865

Richard Furman Lawton
Class of 1862

Interior of the Citadel

James Drayton Nance (1837-1864) (Citadel '56) Attorney in Newberry. Served as Capt., Co. E (Quitman Rifles) 3rd SC Infantry and later as its colonel.

Oliver Johnston Youmans (1838-1864) (Citadel '59) Attorney in Columbia. Served as Pvt., Co. C (Columbia Grays) 2nd SC Infantry.

Washington Pinckney Shooter (1837-1864) (Citadel '59) Attorney and editor in Marion. Served as Lt. Col., 1st (Gregg's) SC Infantry.

William Campbell Preston, Jr. (1838-1864) was a relative of Gen. Wade Hampton.

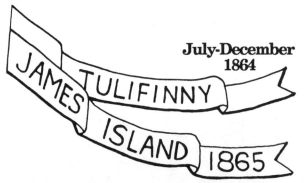

In early July, the Arsenal Cadets were called to Charleston to help man the defenses, seriously weakened by the recent reinforcements sent to Lee's army in Virginia. The Citadel Cadets were also called out on July 3 to guard the 140 prisoners taken in the bluecoats' unsuccessful attack on Ft. Johnson. Earlier in the day, approximately 1,000 Federal troops assaulted the fort manned by a Confederate garrison of 139. After the prisoners had been transported to prison camp, the Cadets were marched further down James Island and placed in charge of fortifications, remaining there over a week. They also performed guard duty at the "New Bridge," near the present bridge across the Ashley River, as well as at the provost marshal's office.[228]

During that summer, Citadel Cadets acted as escorts for the funerals of Capt. John C. Mitchel and Brig. Gen. Clement H. Stevens. Mitchel was commandant of Ft. Sumter when he was struck and mortally wounded by a piece of shrapnel while observing movements of the blockading squadron. Stevens, older brother of Peter F. Stevens, who had commanded the Cadets at the firing on the *Star of the West*, was commanding a brigade of Georgians and South Carolinians when mortally wounded at Peachtree Creek outside Atlanta. Both had been wounded on July 20th, Mitchel dying within four hours while Stevens lingered on for five days.[229]

---

[228] Patrick, 169; Johnson, 218; DuBos, 126; Inglesby, 14; Kershaw, 148.
[229] Barnwell, 165; CV, IV, 7. John C. Mitchel (?-1864) was a recent Irish immigrant who commanded Co. I, 1st Regiment

In January 1864, some fifteen veterans had been detailed, without pay, to the Arsenal by Gen. Beauregard who expected them to take advantage of the academic atmosphere. When their detail expired in late July, the new commander of the department, Maj. Gen. Samuel Jones, refused to extend the luxury of education when the Confederacy desperately needed soldiers to fill the ranks, and the young men were returned to their units.[230]

Cadet details were occasionally sent to convey prisoners to the prison camp at Andersonville, Georgia, chosen originally as a temporary holding pen for Union prisoners of war awaiting exchange. Since exchange of prisoners had been stopped by Gen. Grant who tried thereby to further strain Southern resources by forcing them to feed and house numerous prisoners, the unintentional prison camp had slowly degenerated as more and more prisoners arrived. Although Grant's brutal military logic prevailed, even after the Confederate government offered to return the prisoners without exchange if only Federal authorities would provide transportation, it created intense suffering among his own soldiers, especially those confined at Andersonville. The sight of the prison would make an everlasting impression on Alexander McQueen Salley, a seventeen year old Cadet from Orangeburg. The journey was made in box cars which had previously been used to haul cattle. Before the prisoners were put into the cars, Cadets scraped out the filth with hoes. In after years, Salley

---

SC Artillery. He had commanded Battery Simkins and the artillery at Ft. Johnson before being ordered to Ft. Sumter on May 4th.

Clement Hoffman Stevens (1821-1864), older brother of Peter F. Stevens, had designed the ironclad battery which served during the bombardment of Ft. Sumter. He served on the staffs of Gens. Barnard Bee and Roswell Ripley and later led the 24th SC at Secessionville, Vicksburg, and Chickamauga. He commanded a Georgia brigade during the Atlanta campaign, having been promoted to Brig. Gen. in January 1864.

[230] Patrick, 230.

would often recall: "If Hell could ever be described, or pictured, I think Andersonville Prison would best describe that place."[231]

On another occasion, Cadets guarded a number of Federal officers quartered in a house near Broad Street in Charleston. The officer prisoners were placed there, within range of Federal guns, in retaliation for a group of Confederate officers, afterwards known as the "Immortal Six Hundred," being held within range of Confederate guns on Sullivan's Island and James Island. Once during this time, the Cadets guarded a company or two of seasoned Confederate soldiers on their way to one of the islands. Possibly these were "Galvanized Yankees," Federal prisoners who had taken an oath of allegiance to the Confederate government.[232] Cadets also performed guard duty and pulled provost duty on railway trains to arrest any soldiers not carrying passports. The boredom of this duty was broken briefly by a dress parade on July 22nd, the music provided by the Ft. Sumter band. The Cadets remained on duty throughout much of the summer until relieved in late September after which they were furloughed.[233]

In late September, Lt. Patrick caught wind of an impending duel between two Arsenal Cadets. A challenge had been issued and accepted to settle their differences with pistols, the muzzles of which would be

---

[231] Kershaw, 148; Chapman, 502; UDC, LXIII, 96-97. James Y. Culbreath - See Appendix B.

[232] Kershaw, 148; UDC, LXIII, 96. It is possible that these Confederate troops under guard were members of Brooks' Battalion, a group of Federal prisoners from Florence who volunteered to fight in Confederate service rather than endure prison life.

In June 1864, Federal guns began bombardment of the city of Charleston, placing many civilians in danger. Confederate Gen. Sam Jones placed a number of Federal prisoners in a house in the lower part of Charleston. In retaliation, some 600 Confederate prisoners (the Immortal 600) from Ft. Delaware were transferred to Charleston and placed in a stockade on Morris Island under the fire of the Charleston batteries.

[233] Kershaw, 148-149; *Charleston Mercury*, July 22 & 23, 1864; Thomas, 211; UDC, XXXVII, 82.

touching. Patrick called the two young men together and was able to resolve the matter equitably. On October 4, the entire Corps was in attendance as President Jefferson Davis addressed the citizens of Columbia outside of Gen. Chesnut's residence. Davis expressed optimism about the Confederate cause and "urged all to the discharge of their duties."[234]

The Cadet Rangers spent a hard summer and fall, countering Grant's bloody, unrelenting drive on the Confederate capitol city as the Federal commander used his vast superiority in manpower and resources to bleed Lee's army to death. The constant picketing and patrolling by the Cadet Rangers was punctuated by frequent cavalry battles as the bluecoated squadrons probed Lee's mounted screen, the enemy constantly seeking a weak spot for Grant to exploit.

On July 30th, Gen. Butler lead a foraging expedition around the left of the Yankee lines to secure a large quantity of oats and hay. Sending Col. Miller with seven companies of the 6th South Carolina Cavalry along with one dismounted company to guard the crossing at Lee's Mills, Butler led the other two regiments of his brigade along an adjacent line to protect his wagon train.

At the same time, Federal Gen. D. McM. Gregg was raiding southward toward Weldon, North Carolina attempting to gain and harass the rear of Lee's army. Gregg planned to cross the swamp at Lee's Mills which he thought was unguarded. Arriving there about 3:00 p.m., he bumped up against Col. Miller with the 6th South Carolina Cavalry who had arrived in mid-morning. The men of the 6th, after cutting the mill dam, had settled down to fishing in the mill pond and broiling their catches.

Although Miller beat off Gregg's initial attack, delaying him for nearly two hours, numerical superiority eventually prevailed when Miller was outflanked and began retreating. Butler with the remainder of

---

[234] Patrick, 238-239. Jefferson Davis, President of the Confederate States, made an inspection trip to GA and SC from Sept. 20 to Oct. 15, 1864.

the brigade had, by this time, succeeded in loading the wagons with the much-needed forage when he stumbled into the running engagement. Butler poured in a heavy musketry fire, then led both mounted and dismounted charges, giving Miller time to withdraw orderly.[235]

Of the Cadet Rangers, Corp. Edward C. Dozier was wounded in the engagement, and Pvts. Marshall F. Davis, Joseph F. Gladney, and John M. Kirkland were captured and confined at Elmira Prison.[236] Dozier received his painful wound during a lull in the engagement when he and a group of troopers found a millpond and, leaving horseholders, plunged in the cool water. Federal troopers, intent on capturing their horses, advanced, but Dozier and his fellow swimmers were alerted to the danger and quickly retrieved their clothes and weapons and raced to the roadway. Dozier reached the roadway before the bluecoats and mounted a stump from which he dispatched the leading Yankee. Momentarily confused by the loss of their leader, the Yankees regrouped and forced the Rebels to retreat, inflicting a severe wound on Dozier's left arm and side which disabled him from further service.[237]

On August 14, Hampton was directed by Lee to return to Richmond from his position near Culpeper. Hampton reached White Tavern on the Charles City Road on the morning of the 16th and pressed forward to assist Fitz Lee's division which was seriously engaged by a Federal expedition attempting to slip around the Confederate left to break up the Virginia Central Railroad. Lee was being forced back, and Brig. Gen. John R. Chambliss had just been killed while rallying his Virginians when the division, now commanded by Butler, came on the field.

---

[235] Brooks, 301-302.
[236] CSR, 6th SC Cavalry; Thomas, 218. Edward C. Dozier, Marshall F. Davis, Joseph F. Gladney, and John M. Kirkland - See Appendix A.
[237] Dozier, 41.

Butler's Division, fighting dismounted, attacked the right and rear of the enemy line, while a frontal assault drove the Federals back from their position. When the bluecoats were reinforced the next day, Hampton retired to the south side of the river.[238]

In the next few days, Federal troops under Maj. Gen. Gouverneur K. Warren and Maj. Gen. Winfield S. Hancock secured a position across the Weldon Railroad at Ream's Station, about 6 miles from Petersburg, and began destroying the track. Ream's Station, situated on the Petersburg and Weldon Railroad, was one of the two depots Gen. Lee maintained to supply his army. When the railroad was cut, Lee continued the supply of his army by organizing wagon convoys to haul supplies from Stony Creek Depot, now the northernmost railhead, located twenty miles south of Petersburg. Lt. Gen. Ambrose P. Hill attacked the Federals on the 21st, and despite taking numerous bluecoated prisoners, failed to dislodge them.[239]

Early on August 23rd, Butler crossed Gravelly Run to relieve Barringer's North Carolina Brigade which was on outpost duty. Colliding with an enemy cavalry brigade and, after some initial setbacks, Butler succeeded in driving them back. The fight continued un-

---

[238] Hampton, 270-273; Calhoun, 135-136. John Randolph Chambliss (1833-1864) (West Point '53) was a planter and militia officer. He led a regiment, then rose to Brig. Gen., commanding a cavalry brigade. Boatner, 136.

[239] OR, XLII, pt. 1, 428-430, 851; pt. 2, 260; Clark, V, 207; Brooks, 303. Gouverneur Kemble Warren (1830-1882) (West Point '50) commanded the V Corps from early 1864 to the end of the war.

Winfield Scott Hancock (1824-1886) (West Point '40) commanded the II Corps from mid-1863 to November 1864. His men occupied the center of the Union line at Gettysburg and met the brunt of Pickett's charge. In 1880, he was an unsuccessful candidate for President.

Ambrose Powell Hill (1825-1865) (West Point '47) served in the Mexican and Seminole Wars, then accepted command of a Virginia regiment. He rose to Lt. Gen. in command of a corps, being killed on April 2, 1865, just before the surrender. Boatner, 400.

til dark when the opposing forces improvised breastworks. Losses on both sides had been severe.
However, at the close of the initial day's fighting, the
Federals were neither able to turn Lee's right nor dislodge Barringer's picket line.

At the height of the battle, one Rebel trooper of the
5th South Carolina Cavalry, lying with his comrades
behind hastily constructed breastworks, had complained to his company commander: "Captain, my
gun is foul and will not fire." Sarcastically, the officer
replied, "Never mind, sir, the man next to you will be
killed directly and you can get his gun." To the
amazement of the others, the man held his place in
line, patiently waiting to replace his rifle.[240]

On the 24th, Brig. Gen. John Dunovant, former
colonel of the 5th South Carolina Cavalry, assumed
command of the brigade to replace Butler who now officially succeeded Hampton in command of the division. During the turnover of command, Butler remarked to Dunovant: "I have never seen a man of
more fortitude than Capt. Humphrey."[241]

A.P. Hill joined up with Hampton and assaulted
the enemy in front of Ream's Station at daylight the
next morning. After a severe fight lasting much of the
day, Hill launched a frontal assault with three
Carolina brigades. As the three brigades charged
across the open field and through the abatis in their
front, Butler closed in on the Federal rear, which successfully broke their line. The rout was the final action of the afternoon as Hancock retreated back to
Grant's lines.[242]

During the engagement, Brig. Gen. Samuel
McGowan's South Carolina Brigade had captured
some Union cannon but had no gunners at hand to
man them. As the infantry men watched the blue-

---

[240] Hampton, 284; Brooks, 284-286, 303.
[241] *Sunny South*, May 26, 1896. John Dunovant (1825-1864)
became Col. of the 5th SC Cavalry in 1862 and commanded it
until appointed Brig. Gen. in August 1864. He was killed on
the Vaughn Road on October 1, 1864 while leading his brigade.
[242] Brooks, 303-304; Clark, V, 208-209; Calhoun, 139-140.

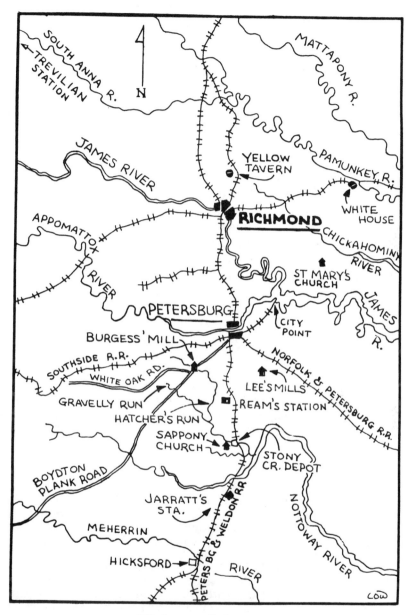

Richmond Area

coats retreat, a freshly captured Federal sergeant piped up, "If you boys will allow me, I can mow those Yanks down while they are running up the hill." Given permission, he helped turn the guns and fire them on his recent friends.[243]

Federal losses were between 600 and 700 killed, as well as 2,150 prisoners, 3,100 small arms, 12 stands of colors, and nine guns and caissons. Confederate losses, principally in Lane's North Carolina Brigade, were about 720 killed and wounded.[244]

Hill, commenting on the combined operation, lyricized in his report: "The bayonet and the sabre shook hands on the enemy's captured breastworks."[245] Gen. Lee, writing to congratulate Gov. Zeb Vance on the services of the North Carolina troops in the affair, also commended his mounted arm, "The operations of the cavalry were not less distinguished for boldness and efficiency than those of the infantry."[246] Hancock, on the other hand, was deeply disturbed by the affair, commenting to friends that he would rather have died than to have witnessed his corps in such a rout.[247]

Some three weeks later, on September 16, 1864, acting on information provided by his scouts, Hampton conducted his famous cattle raid at Coggin's Point, bringing back to his lines about 2,500 cattle while sustaining 50 casualties and inflicting 400 casualties on the enemy. A small portion of the 6th South Carolina Cavalry participated in this raid.[248]

---

[243] Brooks, 306. Samuel McGowan (1819-1897) took command of Maxcy Gregg's brigade after the latter's death at Fredericksburg and led it through the end of the war. Postwar, he was a legislator and SC Supreme Court Justice.
[244] Clark, V, 211; Brooks, 305-306.
[245] Wells, 76; Brooks, 305-306, 311-312; CV, XXII, 408.
[246] Clark, V, 212. Zebulon Baird Vance (1830-1894) served as Capt. and later Col. of the 26th NC. In January 1863, he became Governor of NC and was re-elected two years later. After the war, he served a third-term as governor, then was elected to the US Senate.
[247] Brooks, 306, 312.
[248] Hampton, 287-303; Calhoun, 141; Brooks, 314-324; Wells, 287-305; Stories, 366-367.

The following month, Grant, finding that Petersburg and Richmond could not be taken by direct assault, determined to extend his lines westward to cut the Southside Railroad, hoping thereby to make the two cities untenable. At the time, Hampton's Cavalry Corps was on the extreme right of Lee's army, screening from Hatcher's Run ten miles south of Petersburg to Stony Creek and beyond. His outposts protected both the Southside Railroad and the Boydton Plank Road which were vital supply routes to the country from which Lee subsisted his army.

On a cold, rainy 27th of October, Federal troops under Gen. Hancock set out to extend their lines around Lee's right to seize the Southside Railroad and force the evacuation of Petersburg and Richmond. In conjunction with this movement, Maj. Gen. Benjamin F. Butler, alternately nicknamed "Beast" by Southerners for his ungallant conduct toward ladies of occupied New Orleans, or "Spoons" because of his confiscation of their silver tableware, was to make a strong diversionary attack on the north side of the James River.

About sunrise on the 27th, 80 dismounted men of the 6th South Carolina Cavalry under Lt. James M. Hough, camped north of Hatcher's Run near Burgess' Mill, were awakened by a courier exhorting them to double-quick to a line of breastworks down the creek. Even then, Hampton's pickets were being driven in along a two mile front from Armstrong's Mill to Monk's Neck Bridge. Once behind their breastworks, men were placed about five paces apart and held in position for about three hours until reinforced.

As the pickets were being pressed in, the 6th South Carolina Cavalry mounted, forming a battle line in a field beyond their sutler's tent. As the Federals pressed further, they forced the Confederates back to the vicinity of the sutler's tent. There, Lt. William J. Nettles of the Cadet Rangers fell, his head "...carried off by a round shot," the same shot killing Pvt.

Summers.[249] The bluecoats forced Butler back to a position on the White Oak Road, where he checked their advance.

In a coordinated attack with Hampton late in the afternoon, Maj. Gen. Henry Heth of Hill's command advanced his infantry across the creek. Butler took position on the west side of an open field, his left resting on the Burgess' Mill pond. Butler's dismounted division, having thrown up improvised breastworks, was ordered forward to attack a Federal infantry division. Advancing under a heavy, galling fire across an open field toward the enemy on the far side, Butler led his entire line forward and drove the Yankees back onto Fitz Lee's Division, now advancing down the Boydton Road.[250]

Lt. Thomas Preston Hampton, the cavalry chief's youngest son, along with Lt. Oliver N. Butler, younger brother of Matthew Butler, were riding forward with the line encouraging the advancing troopers when Preston was shot in the groin. Quickly, Hampton rode to his son's side, knelt and tenderly kissed him, and then informed the surgeon that it was too late to help. Wiping away his tears, the General ordered an ambulance to carry his dying son off, then rode to another part of the field where Lt. Francis M. Bamberg was engaged with two guns of Hart's Battery in an artillery duel with some masked Federal batteries. Hampton directed their fire until after dark, giving particular instructions on the firing and elevation of each piece.

The combined attack of Butler and Lee had driven the Yankees back to the cover of a dense pine thicket where, with artillery support, they were able to stop

---

[249] Hampton, 324, 326-327; Brooks, 351, 355, 382; Calhoun, 147; CV, XXII, 408; Thomas, 218. James M. Hough from Lancaster was 3rd Lt. in Co. K. 6th SC Cavalry.

William Joseph Nettles and George T. Summers - See Appendix A.

[250] Hampton, 330-334. Henry Heth (1825-1899) (West Point '47) commanded a division under Gen. Hill. His skirmishers had engaged the Federals on July 1, 1863, to precipitate the Battle of Gettysburg.

the Confederate advance. Convinced of his inability to
flank Lee's lines and unable to maintain contact with
cooperating corps on his right, Hancock withdrew
during the night, rather than face the possibility of being cut off.[251] Federal losses in the engagement came
to about 1,902, of which 1,365 were prisoners.[252]

Lee continued to use Stony Creek as the terminus
for his rail communications, transferring his supplies to wagons for the twenty mile trip into
Petersburg. Stony Creek also served as the dead line
camp for troops who were dismounted and for mounts
needing rest and recuperation. This late in the war,
the availability of horses was critically short, both in
quantity and quality. On December 1st, 113 men of
Butler's Brigade, 28 from the 6th, including 5 Cadet
Rangers, were waiting at Stony Creek. On that day, a
Federal reconnaissance in force overran the depot in
a surprise attack, capturing the entire garrison. The
five captured Cadet Rangers were Pvts. Herman
Schipman, Logan Mabry, John W. Davis, Alfred
Harris, and William A. Huskey. Although Butler
pursued and attempted to overtake the Federals, the
enemy managed to escape.[253]

As a result of the successful reconnaissance,
Grant resumed his plans to destroy the railroad as far
south as Hicksford or Bellefield on the Meherrin
River, some twenty miles south of Stony Creek. On a

---

[251] Brooks, 352-354, 568-569; Hampton, 333-339. Thomas Preston
Hampton (1842-1864) was the second son of Gen. Wade
Hampton, serving as his aide.

Oliver Nathaniel Butler (1844-before 1900) was younger
brother of Gen. M.C. Butler. Lost an arm just before
Appomattox.

Francis Marion Bamberg (1838-1905) served as 2nd Lt. of
Hart's Battery, which participated in 142 engagements during
the war. Bamberg was present in all of them. Postwar, he was
a merchant and banker in Bamberg and founder of Bamberg
County.

[252] Hampton, 342-343.

[253] Hampton, 370-375; CSR, 6th SC Cavalry; *Charleston Tri-
Weekly Courier*, December 10, 1864; Calhoun, 167-168. Herman
Schipman, Logan C. Mabry, J.W. Davis, Alfred Harris, and
William A. Huskey - See Appendix A.

sleeting and rainy December 7th, Gen. Warren, with a large force of 34,000 troops and 5 batteries, started southward for Stony Creek. At the same time, Brig. Gen. Nelson A. Miles led a heavy column against the Confederate right flank but could not dislodge the few but stubborn defenders who managed to hold their position at Hatcher's Run.[254]

Hampton, upon gaining information of the movement, started in pursuit with two divisions. He planned to pass around Warren's left flank, get in front of it, and then delay. Finding the fords across the Nottoway River impassable, however, Hampton withdrew and passed around Warren's rear instead, gaining the enemy's front at Bellefield by the next morning. Once facing the enemy, Hampton directed Butler to barricade Clark's Ford, three miles south of Hicks, to deny it to the Federals. Some 600 men of the 6th South Carolina Cavalry cut trees across the ford and rolled rocks and other obstructions into the river to preclude its use. These troopers then rejoined Hampton who, having coordinated with A.P. Hill, now planned to strike with his infantry from Jarratt's Station, ten miles north.

At the bridge over the Meherrin at Hicks' Ford, a small infantry force supported by a few siege guns and two batteries repulsed the Federals. Thus, with streams swollen and fords barricaded and defended, Warren decided to withdraw, having destroyed some 17 or 18 miles of track and several bridges. Hampton followed and harassed him, capturing about 300 prisoners as well as some abandoned wagons, and many small arms. Warren claimed his expedition was a success, since he thought the track and bridges could not be rebuilt. However, Hampton put Butler in

---

[254] Hampton, 375-377; Brooks, 411. Nelson A. Miles (1839-1925) rose from 1st Lt. to corps command. He was awarded the Medal of Honor for his service at Chancellorsville. Postwar, he remained in the Army, and rose to be the General-in-Chief during the Spanish-American War and Moro insurrection. Boatner, 550.

charge of rebuilding the railroad and, within two weeks, the job was completed.

During the rest of December, there were no serious enemy movements, and the time was spent on picket duty. The Confederates returned to Bellefield and erected temporary winter quarters in log huts. Men and horses were afforded a much-needed rest.[255]

While the Citadel Cadets were on furlough in the late fall, a small detail was maintained as a guard. These guards regularly climbed onto the roof of the school where they had an excellent view of the shelling of the city. Occasionally, shells would land nearby. Once, just after the Cadets had come down from their vantage point, a shell landed in nearby Calhoun Street, cutting the gas main and extinguishing all lights in the building. Another shell, aimed at the tall steeple of the Citadel Square Baptist Church, descended through the roof of a room on the northwest angle of the Citadel building, passed through the outer wall, and knocked down a small house across Meeting Street.[256] When the Cadet Corps returned from their brief furlough, they spent only a night or two at the Citadel. Then, due to the continuing danger from the bombardment and with a threat of yellow fever, they were ordered into a camp near Magnolia Cemetery on the outskirts of Charleston and, subsequently, on November 20th, at Orangeburg.[257] Once there, new undress uniforms of Confederate gray were issued, of better quality than those distributed earlier in the year. While stationed in Orangeburg, a group of Cadets raided a flock of turkeys. The Corps was called together and condemned for the action, though not before some tempers rose.[258]

On October 6th, the Arsenal Cadets were ordered out to guard a large number of prisoners at the Charleston railroad depot in Columbia. They guarded

---

[255] Hampton, 384-385; Brooks, 384-387, 412-413; Calhoun, 168-169; OR, XLII, pt. 1, 444, 613, pt. 3, 1271.
[256] Kershaw, 149; Citadel News, 103.
[257] Thomas, 211; Kershaw, 150; Barnwell, 169.
[258] Barnwell, 174.

the Yankees overnight and, the next morning, marched them to Camp Sorghum, a new prison for Federal officers located on the west bank of the Congaree River across from Columbia. Prisoners began arriving on October 6, 1864, and numbered over 12,000 within a week. The prison was deactivated in mid-December as Sherman's army approached Augusta.[259] Because of the shortage of men, the Cadets stayed on guard at the prison, serving eight hour shifts during each 24 hour period. Lacking permanent quarters, they built brush huts to protect themselves from the rain and cold until they returned to their studies on the twelfth.[260]

Cadets were also detailed for guard duty at the Confederate prison at Florence, South Carolina. John McElroy, a private in the 16th Illinois Cavalry, recalled one Cadet who called the roll there.

> "...though an in-born young aristocrat who believed himself made of finer clay than most mortals, he was not a bad fellow at all. He thought South Carolina aristocracy the finest gentry, and the South Carolina Military Institute the greatest institution of learning in the world; but that is common with all South Carolinians." After roll call one day he taunted the prisoners, "Now you fellers are all so damned peart on mathematics and such things, that you want to snap me up on every opportunity, but I guess I've got something this time that'll settle you." Indicating that none of the officers had been able to solve the problem, he questioned, "...what is the length of a pole standing in a river, one-fifth of which is in the mud, two-thirds in the water, and one-eight above the water, while one foot and three inches of the top is broken off?"

---

[259] Patrick, 240; Bond, 76; UDC, XXXVII, 82.
[260] Obear, October 15, 1864.

The Cadet was amazed when, within a minute, a dozen answered, "One hundred and fifty feet." One of the prisoners comtemptuously added: "Why, if you South Carolina Institute fellows couldn't answer such questions as that they wouldn't allow you in the infant class up North."[261]

One Confederate officer would later comment on the Confederacy's waning ability to uphold its cause at this time:

"The troops were ready to fight 'at the drop of a hat,' there was little of the 'pomp and circumstance of war' remaining with us. With fast thinning columns and rapidly shortening lines, we were grappling, almost hopelessly, with an enemy far superior in point of numbers, in equipment and in every resource.

We had taxed invention, practiced economy and resorted to every known device to maintain our footing and continue the unequal contest. Much that was essential in time of war or peace, and many things absolutely indispensable in war, were becoming exceedingly scarce."[262]

---

[261] McElroy, 307-308. John McElroy (1846-1929) was a Pvt. in Co. L, 16th Illinois Cavalry who was confined at Andersonville, Florence, and Richmond.
[262] *Sunday News*, Sept. 2, 1897. A Gallant Soldier's Story. Benjamin Stuart Williams (1843-1924) enlisted as Pvt., then served as Corp., Sgt., and Lt. of the 25th GA Regiment. He was promoted to Adjutant of the 47th GA Regiment. After the war, he wrote a number of articles on the war, primarily the engagements at Honey Hill and Tulifinny Creek. Postwar, he was auditor, sheriff, and state legislator. Snowden, V, 91-92.

On the 5th of December, Gen. James Jones, Chairman of the Board of Visitors, in his annual report, declared:

> "The continued bombardment of the City of Charleston by the enemy has rendered the Citadel in that city a dangerous habitation, and wholly unfit for the academic duties of the Cadets; they must therefore be removed from that area."[263]

No matter how dangerous, though, the Citadel Cadets did not have the luxury of enjoying their quarters, as they spent the remainder of the war in the field. Unbeknown to them, their academic studies were over for good! With the Confederacy then "robbing the cradle and the grave" to put troops in the field, the Cadets' service was essential.[264]

The Charleston and Savannah Railroad was a part of one of the three railway trunk systems serving the Confederacy. Its rails traversed the heavily-wooded swamps on causeways built up for extended distances. The swamps covered much of the area between the two port cities from which it took its name. The safety of this road which ran parallel to the coast was vital if the Confederacy was to defend the ports of Charleston and Savannah since troops and equipment could be easily shifted over it between the two cities in a short time. From their foothold in Beaufort and Hilton Head, various Union commanders had attempted to cut the railroad on several occasions. However, due to the relative ease with which threatened points could be reinforced, it was never cut or destroyed.[265]

On November 30, 1864, Maj. Gen. John G. Foster, commanding the Federal Department of the South,

---

[263] Thomas, 176.
[264] Bond, 76.
[265] Robinson, 3-4. The Charleston and Savannah Railroad connects the two port cities through Coosawhatchie, running approximately 110 miles.

ordered Maj. Gen. John P. Hatch to advance from Hilton Head to Boyd's Neck to secure a position where he could eventually link up with Maj. Gen. William T. Sherman's troops who were then approaching Savannah at the end of their destructive "March to the Sea." Hatch's advance would also prevent Confederate reinforcements in South Carolina from reaching the threatened city. His plan was to capture the Charleston and Savannah Railroad near Coosawhatchie and destroy the bridge over Tulifinny Creek, some thirty-two miles northwest of Hilton Head. This would bottle up Gen. Hardee's troops along with much scarce rolling stock in Savannah.[266]

Advancing on November 30 with about 5,500 men and 10 guns, Hatch encountered Gen. Gustavus W. Smith with some 1,400 Georgia militia at Honey Hill, three miles south of Grahamville Station. There, Smith repulsed Hatch, losing about 50 men, while Hatch, reporting losses of 755, retreated back to his position at Boyd's Neck.[267]

On the same day that this brilliant small action took place, Major James B. White received orders to

---

[266] OR, XLIV, 416-425. John G. Foster (1823-1874) (West Point '46) served under Maj. Anderson during the bombardment of Ft. Sumter. He commanded the Dept. of the South from May 1864 to February 1865.

John P. Hatch (1822-1901) (West Point '45) was a cavalry commander assigned to the Dept. of the South in early 1864.

William Joseph Hardee (1815-1873) (West Point '38) rose from Col. to Lt. Gen. He commanded the Dept. of SC, GA, and FL from Sept. 1864 and joined Johnston in NC. Boatner, 374.

William T. Sherman (1820-1891) (West Point '40) served in the Mexican War before resigning to become a banker, lawyer, and superintendent of a military school. He initially commanded a regiment, then rose to corps and army command. Postwar, he rose to be General-in-Chief of the army. Boatner, 750-751.

[267] OR, XLIV, 415-416. Gustavus W. Smith (1822-1896) (West Point '42) commanded the Army of Northern Virginia in mid-1862 and was replaced by Robert E. Lee when he suffered paralysis during the Peninsula Campaign. He resigned from the army when six general officers were appointed over him. In June 1864, he became commander of GA militia.

proceed with his Cadets from their encampment at Orangeburg to the nearest Confederate General for service in the field. As the train carrying the Cadets stopped briefly at Branchville, he received orders from Gov. Bonham to assist in the defense of the Charleston and Savannah Railroad. At Charleston, the Citadel Cadets were joined by the Arsenal Cadets who had entrained in Columbia earlier that day in fine spirits. The entire Cadet Battalion, some 343 strong, spent several days at the Citadel barracks before being ordered to move to Coosawhatchie.[268]

About midnight on December 3rd, the Cadets were summoned to the quadrangle and ordered to prepare to march in thirty minutes. Soon assembled with their arms, accoutrements, knapsacks, and blankets, they marched out of the sally port to the lively tune of a fife and drum, their Corps flag flying over them. Their colors, "Of blue Lyons silk, displaying on one side the arms of the State of South Carolina and the name of the Institution, and on the other side an elaborate wreath of oak leaves, enfolding the inscription— Fort Moultrie, Cowpens, King's Mountain, Eutaw Springs, and below, 'Our Heritage',", had been a prewar presentation from the Washington Light Infantry. The Cadets marched toward the Charleston and Savannah depot on the southern side of the Ashley River where they entrained. Early the next morning, they arrived at Pocotaligo, sixty miles away.[269]

The Cadets were clad in their gray wool and cotton uniforms, their cartridge boxes held in front and behind by crossed straps. Cap boxes were on their waistbelt in front on the right side with their bayonet scabbard on the left. Each Cadet carried an Enfield muzzle loading rifle, weighing, with bayonet, about ten pounds. Faculty officers had, early in the preceding year, finally given up their Federal-style blue uniform and now wore the standard Confederate uniform with green facings. Many Cadets were without

---

[268] Thomas, 206; Patrick, 246; Barnwell, 173-174.
[269] Citadel News, 99, 103-104; Sams, 3; Thomas, 202-203.

overcoats and blankets.[270] Still, the natty, young soldiers were in marked contrast to the veterans stationed on the coast, many of whom were poorly clothed and some without shoes. Rations were meager, and this hardship, combined with the low, unhealthy climate, laid out many of the troops.[271]

As the Cadets took the field, the Battalion was reorganized. Faculty officers of the Academy assumed direct command of the companies while Cadet officers acted as noncommissioned officers and Cadet sergeants and corporals were reduced to the ranks.[272]

On the evening of December 5th, Maj. Gen. Samuel Jones, concerned over enemy attempts to land and gain a foothold in the area, ordered Brig. Gen. James Chesnut, commanding the Reserve Forces of South Carolina, to have the 47th Georgia and a section of Bachman's German Artillery battery board a train. They were then to be held at Coosawhatchie until needed to reinforce any threatened point along the railroad. In his reports, Jones would blame later problems on the failure of his subordinates to promptly obey this order.

On the same day, Gen. Hatch had ordered his troops to withdraw from their entrenchments on Boyd's Neck and proceed to Boyd's Landing by transport. About 7:00 a.m. on the morning of the 6th, his troops began their movement. Debarking at Gregory's Plantation, this reconnaissance in force moved up the dirt road, marching north toward the Coosawhatchie and Beaufort Turnpike. When still a quarter mile from the turnpike, the Federals encountered Confederate pickets and quickly drove them in. The enemy then deployed into line of battle, centering on the road, with their right extending into an open field

---

[270] Kershaw, 147; Bond, 77; Patrick, 176. Coffin says the Cadets carried Springfield rifles, however, other sources confirm that they were equipped with Enfields.
[271] Southern Bivouac, 325.
[272] Barnwell, 175; Bond, 76.

perpendicular to the road, with their left refused or canted rearward to cover that flank.[273]

Col. Charles P. Daniel with his 5th Regiment Georgia Infantry met the initial Yankee advance and repulsed several attacks. Meanwhile, some 700-800 Confederate troops were ordered to the scene under the immediate command of Col. Aaron C. Edwards of the 47th Georgia Infantry to reinforce the beleaguered defenders. Edwards had at his disposal about 200 men of his own regiment under Capt. J.C. Thompson, two companies of the 32nd Georgia, the Augusta Battalion (local defense troops), a company of the 1st South Carolina Regulars under Capt. Mitchell King, about 130 South Carolina militia under Lt. Col. Bacon of the 32nd Georgia, and the Cadet Battalion under Maj. White.[274] Confederate Brig. Gen. Lucius J. Gartrell, commanding a brigade of Georgia Reserves, had also started toward Coosawhatchie with his troops.

The Yankees, having landed in much greater numbers than previously believed, pressed forward to the Coosawhatchie Road. At the same time, the Confederates advanced the left of their line, sheltered by some woods on the north and a heavy skirting of trees and hedge on the south, to the vicinity of the turnpike. This line now moved into a field, driving the

---

[273] OR, LVI, 438-439, 443. Samuel Jones (1820-1887) succeeded Gen. Beauregard as commander of the Dept. of SC, GA, and FL. He was relieved in October 1864 due to poor health, and assumed command of the SC coast.

[274] OR, LVI, 443-444, 447-448. Charles P. Daniel rose from 1st Sgt. to Col. of the 5th GA Infantry.

Aaron Coon Edwards (1833-1868) was Capt. and Maj. of the 11th Bn. GA Infantry and Lt. Col. and Col. of the 47th GA Infantry.

Joseph C. Thompson was Capt. of Co. C (Bullock Guards), 47th GA.

Mitchell King (1841-1916) (ex-'60) graduated from the College of Charleston '61. He enlisted as a Pvt. in the Marion Artillery, then commanded Co. A, 1st SC Regulars. He was Regimental Adjutant when captured at Bentonville. CV, XXV, 32.

Augustus Octavius Bacon (1839-1914) was a pre-war lawyer who became Capt. of Commissary. Postwar, he was a GA legislator and US Senator.

Federals in that area back some 100 or 150 yards. Having become extended and disorganized in its advance, four companies of the 127th New York were now able to attack and break the Confederate line, the grayjackets fleeing before this renewed Federal initiative. The 56th New York joined in the attack, overcame some stubborn resistance, and drove the 5th Georgia back from their position so quickly that they captured that regiment's battle flag.[275] The Georgia Reserves arrived and were ordered up along with a section of artillery to support the 5th Georgia, but they came too late. The entire Confederate line now gave way and fell back in confusion across the Coosawhatchie River, partially destroying the bridge.[276]

The Cadet Battalion, whose train had arrived late on December 4th, camped just beyond the trestle over Tulifinny Creek. Pickets having been posted and after a scanty supper of bacon and hardtack, the Cadets turned in for the night. They spent the 5th distributing a cartload of sweet potatoes while awaiting orders.[277]

On the afternoon of the 6th, the noise of fighting three miles away was clearly evident. Maj. John Jenkins of the 3rd South Carolina Cavalry was in command of the immediate vicinity. Reconnoitering the area, he ordered the Cadets forward to support the 5th Georgia by striking the Federal right flank, now exposed by their rapid advance. The Cadets were hurried at the double-quick in the direction of the battle, as balls whistled harmlessly around them. Reaching the battle scene only to find that the Federals had retired, Maj. White ordered his youthful battalion back to the trestle where they remained in readiness along the embankment. Fatigued by all the marching and

---

[275] Fisk, 62; OR, LVI, 439. Lucius J. Gartrell (1821-1891) served at First Manassas and was soon elected to the Confederate Congress. He was appointed Brig. Gen., commanding a Reserve Brigade, in August 1864 and was wounded at Coosawhatchie. CMH, VI, 418-420.
[276] OR, LVI, 444.
[277] Citadel News, 99-100; Bond, 77.

countermarching in the rain, the Cadets lay down on the cornrows in the nearby field and slept on their arms that night. Cadet George Coffin placed his plate canteen over his face to keep off the rain.[278]

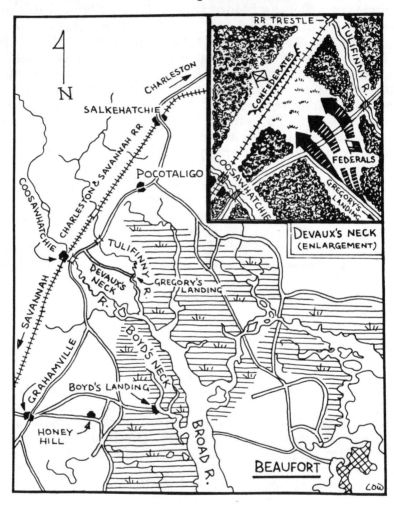

Devaux's Neck

[278] Sellers, 1-2; Citadel News, 100, 105; Bond, 74. George Coffin - See Appendix B.

A mile away, the Federals encamped on the edge of the battlefield. Tensions remained high on both sides during the night. At one point, a skirmish fire from the picket lines caused the entire Cadet Battalion to be formed in line for battle. Another time, as the Cadets rested during the night, a train thundered across the trestle. Confused and startled by the strange noise, Cadet Daniel A. Miller of Company B stumbled about in the cold night and fell into the icy creek.[279]

Later that night, Gen. Jones concentrated all the troops he could collect, adding a battalion of North Carolina Reserves and Bachman's battery to his meager force. Col. Edwards, of the 47th Georgia, the senior colonel, was ordered to attack at dawn. Gen. Gartrell was to make a demonstration from Coosawhatchie as soon as Edwards' guns were heard. If Edwards' attack was successful, Gartrell was to attack vigorously.[280]

At sunrise on the 7th, the skirmish line, composed of the Citadel Cadets and three companies of the 5th Georgia, all under the command of Maj. White, advanced to test the strength of the enemy occupying a fortified hill. The Arsenal Cadets followed, with the 47th Georgia on the right and Col. Bacon's militia on the left. The skirmishers advanced swiftly and steadily across a field of brown broom grass and into a wooded area while "a light frost made the air strike sharply on our faces...."[281] As the skirmishers reached the far edge of the woods in front of the Federal position, they encountered a brisk fire. Farish Furman, a Third Classman from Greenville, later remembered "...marching through the woods when I saw a stream of fire shoot out from the bushes in front of me, accompanied by the sharp crack of a rifle...I was the second man shot at by the enemy. The first

---

[279] Sellers, 2; Citadel News, 99-100, 105. Daniel A. Miller - See Appendix B.
[280] OR, LVI, 444.
[281] Bond, 74; Sellers, 2; Coffin, 100; OR, LVI, 447-448, Citadel News, 100.

had his jacket cut, and the third (Green) was shot in the face. The ball fired at me missed my head a few inches and buried itself in a tree close by."[282] The Confederate front was shifted until it crossed the road at right angles, thus engaging the entire Yankee line. Fighting became general against the Federals who had deployed four or five regiments in a strong line. The Cadets, partially sheltered by the trees, poured a heavy fire into the enemy.[283]

Hungry, shoeless and thinly clad, the Georgians proceeded, in conjunction with the Cadets, through the lagoons and swamps, pushing the Yankees back over the Old Pocotaligo Road until the ragged gray line was flanked within a hundred yards of a Federal battery they had been driving toward. A fierce storm of grapeshot now forced them back across the road where they sought cover behind the railroad embankment. A battalion of Georgia reserves, sent to reinforce them, proved useless by fleeing at the first shots.[284] Cadet Joseph Barnwell picked up a discarded enemy haversack as he crossed the roadway. Upon reaching the relative safety of the woods, he opened it and found a piece of relatively fresh bread. Amazed, he yelled to his company commander, Capt. Hugh Thompson, "Captain, they feed those fellows better than our people do us for see this bread and we have only hardtack and not much of that." Thompson laughingly declined a piece of the booty.

Just then a bullet struck Barnwell above his left knee, knocking him to the ground. Lt. Amory Coffin, Assistant Professor and the Adjutant of the Cadet Battalion, ran up, calling out to the Cadets, "Don't let us abandon our boys." As he spoke, a bullet struck him in the forehead. Coffin was knocked unconscious but escaped serious injury because he was wearing

---

[282] Furman, December 28, 1864, Citadel News, 100-101. Farish Furman - See Appendix B.
[283] OR, LVI, 448; Sellers, 2; *Sunday News*, Sept. 2, 1897; Citadel News, 101.
[284] *Charleston Courier*, Dec. 23, 1864; OR, XLIV, 439; Furman, Dec. 28, 1864.

two military caps, the visors of which saved him from anything more serious than a deep cut in the forehead. For now, his companions thought he was killed, and he was solemnly borne to the rear by Cadets Eugene Stone and Charles E. Coffin, a younger brother. There, he regained consciousness in the ambulance.

Meanwhile, Cadets Lee Hagood, Bob Hayne, and others came up to help the crippled Barnwell to the rear. He removed his belt and cartridge box but requested that his rifle be brought off with him. Two surgeons examined the leg and advised that they would have to amputate. Barnwell implored them not to if there was any way to save it. Reluctantly, the doctors chloroformed him and removed the bullet while leaving his leg intact. Eventually, he was evacuated to his home in Charleston where he recovered, keeping his leg until his death sixty-one years later.[285]

The Cadet skirmishers, having been engaged since dawn, were now ordered to reinforce the Georgians behind the embankment. As they lay behind the embankment, one of the Georgians pointed out to his comrades, "Look, there comes the Cadets!" Advancing in their new uniforms, the Cadets appeared to the tough veterans as if they were on dress parade.[286] As the Federals prepared to charge their position, Maj. White rode his horse up and down the line and cautioned, "Steady, Cadets! Let them come well up" while admonishing them to remain concealed behind the breastworks.[287]

Lt. Ben S. Williams, Adjutant of the 47th Georgia Regiment, recalled the Cadets' bearing under fire when, despite all their training and discipline, the youngsters kept popping their heads above the breastworks to take a look at "the Yankees." Their of-

---

[285] Barnwell, 176-177. Eugene Earle Stone, Charles Edmonston Coffin, Lee Hagood, & Robert Brevard Hayne - See Appendix B.

[286] *Sunny South*; Citadel News, 105; Teague.

[287] Sellers, 3; Boy Soldiers of Tulifinny. Teague. Benjamin Hammet Teague (1846-1921) was a private in Co. B, Hampton Legion. Postwar, he was a dentist and Aiken city alderman.

ficers kept commanding the Cadets, "Down Mr. -----, down Mr. -----," calling out the names of the offenders, prefacing each with the title "mister." The veterans of the 47th, who hadn't been called "mister" in almost four years were highly amused, one remarking, "Them Charleston people is the damdest politest officers to their men I ever struck up with in the army."[288]

As the enemy, their bayonets fixed, emerged from the swamp in front of the Cadets and advanced into the open field, Maj. White rose in his stirrups and gave the order, "Attention battalion, ready, aim, fire." At the command "Attention battalion," the Cadets sprang to their feet, and the order "fire" caused the three hundred plus rifles to belch forth a staggering wave of lead. The advancing Federal line quickly broke, and both Georgians and Cadets advanced to turn their enemy's retreat into a rout.[289]

Company A, the Citadel Cadets, had exhausted its ammunition in the three hour skirmish and was now ordered to retire to replenish its supply. Company B, the Arsenal Cadets, had been held in reserve until now and were moved to relieve them during the brisk fire. To avoid the shell and musketry fire, they had been lying down on the swampy ground.

In the confusion of the movement, many of the Arsenal Cadets forgot whether they were no. 1 or no. 2 in the firing order. Their commander, Capt. John P. Thomas, rushed to their front with his sword drawn and gave the command, "Halt!", "Fall in!", according to height, and when the line was formed, the commands, "Front!", "Dress to the right," "Count off from the right," were given and then, their discipline restored, the Cadets double-quicked to their positions on the skirmish line.[290]

Fighting continued for several hours as the Confederates steadily advanced, retaking the road and pushing the Federals back to their entrench-

---

[288] *Sunday News*, Sept. 2, 1897.
[289] Sellers, 3; Citadel News, 101; Teague; Thomas, 179-180.
[290] A Confederate Soldier's Memoirs.

ments.[291] Adjutant Williams, who had carried the order sending them into action recalled "...the splendid bearing of the Cadets under fire...Never did they cross their Citadel square on drill or dress parade with firmer tread or prouder bearing than when advancing on the enemy at Tulifinny." One of the 47th Georgia veterans, noting the Cadet advance exclaimed: "them youngsters'll fight like hell."[292] Robert Heriot, a gunner in Bachman's Battery and former Arsenal Cadet, was also impressed by his former schoolmates, "The Cadets fought as if on dress parade. Their firing could be distinguished above the roar of battle by the regularity of their discharges."[293]

As the Cadets were preparing to attack, another grizzled veteran of the 47th Georgia approached Williams and asked: "Captain, do you reckon them Dandy-Jim looking kids will stand square up to the rack when they strike the Yanks?" "Morgan," Williams responded, "that is South Carolina blood. You don't know it." "The ---- I don't," replied Morgan, "What was the colonel who made up this regiment? Why, durn it, my daddy and mammy was both born and married somewhere in this little old hot fool State and didn't move to Georgy till I was most big enough to wear breeches." After the engagement, Williams elicited Morgan's opinion of the Cadets' conduct under fire and got the terse answer: "Damned if they didn't fight like Hood's Texicans."[294]

Maj. White later proudly reported, "Every Cadet acted with conspicuous gallantry and showed that the discipline of his Academy had made him a thorough

---

291 OR, LVI, 442, 446; Thomas 180; Sellers, 3; Citadel News, 101.
292 *Sunday News*, Sept. 2, 1897.
293 CV, XXX, 415. Robert Heriot (1847-?) (ex-'66) enlisted with Capt. J.K. Bachman's Charleston Battery in August 1864 and served through the remainder of the war. Alive in Little Rock, AR 1917.
294 *Sunday News*, Sept. 2, 1897; A Confederate Soldier's Memoirs.

soldier for the battlefield."[295] Maj. Gen. Samuel Jones complimented the "gallant body of youths ...who, for the first time felt the fire of the enemy, so bore themselves as to win the admiration of the veterans who observed and served with them."[296]

One of the Cadets exhibited this brand of discipline during the battle when he escorted a prisoner to Col. Bacon, commander of the left of the line. The prisoner was finely equipped, a matter quickly noted by the Colonel. "Young gentleman," the Colonel addressed the Cadet, "take anything the prisoner has on." Solemnly, the youth replied, "No, Colonel, I never rob a prisoner." A fellow Cadet, Lee Hagood, carried in his pocket during the engagement a tiny mascot, a tame flying squirrel, which had been presented to him by a young lady friend. Both the pet and Hagood were commended for their cool behavior.[297]

Breaking off contact late in the afternoon, the Federals retreated back to Devaux's Neck where the sound of axes and spades could be heard throughout the night as they entrenched. As the Federals withdrew and the Confederates were preparing to return to their own encampment, three Cadets spotted what they took to be a Federal soldier standing under an oak tree about a hundred yards distant. Each of the three took a shot, but the Yankee held his ground and did not move. Though regarding themselves as excellent marksmen, the Cadets did not know what to make of the obstinate Federal who refused to move or be shot down. The three determined to charge this enemy who still stood his ground throughout their grand dash. The object of their attention turned out to be a Federal soldier's overcoat hanging on the limb of the tree, pierced with three bullet holes.[298]

That night the Cadet Battalion was withdrawn from the line and went into camp with fires to warm their soaked uniforms and heat their meager meal.

---

[295] Thomas, 207.
[296] OR, LVI, 445.
[297] CV, XXX, 415; Meet, 40.
[298] Dozier, 43.

The Cadets had not had anything but hardtack and bacon the night before. While stationed at Tulifinny Creek, the Cadets did their own cooking, a practice which resulted in Cadet George M. Coffin, a Citadel Fourth Classman from Charleston, being laid out under the trees when he got sick from making biscuits without "rising." Lacking tents or shelter, they lived in the open air.[299] They had been called out on such short notice, they had not gathered the supplies necessary for field service. Thus, in the December 10th issue of the Charleston newspapers, Chaplain Edwin T. Winkler and Surgeon Robert W. Gibbes, Capt. Thomas' father-in-law, appealed on behalf of the Cadets for spirits, tea, coffee, sugar, and rags for hospital use or any other items which soldiers needed.[300]

During the engagement on the 7th, the Battalion of State Cadets had suffered eight casualties. Lt. Amory Coffin received a slight head wound. Cadet William Bailey Patterson of Company A was mortally wounded, and Cadets Joseph W. Barnwell and Edward C. McCarty of Company A were severely wounded. Cadets Stephen F. Hollingsworth, Allen J. Green, Albert R. Heyward, and William A. Pringle of Company A were slightly wounded.[301] Other Cadets were likewise struck, but were lucky not to suffer injury. Citadel Fourth Classman James H. Boatwright of Richland District was struck, the ball penetrating and lodging in a small Testament in his breast pocket. Cadets Jacob C. Lyons and Waddy Thompson

---

[299] Bond, 77; Sellers, 3.

[300] *Charleston Daily Courier*, December 10, 1864; *Charleston Tri-Weekly Courier*, December 10, 1864. Edwin Theodore Winkler (1823-1883) was a Baptist minister in GA, Charleston, AL, and an editor. A son attended the Citadel.

Robert Wilson Gibbes (1809-1866) was a physician in Charleston, Columbia, and VA. Writer. During the war, he was Surgeon-General of SC.

[301] Thomas, 207-208; Citadel News, 101; *Charleston Mercury*, December 19, 1864; Barnwell, 175-176; Coffin, 101. E.C. McCarty, S.F. Hollingsworth, and W.A. Pringle - See Appendix B.

were likewise hit.[302] The Confederates had lost 52 in the engagement, while the enemy reported losses of 300 killed and wounded.[303]

The 8th passed quietly while Federal engineers made a survey, and enemy troops spent the day improving and strengthening their position.[304] Brig. Gen. Beverly H. Robertson, a one time cavalry commander under Jeb Stuart, was given command of the troops from Bee's Creek to Pocotaligo. He ordered the Cadets to the left of the line where they spent the day throwing up breastworks parallel to and on the east side of the railroad.[305]

On the morning of the 9th, enemy pioneers busily fell trees to clear a field of fire for their artillery, exposing the railroad another half mile in front. The Federal artillery, some eight guns, opened a rapid and continuous fire on the Confederate left. This was around nine in the morning and, after an hour, enemy skirmishers advanced on the Confederate breastworks, hotly engaging the left of the Rebel line. After driving in Confederate pickets, the Yankees continued to advance until a severe fire forced them to seek cover behind a low knoll. As artillery fire continued to plow the ground around them, another Federal effort to turn the left failed when it bogged down in the swamp. The enemy advance stalled, and with night approaching, the Yankees withdrew.[306] Out of range of the fighting, the Cadet Battalion had spent most of

[302] *Charleston Daily Courier,* December 23, 1864; Boatwright Family. James H. Boatwright, Jacob C. Lyons, and Waddy Thompson - See Appendix B.
[303] OR, LVI, 446-448.
[304] McGrath, 135, Naval OR, XVI, 107.
[305] OR, LVI, 444, 446; *Charleston Daily Courier,* December 23, 1864; Sellers, 2-3. Beverly Holcombe Robertson (1826-1910) (West Point '49) began the war as a Col. of Cavalry and rose to Brig. Gen. in June 1862. He served briefly in SC before being ordered to Knoxville. He returned to SC in 1864 and was with Gen. Johnston until the surrender. Postwar, he was a businessman in Washington.
[306] McGrath, 135-137; Southern Bivouac, 326.

the day marching and countermarching, prepared to give support wherever necessary.[307]

Abandoning any further direct attempts to cut the railroad, the Federals began establishing batteries within range of the tracks in order to dominate them. By allowing trains to move toward Savannah, they planned to bottle them up there to deny any future use in reinforcing and supplying Savannah from Charleston, as well as the eventual evacuation of the Georgia port.[308] While the Federals did threaten the railroad with artillery, they never seriously damaged it nor did they capture it until Sherman's march into South Carolina the next month.

The Cadets spent the next few weeks in a camp near the railroad in the woods adjoining a "broom grass" field. They lived in the open air with no tents or other shelter except "the clouded canopy of the heavens."[309] Rations were short, and generally just one meal, supper, was prepared. Drinking water came from a ditch by the side of the track, the same ditch also serving for washing and other purposes.[310] Some of the pay Cadets were fortunate in having servants accompany them in the field.[311] In a letter to his mother on December 18th, Farish C. Furman wrote from their camp near Coosawhatchie: "To give you some idea of the life we lead I will tell you that I have not pulled off my clothes for fourteen days."[312]

The incoming fourth class of the Arsenal joined the Battalion toward the end of December, the boys aged 15-18 years. The Cadets of the Arsenal were promoted to the Citadel. Much of the time thereafter was spent in drilling the new recruits.[313] A militia company from Marion District and a youthful com-

---

[307] *Charleston Daily Courier*, December 23, 1864; Citadel News, 102.

[308] CV, XXX, 415; Thomas, 181; Sellers, 3; Citadel News, 101-102; *Charleston Daily Courier*, December 23, 1864; UDC, XXIV, 110.

[309] Bond, 77; Sellers 2; Kershaw, 150.

[310] CV, XXX, 415.

[311] Adger-Smyth-Flynn Family, December 25, 1864.

[312] Furman, December 28, 1864.

[313] Bond, 77, 81; Patrick, 248-249; CV, XXIX, 417.

company from Marion District and a youthful company from Abbeville arrived soon after the fighting and camped in the old field to the west of the railroad. The Marion company knew very little of military tactics and was encumbered with pots, kettles, frying pans, bedding, and other paraphernalia. Cadets were detailed to drill these companies which had not yet even learned basic maneuvers.[314]

During this period, Cadet Waddy Thompson, a Citadel Fourth Classman from Greenville, was wounded by the accidental discharge of his rifle.[315] Another afternoon while the makeshift parade ground was covered with Cadets drilling, Federal shells began tearing up the area. Fourth Classman William Dehon "Big Bill" Palmer of Charleston was walking through camp in the act of returning a borrowed fry pan when a shell tore off his left hand. Palmer ran around crazily until he fell unconscious. Fortunately, his brother-in-law, Dr. Peter Gourdin, a surgeon, was close by and ministered to him, amputating the remains of his hand. Despite this obvious military handicap, Palmer remained with the battalion until the end of the war.[316] The Battalion included at least two other handicapped Cadets, incoming Fourth Classman Andrew F. O'Brien of Colleton District, late a sergeant in the 1st (Gregg's) South Carolina, who had lost his right arm at Spotsylvania Court House in May, and Leonard Yancey Dean from Edgefield who had lost an arm while serving in the Hampton Legion. Presumably, they and Palmer would be excused from future infantry drill "under arms." O'Brien would be selected in 1889 as one of the

---

[314] Sellers, 4; A Confederate Soldier's Memoirs; CV, XXIX, 417.

[315] *Charleston Daily Courier*, December 23, 1864.

[316] Bond, 77; Sellers, 3; CV, XXIX, 417-418; UDC, XXIV, 110; Citadel News, 102. W.D. Palmer - See Appendix B.

Peter Gaillard Gourdin II (1832-1876) graduated from Harvard and practiced medicine in Pineville. He was surgeon of Capt. Simons' Company (Etiwan Rangers).

three Confederate soldiers to represent the State of South Carolina at the funeral of Jefferson Davis.[317]

These new Cadets, however badly maimed, were fortunate. Sgt. Madison F. Hawthorn of the 12th SC Infantry, scheduled to report on Dec. 3, 1864, had been killed in action on the last day of September near Petersburg. Likewise, Pvt. John C.C. Thompson of the 1st SC Cavalry, scheduled to report at the same time, had succumbed to diptheria the previous June in Ladies Hospital in Columbia. Finally, Pvt. Samuel H. Reid of the 26th SC could not report since he was confined as a prisoner of war at Point Lookout, MD.[318]

Leading an arduous outdoor life, the Cadets continued to drill the new troops as well as spending a good deal of time on picket duty. Cadet George Coffin had time to contemplate his aversion to dying at the age of 17 as he stood in an open field watching for the ever-present enemy sharpshooters. One morning the Cadets were rushed to the breastworks on the other side of the railroad to fire several volleys at an unseen enemy, but were soon withdrawn, a select few being detailed to remain in place as sharpshooters.[319]

The officers and 114 new Cadets of the Arsenal were ordered back to Columbia soon after the engagements at Tulifinny to commence their academic and military work. The Citadel Cadets remained in camp until Christmas Day when they were ordered to James Island, encamping near Battery Number 2, close to Legare's Crossroads and Secessionville. There, they performed picket duty, twenty-four hours

---

[317] Bond, 81; CSR; UDC, XIII, 89. Andrew F. O'Brien and L. Yancey Dean - See Appendix B.

[318] Madison F. Hawthorn (1845-1864) had enlisted in Co. F (Means Light Infantry), 12th Regt. SC Infantry. He had been detailed to the Brigade Sharpshooters when killed.

John Caldwell Calhoun Thompson (1846-1864) was from Anderson District and had enlisted April 1, 1864, in Co. F (Allen Hussars), 1st SC Cavalry.

Samuel Henry Reid (1846-1913) of Cheraw enlisted in Co. E, 26th SC Infantry. He was captured March 25, 1865 and confined until July 1865.

[319] Bond, 77-78.

on and twenty-four hours off. John C. Sellers of
Marion remembered the duty being hard but enjoy-
able, the Cadets now having tents and living in the
open salt water breezes.[320]

Maj. White, in his official report of the activities of
the Cadets, declared:

> "I would take this opportunity to express
> my obligations to the officers under my
> command for the zeal, ability, and
> alacrity with which they discharged their
> duties. Nor can I fail to call to your atten-
> tion those young but noble sons of our
> State. Upon the battlefield, in camp, on
> the march, on picket, or working upon
> defenses, they were ready for every
> emergency; manifesting at all times, and
> under the most trying circumstances, a
> manly and soldierly aspect, not finding
> fault with those in authority, but doing
> their duty cheerfully and well."[321]

---

[320] Thomas, 207; Bond, 78; Sams, 3; Sellers, 4; Kershaw, 150.
John C. Sellers - See Appendix B.
[321] Thomas, 208.

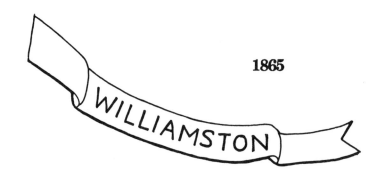

1865

The outlook for the new year was rather bleak for the fortunes of South Carolina and the Confederacy. Savannah, Georgia had fallen to Sherman in late December and, on the 19th of January, his troops began their march northward. While it was uncertain whether their objective was to be Charleston or Augusta, Georgia, the Federals nevertheless made it widely known that they intended to "make South Carolina howl." The Yankee soldiers felt very vindictive toward the Palmetto State, and even Federal Army Chief of Staff Gen. Henry Halleck suggested in a letter to Sherman in Savannah in late December that "...should you capture Charleston I hope that by some accident the place may be destroyed; and if a little salt should be sown upon the site, it may prevent the growth of future crops of nullification and secession." Sherman responded, "I will bear in mind your hint as to Charleston, and I do not think 'salt' will be necessary. When I move, the Fifteenth Corps will be on the right of the right wing, and their position will bring them into Charleston first; and if you have watched the history of this corps, you will have remarked that it generally does its work pretty well." As Sherman moved north, uncertainty over his objective forced the Confederate command to split their troops, some covering Charleston and the rest in the Augusta area. However, with Charleston being a potential trap for any troops then stationed there, preparations were begun to evacuate the port city.[322]

---

[322] Bond, 80; OR, XLIV, 702, 741, 799. Henry W. Halleck (1815-1872) (West Point '39) served as Lincoln's military adviser and General in Chief. When Grant was given command of the

As Sherman moved into South Carolina, Gen. Lee
ordered Gen. Wade Hampton back to his native state.
With him, Hampton was to take the remnants of
Young's and Dunovant's Brigades to face Sherman.
This transfer would also afford the cavalry the opportunity to procure new mounts for an eventual return
to the Virginia theater. On the same day that
Sherman began his move northward, Hampton notified his officers of the transfer and issued the necessary order: "The men will take with them their arms,
their cooking utensils and equipments, and will be
prepared for a winter campaign."

Arriving by train in Columbia in early February,
the veteran troopers received a rousing welcome.
Columbia was gaily decorated in their honor. Bunting
and Confederate flags were draped from balconies
and windows including those of the State House. The
city was filled with old men, women, and children,
many of them ill, mostly refugees from Sherman's
harsh line of march. Accompanying them were numerous hawkers, making money by providing life's
now scarce necessities at exorbitant prices.

The Columbians, nervous at the approach of the
Yankee juggernaut, enthusiastically greeted Butler's
Division as their saviors. The city was still apprehen-
sive though, thinking that Columbia would be the
next Federal objective after Charleston. The city had
few fortifications and was virtually ungarrisoned, except for the Arsenal Cadets and local Reserves. Going
into camp outside of Columbia on the Lexington side
of the Congaree River, Butler's Division dispatched
scouts to make contact with Sherman's advance and
ascertain his movements.[323] As Sherman approached
Columbia, he was opposed only by some minor skirmishing.

Federal armies in March 1864, Halleck was reduced to Chief of
Staff.
[323] Hampton, 388-390; Wells, 79; Brooks, 403; Calhoun, 170;
OR, XLVII, pt. 2, 1071; Kennedy, 56.

Since the Arsenal Cadets had left their Citadel comrades near Tulifinny Creek in mid-December to begin their academic studies, additional Cadets had been arriving almost daily as the Board of Visitors encouraged a large matriculation, hoping to thus provide the nucleus of a State Guard. The new Cadets lacked uniforms and presented a motley appearance when on parade. In addition to their studies, they did provost duty, a difficult task when Wheeler's loosely disciplined cavalry was around. On January 19th, the Cadets were ordered out to guard seven hundred enemy officers confined on the grounds of the State Insane Asylum.[324]

As the enemy approached the capital city, these young men, some no more than fifteen years old, were again called away from their books. This time, they were ordered to support Thomas' Battery, a small 2 gun battery armed with obsolescent 6 pounders, which guarded the Congaree River Bridge at the foot of Gervais Street. Several Cadets who had previously been in artillery service manned the pieces while the remainder of the battalion acted as infantry support.[325] The battery shelled part of the Federal force on the opposite side of the river which caused Sherman in his *Memoirs* to note:

> "This provoked me much at the time, for it was wanton mischief, as Generals Beauregard and Hampton must have been convinced that they could not prevent our entrance into Columbia. I have always contended that I would have been justified in retaliating for this unnecessary act of war, but did not, though I always characterized it as it deserved."

---

[324] Thomas, 181; Bond, 78, 82; Patrick, 252; Lewis, "Arsenal Cadets Before Sherman."
[325] Thomas, 195-196; Sams, 3; Letter of J.P. Thomas to R.J. Davant, December 6, 1865; Lewis, "Arsenal Cadets Before Sherman."

This failure to retaliate was certainly arguable by the South Carolinians whose capital city lay in blackened ruins before his departure.[326]

Lt. Sams echoed Sherman's memoirs, calling the firing a "grave mistake. It may have delayed for a few hours the entrance of Gen. Sherman into Columbia, but it very likely increased his vindictiveness."[327]

The Board of Visitors met in Columbia on February 15, and, among other decisions, communicated to Capt. Thomas that his position as Colonel of a Regiment of Detailed Men was inconsistent with his position as the Superintendent of the Arsenal. Thomas, who had organized a battalion of local troops in 1863 and taken them to Charleston during a crisis in 1864, had assumed the duties with the approval of Gen. Jones, the Board Chairman, and at the request of Gen. James Chesnut, commanding South Carolina's Reserve forces. He had done so with the understanding that it would not conflict with his responsibilities at the Academy. Apprised of the new Board's view regarding the regiment, Thomas turned command of his unit over to the Lt. Col. and devoted his full efforts to the activities of the Arsenal.[328]

On the night of February 15th, Confederate engineers fired the bridge over the Congaree. A small force was left at the battery as it came under fire while the remainder of the Cadets returned to the Arsenal where they were ordered to act as provost guard to Brig. Gen. Evander M. Law (Citadel '56), Acting Provost Marshal Gen. under Gen. Beauregard, who was, on the 16th, appointed to command all troops in South Carolina. Under their commissioned officers, the Cadets patrolled Main Street from City Hall to the State House, trying to maintain some order while stores were broken into and plundered by camp followers and hoodlums.

Soon after daylight on the 16th, Federal skirmishers and artillery appeared on the west bank of the

---

[326] Sherman, II, 279; Harwell, 125; Who Burnt Columbia?, 29.
[327] Sams, 3.
[328] Thomas, 194-195.

Congaree River opposite the city and opened fire upon the Cadet Battery and the city. One shot passed through the third story of the Arsenal while another shell exploded over a chimney of the mess hall where some of the Cadets were dining. In the afternoon,

The different detachments of Cadets who had been patrolling the streets to preserve order were called in, and were drawn up in line, facing the street (Main) our backs to the City Hall, where Gen. E.M. Law had his office. The street was packed with marauders, some drunk, most of them on horseback and loaded with booty taken from stores and residences that had been broken into. Quite a number were drunk and reckless. One, more daring than the rest, was urging his horse against our ranks forcing Capt. Thomas to give the command Charge Bayonets to protect our line and our lives. Gen. Law was notified. Immediately he assumed command. Opening a way through the ranks, his wounded arm in a sling, he went at once to the ring leader of the rabble, seized him by the shoulder, pulled him from his horse, called for a file of Cadets and placed him in jail.

That night, Gov. Magrath, whose 19 year old son and namesake was with the Citadel Cadets now retreating from Charleston, ordered the Arsenal to be evacuated. Officers and men reported to Gen. Albert C. Garlington, Adjutant and Inspector General of South Carolina, now in command of State Troops at Columbia. Near midnight, the 153 Cadets, organized into a battalion of two companies, marched from the Arsenal and joined Garlington's Brigade. The Citadel flag, which had been sent from Charleston along with

most other valuables and property for safekeeping,
was brought out and formally placed in the charge of
a Cadet as the Arsenal Battalion began to slowly move
out of Columbia.[329]

They filed out of Columbia by way of the State
House, and followed Beauregard's retreating army to
White Oak, located on the Charlotte, Columbia, and
Augusta Railroad north of Winnsboro. Capt. Thomas
was a strict disciplinarian and demanded that the
Cadets maintain a military formation during the retreat. On the day after the Cadets left, Federal troops
entered Columbia and plundered and burned the
Arsenal, destroying all the buildings except the officers' quarters. Archives of the Citadel and Arsenal
were both destroyed, the Citadel records having recently been sent there for safekeeping.[330]

Beauregard had anticipated that Charlotte was
Sherman's next objective and ordered Garlington's
Brigade, once it had crossed the Wateree River at
Peay's Ferry, to return to the interior of South
Carolina after the passage of Sherman's troops. On
the 17th, however, Garlington found himself being
pressed by Federal cavalry and realized that his
troops were immediately in front of Sherman's main
force, now advancing on Cheraw rather than
Charlotte.

By the time he reached Lancaster Court House,
Gen. Garlington recognized that his raw troops were
in no condition for active service and disbanded all of

---

[329] Thomas, 196; Sams, 3-4; Lewis, "Arsenal Cadets Before
Sherman." Evander McIver Law (1836-1920) (Citadel '56) was
commissioned from Alabama and served in the Virginia the-
ater and at Chickamauga, having attained the rank of Brig.
Gen. He commanded at Columbia during Sherman's approach
and took command of Butler's cavalry brigade in February
1865.
    Andrew G. Magrath, Jr. (1845-1894) served as a 1st Lt. and
Aide to Gen. James Conner. Postwar, he was a lawyer and
Probate Judge.
[330] Thomas, 196, 229-230; Sams, 5; Thomas Report; Lewis,
"Arsenal Cadets before Sherman"; Lewis, "Their First and
Last Fight"; DuBos, 125; Association of Graduates, 1877, 11.

his brigade, except for Capt. Frederick's cavalry company and the Arsenal Cadets. As the cavalry company rode on to join Lt. Gen. William J. Hardee's retreating corps, the Cadets under Capt. Thomas were ordered to report as soon as possible to the Governor. With Sherman's cavalry within a few miles of Lancaster Court House, Capt. Thomas put his youthful charges into light marching order and managed to cross Lynches Creek before being cut off. Thomas then pressed on to Mt. Croghan in Chesterfield District and rested there briefly while he dispatched a courier to General Hardee for information on the military situation.

Hardee informed Thomas that Sherman was marching toward Cheraw and advised the Cadets to report there. Realizing that the Cadets would be subject to capture before reaching Hardee, Capt. Thomas redirected his march to Ansonville, North Carolina where the ladies of the town fed the tired and hungry boys. The Cadets had now arrived on the left flank of the Federal advance. Marching cross-country from Wadesboro, North Carolina, to the railroad near Charlotte, the Cadets were transported by train to Beauregard's headquarters in Charlotte. Later they continued on by rail to Chester, South Carolina, where they detrained and proceeded across country to Spartanburg Court House, arriving there on the 8th of March.[331]

During their stint on James Island, Citadel Cadet John C. Sellers messed with John C. Tiedeman and James P. Allen of Charleston, along with Lewis Meng of Union. Meng's father sent him a black cook while Tiedeman's father kept the mess supplied with groceries and Allen's father, a local truck farmer, provided fresh vegetables. Combined with their normal rations, they ate so well that Sellers was soon able to

---

[331] Thomas, 197-198; Sams, 4; Lewis, "Arsenal Cadets Before Sherman."

button only the top button of his uniform coat.[332] While these three Cadets were well provisioned, others did not subsist quite so well. Farish Furman wrote his mother on February 1, 1865, that "Living here is terribly expensive to those who depend upon the rations issued them by the government. The soldiers say that rations have gradually dwindled away until not more than half of a sufficiency is issued."[333]

Mid-February 1865 had found the Citadel Cadets still picketing the lower end of James Island in the direction of the Stono River. On the afternoon of the 16th, Cadet Sellers and his comrades could plainly see Federal pickets and the movements of Federal transports. That night, the last Cadets burned their tents and destroyed extraneous supplies as they were removed from the line and hastily marched to the long bridge over the Ashley River to catch up with the remainder of the battalion which had crossed earlier. Early the next morning, they reunited with the main body of the Cadet Battalion. Brigaded with other Palmetto units under Brig. Gen. Stephen Elliott, they formed a unit of Lieut. Gen. William J. Hardee's forces, now evacuating the Charleston peninsula.[334]

The Cadets marched to St. Stephen and, after a few days' wait, secured transportation to Cheraw. There, they became the rear guard of the army, actually crossing the bridge over the Pee Dee River into Marlboro District behind their cavalry. While at the bridge, an advancing enemy battery quickly established itself on a hill near a church and opened fire on the withdrawing Confederates. The bridge was burned before the enemy could cross. At a crossroads about a mile and a half from Cheraw, the Cadets were allowed to take their first rest in many hours. Despite artillery fire bursting around him, seventeen year old John Sellers and others were sound asleep in a few

---

[332] Sellers, 5. John C. Tiedeman and J.P. Allen - See Appendix B.
[333] Furman, February 1, 1865.
[334] Sellers, 5; Thomas, 195; Brooks, 441; UDC, XXXVII, 83.

moments.[335] The Cadets' conduct was to cause their brigade commander, Brig. Gen. Stephen Elliott, to comment, "When the danger is in front, I put the Cadets in front and when the danger is in the rear, I put the Cadets in the rear."[336]

The March rains were incessant, swelling the streams and making roads almost impassable as the Cadets trudged across North Carolina, through Fayetteville and Smithfield. On the long, wearying march from Cheraw to Raleigh, Maj. White was often seen carrying as many of the Cadets' muskets across the withers of his horse as he could hold. Many times he dismounted and walked for miles in the mud while two, sometimes three, exhausted boys rode on his horse. Before they reached Raleigh, Gov. Magrath recalled the Cadets, instructing them to meet him at Spartanburg, his new headquarters, since both Charleston and Columbia were now in enemy hands. A group of Federal prisoners captured when Hampton had attacked Kilpatrick's camp were escorted on to Raleigh, and then the Cadets proceeded to Spartanburg.[337]

As the Cadets were evacuating Charleston, Federal troops marched unopposed into the city and raised their flag over the customhouse and the Citadel. Maj. White had left Dr. William Hume in charge of the building there when the Cadets were ordered into the field in December. Hume was the long-time professor of science whose academic achievements lent prestige to the institution but whose military inability was legendary. Once, while acting as officer in charge, he had taken the corps out for a drill. In his proverbially ill-fitting uniform, he had fallen down in front of them, and the Cadets had marched over him, eventually halting against the King Street fence. Hume had gotten up, called the Cadet Captain and, pointing to the sally port, told him

---

[335] Sellers, 6.
[336] Thomas MSS, V, 8; Thomas, 212.
[337] Sellers, 6-7; Brooks, 442; White, 244.

to take the Cadets there as he was going home. Such incidents, as well as his tendency to give commands on dress parade, such as, "Gentlemen, will you be kind enough to *present arms*," had caused school authorities to long ago strip Hume of any real military functions. To this gentle, eccentric scholar, aged sixty-three, now fell the duty of officially surrendering the Citadel buildings. The conquerors, in turn, kept the old gentleman up until 2:00 a.m. as a hostage against the building being blown up.[338]

One of the Yankees was to recall:

> "Soon after reaching the citadel, hundreds—mostly blacks—gathered on the green in front of the building, and all endeavoring to give expression to their joy, cheering, shouting, laughing, doing whatever they could to express their pleasure at seeing the Yanks..."

> "The fine buildings showed the strokes of our guns."[339]

After the shelling of Columbia by Sherman, Confederate forces evacuated the city early on the morning of February 17th. Hampton departed Columbia with Young's Brigade, leaving by the Winnsboro Road while Butler's Division moved out the Camden Road. At Killian's Mill, the commands united and bivouacked for the night. The next day, Butler cut the dam at Killian's, flooding the low ground to impede the advancing enemy 17th Corps, which had appeared on the other side of the mill pond. Beauregard, commanding the department, now ordered a retreat to Winnsboro, thinking that Charlotte was to be Sherman's next objective. Butler was ordered to watch Sherman's right flank. As he

---

[338] Thomas, 240; Walker, 1; Bond, 79-80.
[339] Denison, 298-299.

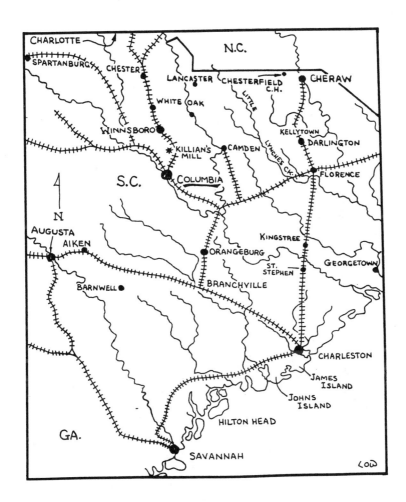

South Carolina

advanced, he encountered Federals on each road leading into Columbia. During the afternoon, however, a captured artificer informed Butler that the supply train to which he had been attached was ordered to camp that night at Rocky Mount on the Wateree River. This indicated to Butler that Cheraw, not Charlotte, was Sherman's real objective.

After sending couriers to Beauregard and Hampton to inform them of Sherman's movements, Butler then withdrew in the direction of Lancaster Court House, where he changed direction, and proceeded east toward Little Lynches Creek. All along their route, his men constantly skirmished with enemy flankers and bummers. Prior to reaching Cantey's Plantation on Little Lynches Creek, Butler decided to make a night attack, but a heavy rainstorm prevented him from getting within striking distance. Early the next morning, Butler reached Cantey's Plantation and found some bluecoats loading 8 or 10 wagons from the barns. Col. Rutledge immediately charged with the 4th South Carolina Cavalry, capturing the loaded wagons along with several prisoners.[340]

During the cold, rainy night of February 22-23, Gen. Butler marched his division in between two Federal corps and quietly camped. Before dawn, he had his troopers in the saddle and moved up in close proximity to an encampment of enemy trains. As the wagons were being hitched up and lined up on the road, Butler charged in and grabbed 19 wagons and 200 prisoners as the others wildly scattered. Butler hurried his captures over the bridge of Little Lynches Creek, then crossed Big Lynches Creek at Pierce's Bridge and turned downstream to Kellytown. When the enemy troops appeared to halt, Butler felt that Sherman might attempt to reach Georgetown where he could obtain much-needed supplies through that city's port. However, Sherman had no such plans, having instead been delayed by the high water in the creeks and rivers from the recent heavy rains.

---

[340] Brooks, 466-471.

As Butler halted for two days at Kellytown, he sent out two reconnaissance expeditions. With about 300 members of the 5th South Carolina Cavalry, Col. Hugh Aiken advanced downriver and a similar force of the Cobb Legion under Maj. Brown marched upstream to determine if the Yankees had passed into Darlington District.

At dark on the evening of the 24th of February, near Dubose's Bridge over Lynches Creek, Aiken encountered a detachment under Lt. John A. McQueen of the 15th Illinois Cavalry en route to release prisoners from the Confederate prison at Florence. Aiken, with Col. Zimmerman Davis of the 5th by his side, led a charge directly into the ranks of the Federal cavalrymen. Aiken was captured but managed to jerk the reins from the hands of his captor and escape. Riding up to Colonel Davis after his momentary capture, Aiken was suddenly hit by a parting shot and cried out, "Davis, I am dying, catch me." His nephew and courier, Willie Aiken of the Cadet Rangers, caught him as he fell to the ground, mortally wounded.[341] The Federals retired while Aiken's force returned to Kellytown to inform Butler of their crossing. Brown reported that the enemy had crossed Pierce's Bridge soon after Butler.

---

[341] Brooks, 422-423, 471, 548-549; McMaster, 4; Aiken, 13. Zimmerman Davis (1834-1910) was a clerk and cotton factor. He enlisted in the Washington Light Infantry, rising to Col. of the 5th SC Cavalry. Postwar, he was active in historical and political organizations, city alderman, and water works company officer. Men of Mark, I, 87-89.

Willie Aiken - See Appendix A.

John A. McQueen (1839-1920) was a Lieutenant of the 15th Illinois Cavalry. He deplored the destruction wrought by Sherman's army and personally saved several houses from destruction. McQueen was wounded in this same engagement and was nursed back to health by Dr. A. Toomer Porter whose house in Columbia had been saved through his efforts.

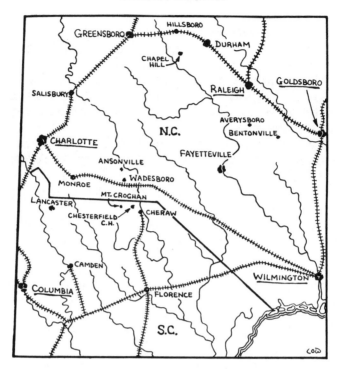

North and South Carolina

Gen. Butler was now convinced that Sherman
was, indeed, heading for Cheraw and, after marching day and night, reached the town just before sunset
on February 26th. There, Butler reported to Gen.
Hardee who had retreated to that point from
Charleston with about 14,000 men. Since the advance
of Blair's XVII Corps was about 12 hours ahead of
any other enemy force and was within just a few
miles of Cheraw, Butler recommended that an attack
the next morning might check Sherman's advance.
Hardee did not think such an attack feasible and instead ordered Butler to picket Thompson's Creek as
well as to make a reconnaissance-in-force in the direction of Chesterfield Court House. Butler moved toward Chesterfield and then retired, fighting a delaying action at every point back to Cheraw.

That evening at a council of war, Butler was asked about Cheraw's evacuation. Butler replied that Hardee needed to get his army across the Pee Dee River at the earliest possible moment. Though some officers in attendance were of the opinion that there was no reason for haste, Hardee ordered the immediate withdrawal of the trains. Butler was directed to bring up the rear and destroy any public stores as well as burn the covered bridge over the Pee Dee River.

The army withdrew during the night, Butler's diligent execution of his orders giving Hardee ample time to remove his heavy trains. Shortly afterwards, Gen. Joseph E. Johnston assumed command of the army.[342]

At dusk on the 9th of March, Capt. Moses B. Humphrey's squadron of the 6th South Carolina Cavalry was acting as advance guard of Hampton's Cavalry Corps. At an intersection of two main roads, Humphrey halted his column and reported to General Butler that signs indicated a heavy mounted column had recently passed. While discussing the matter, a patrol of some 30 troopers galloped down the road into view. When Humphrey denied that he had anyone down that road, Butler rode out and hailed the advancing party: "Who comes there?" "Fifth Kentucky," replied their leader. Realizing that it was one of enemy Gen. Hugh Kilpatrick's regiments, Butler ordered, "Ride up, sir; I want to speak with you." The officer, commanding Kilpatrick's rear guard, along

---

[342] Brooks, 471-474. Francis Preston Blair, Jr. (1821-1875) was a pre-war US Representative. He raised 7 regiments and was commissioned a Col., rising to command of the XVII Corps. Later, he was Democratic V.P. candidate in 1868.

Joseph E. Johnston (1807-1891) (West Point '29) commanded the Confederate Army at 1st Manassas. After a dispute with Jefferson Davis, he was shifted to commands in the West and was relieved in July 1864 after withdrawing before Sherman to the vicinity of Atlanta. He was reassigned to the command of the Army of Tennessee in February 1865, which he led to the surrender at Greensboro, NC, in April 1865. After the war, he was active in the insurance and railroad businesses and served in Congress.

with his orderly, thinking that he was approaching a friend, rode into the midst of Humphrey's men. Pointing his pistol, Gen. Butler demanded their quick surrender, at the same time calling for Humphrey to surround the rest of the enemy. The bloodless encounter yielded 30 prisoners and a stand of colors. When Butler reported the incident to Wade Hampton, the Corps Commander decided to attack Kilpatrick the next morning.

Butler followed Kilpatrick's trail for about four miles. Then, Confederate pickets, probing the perimeter of the area, captured a Federal lieutenant who disclosed the location of Kilpatrick's camp and headquarters in front of a nearby swamp with his rear and right protected by water and his left exposed. Butler then bivouacked without unsaddling or making fires in the cold, rainy night.

Hampton and Butler reconnoitered the enemy camp about midnight and found that Kilpatrick had posted no pickets to guard his rear. Thus, Hampton ordered Butler to move in as soon as Wheeler's Division, still stretched-out on the road, could close on the enemy's rear. Butler would follow Kilpatrick's trail around the head of the swamp and fall on the camp from the west, while Wheeler would move through the woods on the right to attack from the rear. Col. Wright of the Cobb Legion was ordered to charge the camp the next morning with Capt. Bostick's squadron leading. Bostick's orders were to head straight for Kilpatrick's headquarters and hold it until reinforced. The remainder of Butler's Division would follow with Wheeler supporting from the right. Wheeler's horses bogged down in the miry woods, rendering his unit helpless. He finally showed up only after failing to push through the miry woods and rerouting his command to come in behind Butler.

At daybreak, Butler's men charged down the road and into the sleeping camp. Jumping their horses over the slumbering Yankees, Butler's men reached the center of the camp, wheeled about and rode over their enemies again. Kilpatrick not only had no pickets out, but apparently not even a camp guard. About 130-140 recently-captured Confederates, released by their guards during Wright's charge, rushed toward the attacking party, adding to the general confusion. This delay allowed some of Kilpatrick's troopers to recover, seize their rapid-firing Spencer carbines, and attempt to drive Butler back. Butler counterattacked with scattered fragments of his command, but a combination of artillery and carbine fire forced him to retire.[343]

In the initial attack, Capt. Bostick followed his orders and rode up to Kilpatrick's headquarters. Kilpatrick appeared in his nightclothes outside his headquarters, and Bostick, not recognizing him, demanded, "Where is General Kilpatrick?" The little Yankee replied, "Don't you see him running on that horse right yonder?" As Bostick chased an escaping private, Kilpatrick made his escape on his courier's horse. Kilpatrick was to remember years later, "When I heard the Rebel yell in my camp, I threw up both hands and exclaimed: 'My goodness, four year's hard fighting and a major general's commission gone in four minutes.'" Kilpatrick, or "Kill-Cavalry" as he was derisively called by his troopers, took his revenge for his humiliation on the citizens of Raleigh, forcing them to disinter their Confederate dead and burying his own in their place. He survived the war only to drown while serving as ambassador to Chile.[344]

---

[343] Brooks, 443-445; Kennedy, 56. Samuel D. Bostick commanded Co. D, Cobb's Legion.

Joseph Wheeler (1836-1906) (West Point '59) rose rapidly from 1st Lt. to Maj. Gen. by January 1863. He fought aggressively during the Atlanta and Carolinas Campaigns. Postwar, he was a merchant and Congressman. In the Spanish-American War, he served as a Maj. Gen.

Hugh Judson Kilpatrick (1836-1881) (West Point '61) rose from Capt. to Brig. Gen. in the Army of the Potomac. He was transferred to the western theater at Sherman's request and commanded the cavalry force during the Atlanta and Carolinas Campaigns. Postwar, he was active in politics and was Minister to Chile.

[344] Brooks, 428; LaBree, 106-107.

An enemy horse artillery battery, on a slight hill a short distance away, played havoc with Butler's men during the attack. Confederate fire was concentrated on the guns until all the gunners except one lieutenant were either killed or wounded. This lone figure continued to serve the one remaining gun. Finally, Lt. John Deveaux of the 5th South Carolina Cavalry called for men to join him in a charge to eliminate the troublesome cannon. In the noise and confusion, only Capt. Humphrey and Pvt. Glenn Davis of the Cadet Rangers heard his call. As the three gray troopers galloped toward the muzzle of his gun, the doughty Yankee officer pulled the lanyard one last time. Humphrey's arm was shattered by canister, and Deveaux received five superficial wounds. Other men of the command, seeing Humphrey and Devaux fall, immediately charged the battery and pistoled the brave lieutenant as he attempted to reload the piece. At the same time, one trooper mounted Humphrey's horse, a fiery animal named "Yago," and then pulled the badly-wounded young Captain up before him to get off the field.

Humphrey was removed to a hospital in Raleigh where doctors attempted to amputate his mangled arm. Horrified at the prospect of going through life maimed, Humphrey refused to allow them to operate. At first, he seemed to rally and was, on March 18th, even given a furlough to go home. In the meantime, unbeknown to Humphrey, his horse had died from wounds received in the same attack. In the company of "Benny" Schipman, recently appointed a Second Lieutenant for "valor and skill" and who had also been wounded in the attack on Kilpatrick's camp, Humphrey tried to get home. On the way, he suffered a relapse and was readmitted to the hospital on March 20th at Charlotte. Still refusing to allow the surgeons to take his arm, he lingered there until April 30th when he died.[345] Perhaps it was as well.

---

[345] Brooks, 433-434; Marshall, 36-37; Calhoun, 183; Two great Carolinians, May 26, 1896. John Porteous Deveaux (1838-1892)

The gallant young officer had, not long previously, declared that he would rather die than go home to tell his mother and sisters of the Confederate defeat. According to family tradition, he and his horse "Yago" were buried in the same grave.[346]

While the Cadet Rangers were still in the thick of the fighting in Kilpatrick's camp, Pvt. Isaac Harby Moses of Sumter, nicknamed "Lord Shaftsbury" because of his scholarly style of composition, had his horse shot from under him. As he extricated himself from under the dying animal, Moses was confronted by a large bluecoat brandishing a saber. Though small in stature, Moses lowered his head and charged the bluecoat, grabbing him around the middle and wrestling him to the ground. Fortunately, as they scuffled, Corp. Bill Martin came along and "lifted the Yank off of 'Shaftsbury' with his revolver."

In the close fighting, Sgt. Gabriel M. Hodges' horse was killed, and he himself took a shot in the side. Though wounded, he captured another horse and continued in the battle until disabled by another wound in the shoulder. Incredibly, this second bullet entered the same hole made through his coat by a bullet which had hit him at Trevilian the previous June.[347]

At one point as Hampton's troopers charged through the enemy camp, a dismounted Yankee took aim at Capt. Goodwyn of Company C as that officer galloped by. Seeing this, Pvt. Davis of the Cadet Rangers sprang from his horse right onto the Yankee's head, both falling to the ground as the Federal's rifle exploded harmlessly. As the two slugged it out on foot, Davis began to get the worst of it when his antagonist bit off one of his fingers.

---

was 2nd Lt. of Co. D (South Carolina Rangers), 5th SC Cavalry. Postwar, he was a shipsmith in Charleston and county coroner for many years.
    Glenn Edwin Davis - See Appendix A.
[346] Marshall, 37; Stories, 307.
[347] Thomas, 219-220; SHSP, XXIII, 33. Isaac Harby Moses and William Martin - See Appendix A.

However, Pvt. Joe Salley came up and killed the Yankee before he could do any more damage to Davis' anatomy.[348]

Finally forced to retire, Butler's Division carried off 475 prisoners in the attack, then resumed the march, arriving in Fayetteville the next morning. While eating breakfast there, Hampton was informed of the presence of about 100 Federals. Quickly dispensing with his breakfast, Wade Hampton ordered his scouts to follow him and charge the enemy. In the close melee that followed, the Lt. Gen. killed two of the departing Federals with his pistol.[349]

Soon Hampton's Cavalry united with Gen. Johnston's Army of Tennessee to meet Sherman at Bentonville, North Carolina, where 28,000 Confederates engaged Sherman's 90,000 men. However, since Lee had by this time already surrendered at Appomattox, negotiations soon began in Durham to arrange a cessation of hostilities. Before final terms were agreed upon, though, Hampton, Wheeler, and others refused to surrender and left the army to proceed toward the Trans-Mississippi Department hoping to fight on. Butler remained as the ranking cavalry officer with the army and accompanied Johnston to the Bennett House where the surrender took place. As acting chief of cavalry, he signed the muster rolls and surrendered the Confederate cavalry.[350]

Gilmore Simms, who had rejoined the Cadet Rangers prior to the evacuation of Charleston, fell ill while marching home and collapsed into a stream near Chester with typhoid fever. He was nursed in a local residence before returning home by wagon in August.[351] Another Cadet Ranger, Edward J. Dennis, did not participate with his comrades in their final campaign. In late 1864, he had become ill in Virginia

---

[348] Calhoun, 180. Joe Salley - See Appendix A.
[349] Thomas, 198; LaBree, 107; With Hampton in Battle.
[350] Brooks, 475-476.
[351] Manning, V, 12.

and, when he was well enough to travel, was sent home on furlough to Charleston District. By the time his health improved, Charleston had been evacuated, and he had no idea where his unit was located. Therefore, he gathered a squad of six men determined to offer some protection to their home area. Shortly after the Federals advanced into the area, a mulatto leading an enemy detachment notified some young ladies in a nearby mansion that he would dance with them that night at a ball. Dennis was informed of the threat and waited for the Yankees to return that evening. As the raiders approached the house, Dennis dispatched the leader with his first shot and pursued the remainder for several miles.[352]

Soon after Hampton's attack on Kilpatrick's camp, the Citadel Cadets arrived in Spartanburg, South Carolina. Upon their arrival, Maj. White dispatched a letter to Gov. Magrath:

Spartanburg, S.C.
March 21, 1865

To His Excellency Governor A.G. Magrath

Sir:
I have the honor to report to you that I arrived at this place last night with my Command (120) strong.

The Cadets are much in want of clothes and shoes and are worn down by heavy marching.

I would therefore respectfully recommend that the Command be furloughed for fifteen or twenty days.

* * *

Respectfully,

---

[352] Brooks, 93-94.

Your obedient Servant
J.B. White
Major B.S.C.[353]

Gov. Magrath addressed the Cadets at his headquarters, praising them for their soldierly conduct
and trying march. Despite their rapid movements,
the Cadets had returned to the State with arms, colors, and baggage intact.[354]

While the Citadel Cadets were stationed at
Spartanburg, they heard stories about the destruction
wrought by Sherman's hordes. Henry N. Obear
walked to his home in Winnsboro to check on his family. He was so footsore by the time he arrived home
that he was bedridden for several days. Finding his
family well, however, he proceeded back to the encampment at Wofford College where his punishment
for overstaying his visit was a week's confinement in
the guard house. To occupy his time, he penned an
ode on the guard house wall:

> "Alas, the die is cast,
> And in this room I'm locked at last,
> What for? the reason is, that I went
>   home,
> And did from this battalion roam,
> Without permission. But know good peo-
>   ple all,
> Who read what I have written on this
>   wall,
> That I don't care a darn. If truth were
>   told,
> I'd rather be here than my freedom hold.
> No reveille disturbs my rest at morn,
> No drill calls make me wish I'd ne'er
>   been born.
> On dress parade, I am not bound to ap-
>   pear,

---

[353] White, 244.
[354] Thomas, 198.

Nor have I still that tattoo call to fear.
No guard detail comes round to break my
   rest,
No extra roll-calls, which my patience
   test,
But all is peace, and quietness and ease,
And any one who walks in here and sees
The room, and comforts which do me
   surround,
And all the blessed peace and rest I've
   found,
Would say, 'O Stranger, thou who
   dwellest here,
Praise, praise the gods whom thou dost
   fear,
Adore them still, nor heave a sigh,
Because thou in this room must lie.
The Castle of the Indolent. Wherein as
   bards do say,
Men lived, and nothing did the livelong
   day,
Could not with this, thy dungeon's cell
   compare,
In ease, or indolence or in wholesome
   fare.'
But then, some fool may say, 'It is dis-
   grace
To be locked up, nor see a human face.'
I'll answer, 'Tis not punishment, but
   crime
Has brought disgrace, at least, up to this
   time,
And to revisit that dear spot of earth
Whereon is placed our loved ones and our
   hearth
Is not a crime, but duty which man owes,
To where he's seen his childhood's joys
   and woes.'
Enough. For me, kind reader, do not drop
   a tear,
You need not pity.

Henry N. Obear
Co. B Bat. State Cadets"[355]

Citadel Cadet Allen J. Green, seriously ill with pneumonia contracted after his face wound at Tulifinny, was lying on the railroad platform in Columbia when Gen. Beauregard arrived on the last train from Charleston. Beauregard's son, a classmate of Green's, urged his father to have Green sent to a hospital. When advised to evacuate the city, Green found refuge with his mother and relatives in Lancaster where they received harsh treatment from occupying Federal soldiers, including their commander, Col. Smith D. Atkins of the 92nd Illinois Volunteers, who threatened to hang the sick Cadet as a spy. When Atkins, whose headquarters was in the same residence, attempted to interrogate Green's mother about military matters, her evasive answers caused him to explode, "You know less than any woman I ever saw." Next morning, however, Atkins softened and informed the lady he would provide protection for the house. Explaining his soldierly concern about a Rebel soldier possibly feigning illness, a fact now disproven by the surgeon who had verified the Cadet's condition, he told the mother that her son's "...being a Cadet has saved his life. Several of my officers were guarded between Charleston, Florence and Macon by Cadets last summer. They met with so much kindness and courtesy at their hands that we gladly avail ourselves of every opportunity to return their civility. Your Cadet will not be molested by any of my people."[356]

---

[355] Winnsboro, 78-79.
[356] Devereux, 292-299; Jones, 236-239. Mary Boykin Chesnut mentioned a similar story: "They overhauled the Halcott Greens at Lancaster, stripped them bare and threatened to shoot Allen before her very eyes. Some Yankee soldier to whom he had been kind in Charleston recognized him and saved his life." Chesnut, 499.

On March 8, the Arsenal Cadets arrived in Spartanburg and found quarters in the Wofford College buildings. Two days later, they were furloughed to report back in fifteen days. During their absence, the Citadel Cadets, joined by a detachment of militia, arrived and went into camp on the grounds of Wofford. Here, a camp of instruction for boys and young men had been previously established. Thomas A. Johnson of Newberry District in the Citadel 4th Class, died on the 23rd of March of brain fever.

Both Corps of Cadets, now reunited at Wofford, were commanded by Maj. White. In the latter part of March, the Arsenal Cadets marched to Greenville Court House, followed shortly by the Citadel Cadets. The Arsenal Cadets proceeded across country, encamping on the Buncombe Road near Paris Mountain, close by Finlay's Bridge along the line of the Greenville and Columbia Railroad, two miles north of the town. Seeking protection, the Cadets laid out the ground and built several rows of pine pole log houses, shaped like A's, and covered them with dirt and leaves. The huts were quite helpful as there were several protracted rains. April passed drearily with the monotonous camp routines and constant drilling.[357] The Citadel Cadets, in the field since the previous December, were furloughed by the Governor for a month.

The Arsenal Cadets, still in camp, were concerned about rumors of Lee's surrender at Appomattox on April 9th. They called upon Thomas who confirmed their suspicions that the Confederacy was deteriorating. However, Thomas reminded them of their obligation to follow the orders of the Governor. "...It was their duty to stand to their colors, maintain their organization, and accept the usual discipline of the Academy, until formally disbanded in orders from the proper State authorities." Although numerous veterans of Lee's and Johnston's armies were passing

---

[357] Lewis, "Arsenal Cadets Before Sherman"; Lewis, "Their First and Last Fight"; Sams, 4.

their camp each day on their way home, the Cadets stood by their colors and maintained their discipline until the end.[358]

During April, the Arsenal contingent was reinforced by a number of young recruits. "As a result of the disorganized condition of the state," State authorities had determined to use the Cadet Corps as the nucleus of a State guard. The Board of Visitors (Gov. Magrath, Gen. J.W. Harrison, and Col. A.P. Aldrich) met at Greenville on April 27th and resolved:

"...that in view of the present condition of the State, it was expedient to increase the number of Cadets in the two Military Academies to the largest number possible capable of receiving instruction from the Professors of these Academies; that such admissions be made by the Chairman of the Board of Visitors; and that the headquarters of both these Institutions be established at such places as the Chairman, in consultation with the Governor, might select. It was further resolved that it was expedient, as soon as possible, so to arrange the camps of instruction for the commands, that the academic exercises might be resumed."[359]

---

[358] Thomas, 212-213; Smythe, March 20, 1865.

[359] Thomas, 199. J.W. Harrison (1819-1888) was a lawyer, militia Brig. Gen., and legislator. Postwar, he was President of the Blue Ridge Railway and editor of the Anderson Gazette. Senate, 233.

Alfred Proctor Aldrich (1814-1896) served on the staff of Gen. Bonham and, later, Gen. Maxcy Gregg. He was badly injured in a railroad accident and was disabled from further military duty. After the war, he was elected judge of the Superior Court of SC, but was removed by the military commander. He was restored to office in 1876 and served until just prior to his death. His sons were both members of the Cadet Rangers.

Several Citadel Cadets, Francis J. Murdoch, George M. Coffin, and Abner W. Lamar were ordered to remain with the Arsenal Corps as drillmasters. At this time, new candidates for admission to the Citadel arrived. Since the other Citadel Cadets were still on furlough, and with Charleston occupied by Federal troops, the new recruits were attached to the Arsenal Corps which now numbered 153 Cadets and was organized into two companies.

On February 25th, Gov. Magrath of South Carolina had written Gen. Beauregard informing him that a raid led by the Federal Gen. George Stoneman was being prepared to strike the upper part of the State. Magrath had requested that the militia and Cadets be returned as there was no other force with which to protect the area.[360] Troops from the Federal army were already spread over much of the State after guarding Sherman's lines of communications and acting as an occupation force. One Federal brigade commander, William J. Palmer, complained in writing about the activities of these troops:

"(The)...officers (of Brown's and Miller's Brigades) for the most part have lost control over their men. A large number of men and some of the officers devote themselves exclusively to pillaging and destroying property. General Brown appears to have given them carte blanche in South Carolina, and they are now so entirely destitute of discipline that it cannot

---

[360] Bond, 78; OR, XLVII, pt. 2, 1274; Lewis, "Their First and Last Fight." Abner W. Lamar - See Appendix B.

George Stoneman (1822-1894) (West Point '46) commanded the District of East Tennessee, Cumberland, and led a raid into NC and VA in March-April 1865 to support Sherman's Carolinas Campaign. Postwar, he was a politician and Governor of CA.

be restored in the field and while the command is living on the country."[361]

On Sunday afternoon, April 30, the Cadets were picketing along the road leading to Marietta, South Carolina. This type of outpost duty was new to the Arsenal Cadets since they had never previously performed guard duty outside of camp. The pickets, under Lt. A.J. Norris, were formed and set up a post about a half mile from camp in the direction of the mountains. After posting one or two men in advance here, they stacked arms. About 10:00 p.m., the Cadets were awakened by the call of the guard—"Halt! Who comes there?" A reply in forcible language demanded another answer, "Who dared to halt the group?" Quickly, the Cadets grabbed their weapons as officers ran forward, responding to calls: "Corporal of the Guard." As it turned out, the horsemen were some mounted home guards from Greenville who had gone into the mountains near Marietta scouting the location of Federal troops. Their flag of truce had been met by a volley, and they were now returning home. The group was allowed to proceed on through the Cadet lines. Forewarned of the nearness of the approaching Yankees, the Cadet pickets were moved back to camp. There, the remaining Cadets were awakened, formed up, and prepared to march. Since there were no other Confederate troops in Greenville District and no real organized Southern force under arms in the State, Thomas determined to march toward Columbia to avoid being captured. Once in Greenville, the city authorities, fearing retaliation, requested that the Cadets not make a stand against the raiders.

Wagons and equipment being quickly assembled, about 2:00 a.m. on the morning of May 1st, the Cadets moved through Greenville on toward Williamston, marching down the Grove Road very close to the

---

[361] OR, XLIX, pt. 1, 550. William J. Palmer (1836-1909) earned the Medal of Honor for his actions at Red Hill, AL, in January 1865.

Georgia and Carolina railway track.[362] Reaching
Dean's Crossing about sunrise, Capt. Thomas sent a
Cadet back to Greenville to observe any enemy activity
and report it to him as soon as possible. Since Thomas
was expecting an imminent attack, the pace had been
slow. However, now upon receiving the report from
the rear guard, "All quiet, all well," the Cadet
Battalion hastened on toward Williamston, giving a
wide berth to Gen. Simeon B. Brown's Brigade at
Anderson.[363] After a short march, Lt. John F.
Lanneau of the Citadel Corps, which was still on furlough, rode up and again placed the Citadel flag in
the hands of Capt. Thomas for safekeeping. The flag
had been entrusted to Capt. Thomas while in
Columbia and returned to Maj. White in
Spartanburg. This time it was to be seventeen years
before it was again returned to the Citadel Cadets.[364]

His boys being worn out and in need of food and
water, Capt. Thomas halted them near Williamston,
at a comfortable looking farm house by an orchard
near Shiloh Church.[365] The exhausted Cadets broke
ranks and crowded into a shady corner of the yard at
a spot near a curve in the road, leaving only advance
and rear guards. The rear guard, under Cadet Sgt.
Robert M. Pitts, was located well behind. The Cadets,
bone-tired from their long march, were lying down,
many asleep on their arms, when suddenly, one of the
rear guards who had been lying with his ear on the
ground called Pitts' attention to an unusual sound.
Almost immediately, a body of horsemen, led by two

---

[362] Arsenal Cadet; Sams, 4; Lewis, "Arsenal Cadets Before
Sherman"; Lewis, "Their First and Last Fight."
[363] Lewis, "Their First and Last Fight"; Arsenal Cadet.
Simeon B. Brown (?-1893) commanded the 2nd Brigade,
Cavalry Division of East Tennessee, Cumberland, under Gen.
Stoneman.
[364] Thomas, 199; Association of Graduates, 1877. John Francis
Lanneau - See Appendix B.
[365] Arsenal Cadet; Sams, 5.

negroes armed with shotguns, appeared around the bend in the road.[366]

As the intruders broke into view, they cheered, "Hip, hip, hurrah," and began firing. A few younger Cadets bolted at the sudden alarm. Capt. Thomas, however, stepped to the front and loudly ordered, "Rally 'round the flag, boys, rally 'round the flag." Quickly, the Cadets surrounded their leader under the Citadel flag and returned the fire of the charging cavalrymen. Lt. Patrick, attempting to cross over the rail fence, fell back on Cadet George W. Sullivan's leg and almost put both of them out of action.[367]

Armed with repeating carbines, the enemy troopers fired several volleys. Several slugs ripped through Cadet John Spearman's hand, splintering his rifle stock. But the rear guard of the Cadets promptly returned fire with their Enfields, and the horsemen, at a disadvantage against disciplined infantry fire, began to fade away. As the cavalrymen retired, one bluecoat was struck and fell from his horse at the skirt of woods alongside the road. Another horseman picked him up, and the remaining troopers retreated up the White Plains Road. The wounded bluecoat later recovered in a Greenville hospital.[368]

Cadet Ellison A. Smyth, a Fourth Classman from Charleston, later recalled: "Only a few shots were exchanged. When the raiders retired, but one man fell off his horse, and lay on the ground, and was picked up by a comrade and flung across the front of his saddle. We thought he was dead; but the whole affair lasted three or four minutes, though it seemed to us cadets a much longer time." The brief engagement

---

[366] Lewis, "Their First and Last Fight"; Sams, 5; Price. R.M. Pitts - See Appendix B.
[367] Arsenal Cadet; Lewis, "Their First and Last Fight"; Vandiver, February 24, 1921; Sams, 5; Vandiver, March 9, 1921. George W. Sullivan - See Appendix B.
[368] Lewis, "Their First and Last Fight"; Sams, 5; Price. John Spearman - See Appendix B.

was the last recorded unit action of the war east of the Mississippi.[369]

When Capt. Thomas realized that the attacking party had withdrawn, he quickly formed up his Cadets, turned them about and continued the march. Soon the enemy cavalry appeared again, now wearing Confederate uniforms and claiming to be a part of Wheeler's Cavalry. They passed through the Cadet lines and moved rapidly ahead of them to Williamston. There, the raiders set fire to the depot and quartermaster's store house, burned a freight train, and stopped another train on its way from Columbia to Greenville. Its cars were torched after all of the baggage had been carefully rifled.

As the Cadets approached Williamston, the citizens mistakenly assumed that they were bluecoats bent on completing the town's destruction. The Cadets were met under a flag of truce by the Rev. Benjamin F. Mauldin proclaiming that there were no troops in the town to dispute their entry. Explaining to the frightened preacher who they were, Capt. Thomas marched his Cadets into town, where they stacked arms and rested in a grove near the still-smoking depot. Later, the Cadets proceeded on to Belton, reaching the town about sundown without encountering any additional raiders.

Early the next morning, the Cadets marched out of their temporary camp to Honea Path where they drew their first rations since the previous Sunday. After this scanty meal, they moved down the Greenville and Columbia Railroad to Donalds and on into Greenwood. There, a very liberal meal was prepared for them by an unknown gentleman. They then moved into a temporary camp west of the town of Ninety Six where they remained for about a week before moving on to Newberry.[370]

---

[369] Bond, 85. Ellison A. Smyth - See Appendix B. E.B. Long does not mention any other engagement east of the Mississippi, nor does he mention this one. Long, 684-691.
[370] Lewis, "Their First and Last Fight"; Sams, 5. Benjamin Franklin Mauldin (1814-1886), a signer of the Ordinance of

At Newberry, Capt. Thomas ordered Lt. Robert O. Sams to request further orders from Gov. Magrath. After carefully considering the situation, Magrath sent back written instructions to furlough the Cadets. Acting under the Governor's orders, Thomas furloughed the Arsenal Cadets for sixty days, ordering that they reassemble at some location to be designated later. Upon being disbanded, each Cadet was authorized to keep his musket, accoutrements, and ammunition until recalled by the State authorities.[371]

The Arsenal Cadets were never surrendered but simply disbanded.[372] Their engagement with the raiders on the 1st of May has been cited as the last engagement by organized forces east of the Mississippi. Certainly, it was the last one recorded in South Carolina. It definitely was the last achievement for the Arsenal Cadets. Their furlough permanently disbanded the Corps since the Columbia branch of the South Carolina Military Academy, having been physically destroyed in February, was never again reopened.[373] The Citadel Cadets, who had been on furlough since early April, also never surrendered and did not reassemble as an academic institution for seventeen years.

The flag of the Citadel which had been entrusted to Thomas on two separate occasions had again been returned to him. He took the flag on to Columbia and maintained it until 1879 when he presented it to the Association of Graduates.[374]

During this final period of active service, seven Cadets, Alfred O. Brown, R.F. Nichols, R.E. Muldrow, John Culbreath, George O. Buck, Thomas A. Johnson, and Russell Noble, had died from disease

---

Secession, was a farmer and Baptist minister. Postwar, he was paymaster and local agent of the Greenville and Columbia Railroad. May 177-178.

[371] Thomas, 200-201; Sams, 5. Robert O. Sams - See Appendix B.

[372] Sams, 6; Vandiver, March 9, 1921.

[373] Thomas, 200, 202.

[374] Thomas, 202-204.

induced by exposure and the hardships of service.[375] On May 9, Cadet McKenzie Parker and other young men from Anderson County encountered some Yankee scouts. Parker ordered one to surrender, raising his gun. The Yankee likewise called for him to lower his arm, but Parker snapped his gun twice, and it failed to fire. The bluecoat fired, and Parker was dead within a few minutes.[376]

In his report to the Board of Visitors on October 31, 1865, Capt. Thomas noted: "The Cadets of the Arsenal Academy, whilst in the field, behaved well and suffered no casualties." While the Cadets had not suffered severely, the campus of the Arsenal itself had not fared as well. "The Arsenal, fired by order of Genl. Sherman, is in ruins. The officers' quarters detached from the main building, and some out-houses escaped the flames, and are standing." These surviving officers' quarters were later renovated and today serve as the official residence of the Governor of South Carolina.[377]

In a later report to R.J. Davant, Chairman of the Board of Visitors written on December 6, 1865, Thomas eulogized: "Whilst the Confederate forces were disbanding and after the cause had been utterly and irretrievably lost, these young men, with very few exceptions, continued faithful to their colors, and to the last, faithfully discharged their duty to the State."[378]

---

[375] Thomas, 208. Alfred O. Brown, R.F. Nichols, R.E. Muldrow, John Culbreath, George O. Buck, Thomas A. Johnson, and Russell Noble - See Appendix B.
[376] Smith, 213; Marszalek, 440.
[377] Thomas, October 31, 1865.
[378] Thomas, December 6, 1865.

EPILOGUE

The Arsenal buildings in Columbia had been severely damaged by Sherman's troops in February. Only the officers' quarters and several outbuildings were all that remained, and these were in the possession of other persons. "The personal property of the Citadel Academy, consisting of room, mess hall, office and section room furniture, records, text books, astronomical and surveying instruments; chemical and philosophical apparatus, cabinet of minerals and library, containing (8,000) eight thousand volumes, had been removed to Columbia for safety, and were, with all similar property belonging to the Arsenal, consumed in the conflagration of the City." The buildings at the Citadel were not materially damaged, but, upon the fall of Charleston, they were occupied by Federal troops.[379]

During this first twenty-four years of its existence, the South Carolina Military Academy had educated, to some extent, more than 1,800 young men. Of these, some 200 had graduated by the time Ft. Sumter was fired upon while another 40 graduated during the war. Out of 240 graduates, fourteen pre-war alumni had died before the war began in earnest at 1st Manassas. An additional alumnus died during 1861, and an 1863 senior died just weeks after receiving his diploma. Of the 224 left alive and eligible to serve in the war, 209 graduates entered Confederate service. The highest military ranks held by them were:

---

[379] Thomas, 229-230.

Brigadier General   4
Colonel   19
Lieutenant Colonel   11
Major   18
Captain   50
Lieutenant   65
Surgeon   11
Chaplain   2
Not Commissioned   29

The fifteen graduates who did not serve included 5 Ministers of the Gospel, 2 Physicians, 1 railway official, and 2 civilian engineers for the Confederate government as well as 3 who lived in California and 1 studying in Germany. Forty-nine graduates gave their lives for the Confederacy, 36 being killed in action or dying from wounds on the battlefields from 1st Manassas to Five Forks. Seven had died from disease and 6 of wounds or disease contracted while in military service, including one, Alfred Septimus Gaillard ('60), who succumbed to his wounds at Bentonville some five years after the war. At least 94 non-fatal wounds were suffered by alumni and 16 were captured in action. Some 200 former Cadets died in Confederate service, while 12 Cadets had died of wounds or disease in the field. Seventeen seniors, who should have graduated in April 1865, had finished the war with the Battalion of State Cadets. By special act of the General Assembly of South Carolina, they and a classmate who died in service were awarded diplomas with the class of 1886, the first to graduate from the Citadel after the war. Unfortunately, at least six were already dead. Eleven Cadet Rangers who were former Cadets had been wounded and four others had paid the supreme sacrifice.[380]

---

[380] The above information is based upon modern research conducted by Jim D. Moody, Class of 1965, Charleston, SC. It differs radically from the alumni records at the Citadel which

   Throughout most of Reconstruction, the buildings
of the Citadel served as barracks for the occupation
troops. With the return of self-government in South
Carolina in 1876, the financial condition of the State
did not permit the reopening of the school. After considerable political maneuvering between State and
Federal authorities, the buildings of the Citadel were
returned to control of the college's Board of Visitors.
The Arsenal campus was never rebuilt and the few
structures remaining were converted into the present
Governor's Mansion. In 1882, the Citadel reopened its
doors. They have remained open for over a century,
educating thousands of students from South
Carolina, the United States, and the world. The tradition established by an earlier generation of alumni in
the Civil War has continued until the present day
with Citadel alumni paying the supreme sacrifice in
each of America's subsequent wars.
   On December 18, 1942, in commemoration of the
centennial of the establishment of the Citadel, Gov.
Richard M. Jefferies presented to the Corps of Cadets
nine battle streamers denoting as many operations
participated in by the Cadets during the war. All nine
streamers are gray with blue inscriptions, with the
exception of the "Confederate States Army" streamer
which is inscribed in white. The streamers were presented for service at:

Star of the West	January 9, 1861
Wappoo Cut	November 1861
James Island	June 1862
Charleston and Vicinity	July to October 1863
James Island	June 1864
Tulifinny	December 1864

were compiled in the last century. Also, no attempt has previously been made to record the service of ex-Cadets during the
war.

James Island   December 1864 to
                                       February 1865
Williamston   May 1865
Confederates States Army

The streamers continue to fly from the flag of the
Corps of Cadets, a reminder of the proud heritage of
those Cadets who interrupted their education to serve
their country. The Citadel continues to educate young
men of the world to prepare them to better serve their
country.

APPENDIX A

CADET RANGERS

Organized at the Citadel, Charleston, South Carolina on June 9, 1862. Mustered into state service as Captain M.B. Humphrey's Company, SC Cavalry and assigned to Aiken's 1st Regiment SC Partisan Rangers. Mustered into Confederate service as Company F, 16th Battalion SC Cavalry July 23, 1862. Redesignated Company F, 6th Regiment SC Cavalry when its parent organization was increased from battalion to regiment.

* Enlisted at the Citadel on June 9, 1862, unless otherwise noted.

Ranks indicated are as of the date the unit mustered in on July 23, 1862, or the date of enlistment, if later.

Aiken, John W., Pvt. (1804-?) Fairfield. Enl. Co. B (Lyle Rifles), 7th Infantry Battalion at Columbia Mar. 20, 1863. Trans. June 30, 1863. Scout. WIA Burgess' Mill Oct. 27, 1864. Planter.

*Aiken, William David, Pvt. (1846-1925) Fairfield, Enl. Winnsboro May 1, 1864 while a 3rd Classman. Courier for his uncle, Col. Aiken. Farmer.

*Aldrich, Alfred, 3rd Lt. (1845-1919) Barnwell, 2nd Classman. Prom. 2nd Lt. Oct. 27, 1864. WIA three times Trevilian Station June 12, 1864. Paroled Greensboro, NC May 1, 1865. Planter and Treasurer of Barnwell Co. Brother of Robert Aldrich.

*Aldrich, Robert, Pvt. (1844-1911) Barnwell, 3rd Classman. Apptd. 1st Lt. and Adjutant, 6th Cavalry on Oct. 3, 1862. WIA Trevilian Station June 12, 1864. Acting Assistant Inspector General on staff of Brig. Gen. P.M.B. Young 1865. Paroled Greensboro, NC May 1, 1865. Attorney in Barnwell Co. Democratic Presidential Elector, legislator and State Senator. Brother of Alfred Aldrich.

*Anderson, Frank S., Pvt. (1844-?) Edgefield, 3rd Classman.

Appleby, Franklin B., Sgt. (1838-1864) Colleton. Farmer. Enl. Columbia June 18, 1862. WIA and captured John's Island

Feb 9, 1864. Confined Ft. Lafayette and Ft. Delaware. Exchanged Aiken's Landing, VA Sept. 22, 1864. Admitted Jackson Hospital, Richmond the next day suffering from pneumonia. Died Oct. 20, 1864.

Appleby, R. Hiram, Pvt. (1840-?) Colleton. Enl. John's Island Feb. 25, 1864. Detailed light duty in Quartermaster Department on Jan. 3, 1865. Farmer in Colleton Co.

Barker, James H., Pvt. (1839-1926) Enl. Columbia June 18, 1862. Farmer in Great Cypress Township.

*Baxley, Jacob Virgil, Pvt. (1844-1935) Barnwell, 3rd Classman. WIA Trevilian Station June 12, 1864. Cotton factor and commission merchant in Charleston and Blackville.

*Beaty, Benjamin Lewis, Pvt. (1842-1913) Horry, 2nd Classman. Trans. to Co. K (Eutaw Rifles), 26th Regiment SC Infantry Nov. 11, 1862. Rose to Captain. Miller, farmer, and merchant in Horry Co. Legislator.

*Black, Thomas P., Pvt. (1843-1867) Charleston, 3rd Classman. Detailed Signal Corps Sept. 23, 1863. Clerk to Brig. Gen. Thomas Jordan through Dec. 1864 when he returned to the company.

*Blake, Godfrey Mundy, Pvt. (1844-?) Beaufort, 3rd Classman. Prom. corporal Dec. 1, 1863. Detailed Signal Corps and consequently reduced to ranks Jan. 31, 1864. On duty with Signal Corps at Savannah through August 1864. Planter at "Rice Hope" on Savannah River.

Boyd, Robert Watson (1840-1864) Chester. KIA Lee's Mill July 31, 1864. Appears on Memory Roster. CSR shows him in Co. C, 6th SC cavalry.

Brannon, William H. "Willis," Pvt. (1836-1917) Spartanburg. Enl. Spartanburg Mar. 28, 1862 Co. F, 18th Regiment SC Infantry. Re-enl. Cadet Rangers Oct. 15, 1863. Captured John's Island Feb. 9, 1864. Initially confined on Hilton Head, Trans. to Ft. Pulaski Oct. 25, 1864. Farmer and wagoner.

Bridges, Joseph (M.?), Pvt. (1831-?) York. Enl. Columbia July 8, 1862,. Trans. to Co. K (Broad River Guards), 18th Regiment SC Infantry in exchange for E. Morgan Nov. 15, 1862. Teacher in York.

Broughton, John J., Pvt. (1839-?) Clarendon. Enl. Clarendon District July 23, 1862. Farmer in Clarendon Co. Alive 1890.

Brown, Edward, Pvt. (1812-1885) Union. Enl. Columbia June 23, 1862. Trans. to Co. F., 18th Regiment SC Infantry Oct. 15, 1863. WIA May 20, 1864. Captured Farmville, VA, April 6, 1865. Farmer in Gowdyville.

Brown, George, Pvt. (1810-1888) Enl. John's Island Feb. 25, 1864.

Brown, Joseph, Pvt. (1815-?) Spartanburg. Enl. Columbia June 20, 1862. Farm laborer.

Bryan, Harper K., Pvt. (1832-?) Enl. Columbia June 20, 1862. AWOL on muster roll for July-October 1862. No further record. Farm laborer.

*Caldwell, Jacob Andrew, Pvt. (1842-1895) Fairfield. Enl. John's Island Aug. 1, 1863. Detailed to light duty in enrolling office Winnsboro Mar. 15, 1864 on recommendation of Medical Board. Was 3rd Classman at the Citadel when the war began. Served in Co. G (Boyce Guards), 6th SC Infantry. Given a surgeon's discharge. Farmer in GA.

Cantey, Morgan Sabb, Pvt. (1844-1932) Clarendon. Enl. Oct. 27, 1861 Co. I (Sprott Guards), 23rd SC. Trans. to Cadet Rangers Feb. 1863. Farmer in Summerton.

Cave, William Mallory, Pvt. (1834-1901) Enl. Columbia June 21, 1862. Farmer in Red Oak Township.

*Chisolm, Alexander Robert, 2nd Corp. (1845-1868) Charleston, 3rd Classman. Discharged as underage Aug. 4, 1862. Planter at Palmetto Hall, Chisolm's Island in Beaufort Co.

Clark, John Quincy Adams, Pvt. (1835-?) Laurens. Overseer. Enl. Co. A (Carolina Guerillas), 6th SC Cavalry Mar. 1, 1863. Trans. to Cadet Rangers May 1, 1864. Hospitalized for pneumonia summer and fall 1864. Trans. to Co. E, 1st Battalion Invalid Corps 4th quarter 1864.

Cloud, James Franklin, Pvt. (1825-1870) Fairfield. Enl. Church Flats Feb. 18, 1863. WIA slightly Trevilian Station. Paroled Charlotte May 6, 1865. Planter and merchant.

Clowney, Moses, Pvt. (1822-1894) Fairfield. Enl. John's Island Jan. 17, 1864. Previous service with 6th SC Reserves and Co. H, 4th SC State Troops. Planter.

Cohen, Mark Edward, Jr., Pvt. (1839-1865) Charleston. Enl. March 5, 1862 Charleston where he was a dentist. Originally served in Co. D (South Carolina Rangers), 5th SC Cavalry. Trans. to Cadet Rangers Sept. 1, 1862. Trans. to Capt. J.F. Hart's Company (Washington Mounted Artillery), SC Horse Artillery. KIA Bentonville, NC, Mar. 19, 1865.

Coleman, James Henry, Pvt. (1833-1890) Union. Enl. Columbia June 20, 1862. Detailed as a wagoner. Paroled Greensboro, NC May 1, 1865. Merchant and farmer in Jonesville, Union Co.

Connor, Langdon Finch, Pvt. (1844-1877) Abbeville. Enl. John's Island Jan. 1, 1864. Prior service with Co. F (Ripley Rifles), Holcombe Legion. WIA 2nd Manassas. Trans. to Co. C, 6th SC Cavalry. Active in overthrowing radical government in Cokesbury.

Crane, F.C., Pvt. Enl. June 20, 1862 in Columbia. Trans. to Co. E, 6th SC Cavalry June-Oct. 1862.

Crawford, Robert Bryson, Pvt. (1824-1905) Enl. John's Island Jan. 1, 1864. Stone mason.

Cunningham, John B., 2nd Lt. Resigned Jan. 27, 1865.

*Davis, A. James, Pvt. Enl. Adam's Run Mar. 1, 1863. 3rd Classman, Fairfield.

*Davis, Glenn Edwin, Pvt. (1843-1930) Charleston, 2nd Classman. Exchanged for J.E. Saulesbury and trans. to Co. D (South Carolina Rangers), 5th SC Cavalry Nov. 1, 1863. Apptd. Sgt.Major, 5th SC Cavalry. Acting Adjutant, 5th SC Cavalry Jan. 1865. Sheriff of Charleston Co.

Davis, J.A., Pvt. (1843-?) Colleton. Enl. Mar. 1863 in Co. I (Rebel Troop), 3rd SC Cavalry. Exchanged for J.O. Willson and trans. to Cadet Rangers Dec. 1, 1863. Deserted into Union lines Charleston Mar. 9, 1865. Took oath of allegiance and released.

Davis, Jacob (N?) W., Pvt. (1810-?) Spartanburg. Enl. John's Island Feb. 1, 1864. WIA June 1864. Captured near Stony Creek Dec. 1, 1864. Confined Point Lookout. Took oath and released June 25, 1865.

Davis, Marshall F., Pvt. (1839-?) Spartanburg. Enl. Adam's Run Feb. 27, 1863. Captured at Lee's Mills on July 30, 1864. Confined Elmira. Took oath and released June 19, 1865. Student.

*Davis, Ross, Pvt. (1846-1864) Fairfield. Enl. Columbia June 25, 1862 where he was a 4th Classman at the Arsenal. Exchanged for G.T. Summers and trans. to Co. D (South Carolina Rangers), 5th SC Cavalry 1863. Apptd. 2nd Lt., Co. I (Dutch Fork Guards), 15th SC Infantry, KIA Petersburg June 1864.

Davis, William H., Pvt. (1833-?) Anderson. Enl. Adam's Run Feb. 15, 1863.

*Dennis, Edward James, Pvt. (1844-1904) Charleston, 3rd Classman. Sent to Kittrel Springs Hospital Sept. 10, 1864. Attorney and planter in Berkeley Co. Legislator, State Senator, and Militia General.

Douglass, Alexander Scott, Pvt. (1833-1914) Fairfield. Enl. Columbia Aug. 25, 1862. Brother of C.B. Douglass. Attorney

Douglass, Charles Brown, Pvt. (1825-?) Fairfield. Enl. Columbia Aug. 25, 1862. Brother of A.S. Douglass. Planter in Jenkinsville.

*Dozier, Anthony White, Jr., 1st Lt. (1842-1874) Williamsburg, 2nd Classman. WIA and captured John's Island Feb. 9, 1864. Confined Ft. Delaware. Released to await exchange Feb. 2, 1865. Attorney and school teacher in Marion. Removed to CA in 1869 where he was a school principal. Brother of E.C. Dozier. Died from effects of imprisonment.

*Dozier, Edward Charles, 1st Corp. (1843-1919) Williamsburg, 3rd Classman. Prom. 5th Sgt. Apr. 1, 1863 and 2nd Sgt. Feb. 9, 1864. WIA Lee's Mills Aug. 8, 1864. Plantation manager in Williamsburg Co. Removed to CA in 1869 where he was a ranch manager and rancher. Brother of A.W. Dozier.

*Dutart, John Steele, 4th Sgt. (1843-1864) Charleston, 1st Classman. KIA John's Island Feb. 9, 1864. Cousin of G.A. McDowell.

*Earle, Baylis John, Pvt. (1843-1928) Greenville, 2nd Classman. Orange grower in FL. Brother of E.D. Earle.

*Earle, Elias Drayton, 1st Sgt. (1841-1894) Greenville, 1st Classman. Reduced to ranks Apr. 1, 1863. Physician in FL. Brother of B.J. Earle.

Eaves, Ulysses Montgomery, Pvt. (1844-?) Barnwell. Enl. Columbia June 20, 1862. Paroled as a patient at General Hospital No. 10, Salisbury, NC May 2, 1864. Farmer in Buford's Bridge.

Eison, Napoleon Bonaparte, Pvt. (1838-1919) Colleton. Enl. Columbia June 20, 1862. Prior service with Co. E (Marion Volunteers), 1st (Gregg's) Regiment SC Infantry and Co. B, 18th Regiment SC Infantry. Trans. to Co. K (Mountain Ranger), 5th Regiment SC Cavalry. Salesman and farmer in Jonesville.

*Farr, David Alexander Thomas, Pvt. (1844-1905) Enl. Adams Run Nov. 1, 1862 while he was a 4th Classman at the Arsenal. Farmer in Jonesville.

*Fleming, Donald, Pvt. (1844-1875) Richland, 3rd Classman. Trans. to 22nd Regiment SC Infantry Feb. 5, 1864 and commissioned 2nd Lt. Merchant in Spartanburg.

Fowler, E.F., Pvt. (1830-?) Enl. Columbia June 20, 1862. Discharged, no reason given, Jan. 1863. Farmer in Jonesville, Union Co. in 1890.

Fowler, George A., Pvt. (1845-1926) Spartanburg. Enl. Pocotaligo Dec. 3, 1862. Manufacturer in Reidville.

*Fowler, William Dixon, Pvt. (1844-1922) Laurens. Enl. Pocotaligo Dec. 3, 1862 while a 4th Classman at the Arsenal. Draymaster in Spartanburg.

Gaffney, Thomas E., Pvt. (1842-?) Spartanburg. Enl. Adam's Run Dec. 1, 1862. Prior service with Co. G (Pacolet Guards), 5th SC Infantry. Farmer.

Gale, F.B. (P?), Pvt. Enl. Winnsboro May 1, 1864.

Gilbert, Danuel Pinckney, Pvt. (1833-1917) Spartanburg. Enl. Pocotaligo Dec. 3, 1862. Prior service with Co. C (Morgan Rifles), Holcombe Legion. Farmer and carpenter in Spartanburg.

Gilchrist, Daniel E. "Van," Pvt. (1841-1903) Marion. Enl. Columbia June 23, 1862. Serving with Co. F (E.M. Dragoons), 4th SC Cavalry at close of war. Never married. Railroad agent for Atlantic Coast Line RR at Nichols. Also schoolteacher in Marion.

Gladney, David Becket, Pvt. (1815-1868) Fairfield. Enl. Monticello Aug. 29, 1861. Transferred to Co. D, 6th SC Cavalry. Trans. to Cadet Rangers May 1, 1864. In AL.

Gladney, Hugh Yongue, Jr., Sgt. (1841-1883) Fairfield. Enl. Columbia June 15, 1862. Prior service in Co. E (Monticello

Guards), 15th SC Infantry. Prom. Corporal April 1, 1863 and Sgt. Feb. 9, 1864. WIA Trevilian Station June 12, 1864.

Gladney, James Patrick, Pvt. (1834-1910) Fairfield. Enl. John's Island Jan. 1, 1864. With disabled horses at Lynchburg. Paroled Augusta, GA May 19, 1865. Moved to Claiborne Parish, LA. Brother of J.P. Gladney. Planter.

Gladney, Joseph Patrick, Pvt. (1846-1883) Fairfield. Enl. Winnsboro June 1, 1864. Captured Lee's Mills July 20, 1864. Confined Elmira. Took oath and released June 19, 1865. Physician in LA. Brother of J.P. Gladney.

Gladney, Richard Jackson, Pvt. (1816-1899) Fairfield. Enl. John's Island Sept. 25, 1863.

Gladney, William McMilling, Pvt. (1816-1899) Fairfield. Enl. John's Island Sept. 25, 1863. Was discharged in early 1864, providing Robert Crawford as a substitute. In TN. Brother of R.J. Gladney.

Guignard, William Mayrant (1849-1869) Richland. Enl. Columbia Feb. 1865.

Hall, J., Pvt. Enl. Columbia July 20, 1862.

Hall, R., Pvt. Enl. Columbia July 20, 1862.

Hall, S.A., Pvt. Enl. Brooks CH, VA June 1864. Admitted General Hospital, Danville, VA Oct. 5, 1864 for gunshot wound in right arm.

Hardin, Jesse Havries, Pvt. (1818-1910) Fairfield. Enl. Sept. 25, 1863 John's Island. Lawyer, farmer and legislator near New Hope, Chester Co., trustee of Clemson College.

Hardin, Timothy, Pvt. (1822-1896) Enl. John's Island Sept. 1, 1863. Farmer near Winnsboro.

*Harllee, Edward Porcher, Pvt. (1843-1878) Marion, 2nd Classman. Apptd. 2nd Lt. and Asst. Inspector Gen. on staffs of Gens. Joseph B. Kershaw, James Connor, and John D. Kennedy. WIA Cedar Creek. Paroled Greensboro, NC May 1, 1865. Attorney and school-teacher in Marion. Later, a newspaper editor in New Orleans.

Harris, Alfred, Pvt. (1836-?) Spartanburg. Enl. John's Island July 1, 1863. WIA Nov. 1864. Captured Stony Creek Dec. 1, 1864. Farmer in Spartanburg.

Harvin, Arthur, Pvt. (1843-?) Clarendon. Enl. June 25, 1862. AWOL by October 1862. No further record. Farmer in Clarendon.

*Heyward, William Henry, Pvt. (1846-1926) Charleston. Enl. June 25, 1862 Columbia while a 4th Classman at the Arsenal. Not obtaining parental consent, he was discharged August 14, 1862.

*Hill, L., Pvt. Enl. Columbia June 28, 1862. Exchanged for Alexander Williams.

Hix, W.S., Pvt. (1826-1864) Enl. Columbia July 25, 1862. KIA Oct. 27, 1864 Burgess' Mill.

Hodge, Junius A., Pvt. (1844-1895) Clarendon. Enl. Adam's Run Aug. 17, 1862. WIA Ream's Station Aug. 23, 1864. Farmer in Sammy Swamp Township, Clarendon Co.

***Hodges, Gabriel Mitchell,** 3rd Corp. (1841-1892) Abbeville, 3rd Classman. Prom. Color Sgt. Dec. 1, 1863. WIA Trevilian Station June 12, 1864. Farmer in Hodges.

***Holmes, Charles Rutledge,** Pvt. (1845-1915) Charleston. Enl. Simmons Bluff Apr. 20, 1863 while a 4th Classman at the Arsenal in Captain E.L. Parker's Company (Marion Artillery), SC Artillery. Trans. to Cadet Rangers. Paroled Greensboro, NC May 1, 1865. Freighter (draymaster). Brother of J.G. Holmes.

***Holmes, James Gadsden, Jr.,** Pvt. (1843-1926) Charleston, 3rd Classman. Color bearer. Commissioned Adjutant, Dismounted Battalion, Butler's Cavalry Division. Apptd. Capt. and Asst. Adjt. Gen. to Brig. Gen. E.M. Law. Active in veterans affairs. Brother of C.R. Holmes.

***Hook, Joseph F.,** Pvt. (1843-?) Orangeburg, 2nd Classman. Alive 1900.

Horton, Howell F., Pvt. (1843-1925) York. Enl. Mar. 1, 1863 Spartanburg. Captured John's Island Feb. 9, 1864. Confined Ft. Delaware. Exchanged Oct. 31, 1864. Postwar at Sharon, York Co.

***Huger, Francis Kinloch,** Pvt. (1845-1926) Charleston, 3rd Classman. Detailed to Signal Corps Dec. 13, 1862. Returned to company Apr. 1864. Commissioned 2nd Lt., 1st Regiment SC Regulars Aug. 15, 1864. Captured near Fayetteville, NC Mar. 1865 while acting adjutant of his regiment. In railway service.

Humphrey, John Washington, Pvt. (1833-1895) Clarendon. Farmer. Enl. Clarendon Nov. 2, 1861 Co. I, 23rd SC Infantry. Enl. in Cadet Rangers John's Island Oct. 15, 1863. WIA Ladd's Store (Nance's Store) June 24, 1864 with middle finger of his left hand amputated. Paroled Charlotte, NC May 11, 1865. Farmer in Clinch Co., GA. Older brother of M.B. Humphrey.

***Humphrey, Moses Benbow,** Capt. (1840-1865) Clarendon, 1st Classman. WIA John's Island Feb. 9, 1864. WIA Trevilian Station June 12, 1864. WIA Mar. 13, 1865 during attack on Kilpatrick's camp. Admitted to Pettigrew General Hospital, Raleigh, NC Mar. 18, then readmitted to General Hospital No. 11, Charlotte, NC Mar. 20, 1865 where he died Apr. 30, 1865. Younger brother of J.W. Humphrey.

Huskey, William Alexander, Pvt. (1843-1924) Spartanburg. Enl. Adam's Run Mar 1, 1863. Captured Stony Creek Aug. 1, 1864. Confined Point Lookout. Took oath and released June 14, 1865. Farmer in Cherokee County.

Jefferies, Samuel, II, Pvt. (1828-1916) Laurens. Enl. Columbia June 18, 1862. Farmer in Gowdyville.

Jeter, Henry, Pvt. (1834-?) Union. Enl. Columbia June 12, 1862.

Jeter, Richard Gilliam Hobson, Pvt. (1833-1900) Union. Enl. June 23, 1862 Columbia. WIA Dec. 1864. Farmer in Santuc, Union Co.

Jones, D.P., Pvt. (1843-?) York. Enl. Columbia Aug. 25, 1863. Deserted Sept. 15, 1863.

Jordan, John Walker, Pvt. (1842-1864) Fairfield. Enl. Columbia June 15, 1862. Prom. Corp. Feb. 23, 1864. Captured Trevilian Station June 11, 1864. Initially confined Point Lookout, Trans. to Elmira July 25, 1864. Died there of "chronic diarrhea" on Sept. 22, 1864.

Kennedy, Arthur B., Pvt. (1826-1884) Fairfield. Enl. Columbia July 20, 1862. Paroled Greensboro, NC May 1, 1865. Planter in Shiloh Township, Sumter Co.

Kennedy, William Meek, Pvt. (1834-1915) Fairfield. Enl. July 20, 1862 Columbia. Planter and merchant in York.

Kirkland, John Murray, Pvt. (1836-?) Fairfield. Enl. John's Island Oct. 15, 1863. Captured Lee's Mills July 30, 1864. Confined Elmira. Took oath and released June 14, 1865. Planter near Monticello. Alive 1890; apparently dead by 1900.

Legare, Solomon E., Pvt. (?-1865) Charleston. Enl. Nov. 10, 1861 in Capt. J.B.B. Walpole's Company (Stono Scouts), SC Cavalry. Trans. to Cadet Rangers July 28, 1864. Detailed to HQ, Cavalry Corps as scout Sept. 28, 1864. Captured near Petersburg Nov. 7, 1864. Took oath and released June 28, 1865 but was too ill to leave and admitted to hospital and died there of "chronic diarrhea" July 22, 1865. Family history says he reached home and died there.

Lipscomb, David, Pvt. (1836-?) Spartanburg. Enl. Columbia June 15, 1862. Shown as AWOL for period ending Oct. 31, 1862. No further record. Farmer in Spartanburg.

Long, John Fowler, Pvt. (1843-1921) Union. Enl. Columbia June 20, 1862. Last shown as AWOL as of Oct. 24, 1864. No further record. Farmer in Jonesville, Union Co.

Long, William H., Pvt. (1841-?) Marion. Enl. Columbia June 20, 1862. Captured John's Island Feb. 9, 1864. Confined Ft. Delaware. Took oath and released June 10, 1865. Alive 1902 in Jonesville.

Mabry, Logan C., Pvt. (1845-1920) Union. Enl. John's Island Mar. 1, 1864. Captured Stony Creek Dec. 1, 1864. Confined Point Lookout. Took oath and released June 29, 1865. Signed by mark. Farmer in Draytonville.

Martin, Robert Lafayette, Pvt. (1843-1923) Fairfield. Enl. Lightwood Knot Springs Aug. 29, 1861 in Co. E (Monticello Guards), 15th Regiment SC Infantry. Exchanged for W. Moorehead and trans. to Cadet Rangers Jan. 27, 1864. WIA Ream's Station Aug. 23, 1864. Farmer near Monticello.

Martin, William J., Pvt. (1840-?) Fairfield. Enl. Adam's Run Feb. 13, 1863. Prom. Corp. Feb. 13, 1864. "Made famous by passing off as the wife of the late J.D. McCarley on the march home." Farmer near Monticello.

*McDowell, George Archibald, Corp. (1842-1864) Charleston. (Citadel '62). Detailed as clerk to Col. Alfred Rhett Nov. and Dec. 1863. KIA John's Island Feb. 9, 1864. Cousin of John S. Dutart.

McDowell, John Lide, Pvt. (1842-1918) Spartanburg. Enl. John's Island Nov. 15, 1863. Farmer in Campobello.

McDowell, Landrum M., Pvt. Enl. Nov. 1, 1863 John's Island. Farmer in Campobello.

*McIver, Evander Roderick, Pvt. (1843-1904) Darlington, 2nd Classman. Paroled Charlotte, NC Mar. 25, 1865. Attorney and planter in Darlington Co. State Treasurer and legislator.

McJunkin, Dyer (Dire) J., Pvt. (1843-1929) Pickens. Enl. Columbia June 20, 1862. Trans. to Company E, July 30. Trans. to Co. G, Apr. 30, 1864. Farmer in Pickens.

McJunkin, John, Pvt. (1842-?) Pickens. Enl. Columbia June 20, 1862. Trans. almost immediately to Co. E. Farmer in Cleveland Township, Greenville Co.

*Mellett, Peter, Pvt. (1843-1908) Sumter, 3rd Classman. Captured John's Island Feb. 9, 1864. Confined Ft. Delaware. Took oath and released June 10, 1865. Farmer in Wedgewood, Sumter Co. Married sister of Cadets Wm. Odell and Richard M. Cain.

Miller, Cody M., Pvt. (1826-1910) Laurens. Enl. Sept. 5, 1862 Columbia. Farmer in Pickens.

*Miller, William Capers, Pvt. (1845-1932) Kershaw. Enl. at the Arsenal July 15, 1862. Detailed to Brigade Ordnance Staff Sept. 1864. Ex-Arsenal. Graduated College of Charleston. Merchant.

Milling, John McKibben, Pvt. (1825-1864) Fairfield. Planter. Enl. John's Island Jan. 17, 1864. KIA Trevilian Station June 11, 1864.

Mobley, Edward G., Pvt. (1836-?) Farmer in Chester. Enl. Nov. 1, 1862 Adam's Run. Detailed as nurse General Hospital No. 7 by order of Medical Examining Board Aug. 15, 1864. Never rejoined company. Citadel Cadet 1852-1853. Attended Mt. Zion College and SC College. Married and moved to Texas. Farmer.

Moorhead, William A., Pvt. (1823-1874) Pickens. Enl. Columbia July 23, 1862. Exchanged for R. Martin and trans. to Co. E (Monticello Guards), 15th SC Infantry Jan. 27, 1864.

Morgan, Arthur M., Pvt. (1838-?) Spartanburg. Enl. Palmetto Sharpshooters Apr. 13, 1861. Trans. Adam's Run Nov. 20, 1862. Farm laborer.

Morgan, E.A., Pvt. Enl. Co. K (Broad River Guards), 18th SC Infantry Dec. 1, 1861 Columbia. Exchanged for Joseph Bridges and trans. to Cadet Rangers Nov. 15, 1863.

Captured Trevilian Station June 11, 1864. Confined Point Lookout and Elmira. Exchanged Mar. 2, 1865.

*Moses, Isaac Harby, Corp. (1842-1900) Sumter. Recently graduated class of 1862. Detailed as clerk and reduced to the ranks in Brig. Gen. Thomas Jordan's office Jan. 31, 1864. Returned to the company May 10, 1864. Commission merchant New York City.

Murphy, E., Pvt. Enl. John's Island Jan. 1, 1864.

*Nettles, William Joseph, 2nd Lt. (1842-1864) Sumter, 1st Classman. KIA Burgess' Mill Oct. 27, 1864.

Nixon, James P., Pvt. (1844-?) Pickens. Enl. Co. A, 6th SC Cavalry Abbeville CH June 20, 1862. Trans. to Cadet Rangers May 1, 1864. WIA Trevilian Station June 12, 1864. Clerk and farmer in Pickens.

Orr, Joseph A., Pvt. (1828-1864) Farmer in Union. Enl. Columbia June 20, 1862. KIA Burgess' Mill Oct. 27, 1864.

Ott, Lewis M., Pvt. (1830-?) Orangeburg. Enl. John's Island Jan. 4, 1864. Permanently detached to Engineers June 15, 1864 on recommendation of Medical Board. Never rejoined company. Farmer.

Owens, Alexander, Pvt. (1844-1864) Charleston. Butcher. Enl. Co. G, 3rd SC Cavalry Apr. 5, 1862. Enl. Columbia June 20, 1862. Hospitalized in Charleston from Aug. 1863 to Apr. 1864. Rehospitalized for diarrhea and febris in Richmond on Dec. 20, 1864 and apparently died there.

*Owens, Sherod Harvey, Pvt. (1841-1892) Williamsburg, 2nd Classman. Detailed as clerk in Col. Alfred Rhett's office Nov. 23, 1863. Returned to company Apr. 1864. Captured Trevilian Station June 11, 1864. Confined Point Lookout. Exchanged and paroled Mar. 17, 1865. War ended while still in parole camp at Richmond. Turpentine manufacturer in Williamsburg Co.

*Paslay, Buckingham Horlbeck, Pvt. (1843-1917) Laurens, 2nd Classman. Prom. corp. Feb. 23, 1864. Farmer in Hunter Township, Laurens Co.

Paslay, William H., Pvt. (1846-1863) Laurens. Enl. Adam's Run Jan. 1, 1863. Died in hospital of disease Oct. 1863.

Perry, Andrew Jackson, Pvt. (1839-1920) Spartanburg. Enl. Columbia June 18, 1862. Wheelwright and farmer in Cherokee Co. Younger brother of W.L. Perry.

Perry, William L., Pvt. (1837-1887) Spartanburg. Enl. 5th SC Feb. 22, 1861. Enl. Columbia June 18, 1862. Trans. to Co. B (Charleston Light Infantry), 1st Battalion SC Infantry June 29, 1863. Older brother of A.J. Perry. Millwright in Center Township.

Phillips, John, Pvt. Enl. at Adam's Run July 9, 1863. Detailed on Oct. 29, 1864. Probably never rejoined company. Farmer in Spartanburg Co.

*Pinckney, Samuel Gourdin, Pvt. (1843-1902) Charleston, 3rd Classman. Trans. in Dec. 1862 to Co. I (Palmetto Guard),

2nd SC Infantry. Agent for Southern Express Company in Charleston.

*Platt, Daniel H., Pvt. (1846-1909) Charleston. Former Arsenal Cadet. Enl. May 1, 1863 in Co. I (Rebel Troop), 3rd SC Cavalry. Exchanged for M.M. Seabrook Dec. 1, 1863. Deserted into enemy lines on March 6, 1865. Took oath and released Mar. 15, 1865. Surveyor in Collins Township.

Porter, J.H., Pvt. (1842-?) Farm laborer. Marion. Enl. Conwayboro June 12, 1862. Discharged Oct. 4, 1862. Farm laborer. Merchant in Westminster, Oconee Co.

*Proctor, James Toutant, Pvt. (1845-1910) New Orleans, LA. Gen. Beauregard's nephew. Enl. at the Arsenal, where he was a 4th Classman, June 25, 1862. Underage and not receiving parental consent, he was discharged Aug. 25, 1862 and returned to the Arsenal. He left later in 1862 and was Prom. to Lt. for meritorious service at Fredericksburg. Lost a foot at Chancellorsville, VA, then served on his uncle's staff.

Ross, Jacob Brown, Pvt. (1847-1927) Enl. Jan. 1865. Contractor in Blacksburg, Cherokee Co.

Ross, William M., Pvt. (1839-1925) Enl. Co. K, 18th SC Infantry. Enl. Columbia May 1, 1864. Detailed as a blacksmith. Farmer in Blacksburg.

*Salley, Joel Townsend, (1842-1888) Orangeburg, 3rd Classman. Paroled Greensboro, NC May 1, 1865. In Liberty Township.

Sarratt, Henry M., Pvt. (1844-1910) Spartanburg. Enl. Adam's Run Dec. 1, 1862. Memory Roll says WIA Trevilian Station. Furloughed for 60 days on Sept. 20, 1864 by order of Medical Examining Board. Farmer in Limestone Springs.

Sarratt, Iverson G., Pvt. (1842-?) Student. Enl. Columbia June 18, 1862. Captured Trevilian Station June 11, 1864. Confined Elmira. Transferred and exchanged at City Point May 2, 1865. Confined to Jackson Hospital in Richmond for "chronic diarrhea" immediately. No further record.

Sarratt, William A., Pvt. (1840-1864) Spartanburg. Farmer. Enl. Palmetto Sharpshooters Apr. 13, 1861. Enl. Feb. 25, 1864 John's Island. Mortally wounded at Trevilian Station and died June 16, 1864.

Saulesbury, J.E., Pvt. (1835-?) Farm manager in Colleton. Enl. Sept. 1, 1863 Charleston in Co. D (South Carolina Rangers), 5th SC Cavalry. Exchanged for G.E. Davis and trans. to Cadet Rangers Nov. 1, 1863. WIA Trevilian Station June 12, 1864. Farm manager, St. Goose Creek Parish.

*Schipman, Berent Momming, Pvt. (1841-1868) Charleston. Enl. on May 9, 1861 in Charleston, where he was a 2nd Classman at the Citadel, in Co. I (Palmetto Guard), 2nd Regiment SC Infantry. Re-enl. in Cadet Rangers June 9,

1862 at the Citadel. Prom. Corp. Feb. 13, 1864. Prom.
Regimental Sgt. Maj. (for gallantry) Aug. 6, 1864. Apptd.
2nd Lt. (for valor and skill) Mar. 2 to rank from Feb. 17,
1864 and posted to Co. D, 6th SC Cavalry. WIA Mar. 13,
1865 and admitted to General Hospital No. 13 that day and
furloughed on Mar. 19. Planter in Berkeley Co. Brother of
H. & J. Schipman.
*Schipman, Herman, Pvt. (1845-?) Charleston, 3rd Classman.
WIA Ream's Station Aug. 23, 1864. Captured Stony Creek
with disabled horses Dec. 1, 1864. Confined Point Lookout.
Took oath and released June 5, 1865. Farmer and turpen-
tine distiller in Berkeley Co. Brother of B. & J. Schipman.
Schipman, James Harris, Pvt. (1847-1884) Charleston. Name
appears on Memory Roll but not in CSR. Left Citadel to en-
list in 1865. Merchant and turpentine dealer. See also
Appendix B. Brother of B. & H. Schipman.
*Seabrook, John La Roche, 5th Sgt. (1842-1870) Colleton, 1st
Classman. Trans. on Nov. 15, 1863 as a Pvt. in Co. I
(Rebel Troop), 3rd SC Cavalry. Planter John's Island.
Older brother of M.M. Seabrook.
*Seabrook, Marcellus Murray, 2nd Sgt. (1843-1910) Colleton,
2nd Classman. Trans. on Dec. 1, 1863, as a pvt. in ex-
change for D.H. Platt to Co. I (Rebel Troop), 3rd SC
Cavalry. Planter on Edisto Island. Younger brother of J.L.
Seabrook.
*Sheppard, James Oscar, 4th Corp. (1842-1864) Edgefield, 3rd
Classman. Prom. Regimental Sgt. Maj. Jan.-Feb. 1863.
Strongly recommended for commission. KIA Trevilian
Station June 12, 1864.
*Simms, William Gilmore, Jr., 3rd Sgt. (1843-1912) Barnwell,
2nd Classman. Prom. 1st Sgt. Apr. 1, 1863. WIA Trevilian
Station June 12, 1864. Prom. 2nd Lt., Co. D, 1st Regiment
SC Artillery Oct. 31, 1864. Attorney and judge in Barnwell
Co.
Sloan, Robert Easley, Pvt. (1841-1932) Pickens. Enl. John's
Island Jan. 1, 1864. Cotton buyer in Greenville; general
merchant and farmer in Pickens.
Smith, S.G., Pvt. Enl. Adam's Run Dec. 1, 1862.
Smythe, R.L., Pvt. (1842-?) Enl. Columbia June 30, 1862.
Discharged Aug. 14, 1862.
Snelling, William Henry, Pvt. (1823-1864) Barnwell. Farmer.
Enl. June 20, 1862 Columbia. Discharged Aug. 14, 1862.
*Spann, Henry Asbury, Pvt. (1843-1916) Lexington, 3rd
Classman. Captured John's Island Feb. 9, 1864. Confined
Ft. Delaware. Took oath and released June 7, 1865. Farmer
in Leesville.
Sparks, Junius, Pvt. (1837-1910) Union. Enl. Sept. 1862 in Co.
C, 18th Regiment SC Infantry. Trans. to Cadet Rangers
May 1, 1864. AWOL as of Oct. 24, 1864. Farmer in
Draytonville.

Stacey, James Franklin, Pvt. (1846-1920) Spartanburg. Enl. John's Island Feb. 13, 1864. WIA and captured Ream's Station Aug. 23, 1864. Variously confined at II Corps Hospital at City Point, Harewood, and Lincoln General Hospitals, Washington, DC and Old Capitol Prison and Elmira. Took oath and released June 21, 1865.

Summers, George T., Pvt. (1839-1864) Charleston. Enl. Green Pond Feb. 6, 1863 in Co. D (South Carolina Rangers), 5th SC Cavalry. Trans. to Cadet Rangers in 1863 in exchange for Ross Davis. KIA Burgess' Mill Oct. 27, 1864.

Utsey, Jacob C., Pvt. (1832-1907) Charleston. Enl. Adam's Run Nov. 15, 1862. WIA Mar. 13, 1865. Admitted to Pettigrew General Hospital in Raleigh, NC the same day. Farmer in Koger Township.

Vaughn, Richard J., Pvt. (1815-?) Spartanburg. Farmer. Enl. Adam's Run Nov. 20, 1862. Paroled Greensboro, NC May 2, 1865.

Weir, Matthew (also shown as **Wier** and **Ware**), Pvt. (1826-?) Fairfield. Enl. 4th Sgt. of Co. F, 23rd SC Infantry. Enl. Columbia July 9, 1862 in Co. C, 6th SC Cavalry. Trans. to Cadet Rangers spring 1864.

Whitlock, William H., Pvt. (1843-1919) Anderson. Enl. Columbia June 25, 1862. WIA Trevilian Station. Farmer in Anderson Co.

Williams, Alexander, Pvt. Enl. Columbia June 23, 1862. Exchanged for L. Hill.

***Willingham, Joseph**, Pvt. (1839-1864) Fairfield. Enl. June 1, 1864 Winnsboro. No further record after October 1864 when furloughed for disease. KIA at Fayetteville.

***Willson, John Owens**, Pvt. (1845-1923) Charleston, 2nd Classman. Trans. to Co. I (Rebel Troop), 3rd SC Cavalry Dec. 1, 1863 in exchange for J.A. Davis. Attorney, Methodist Minister, and college president in Greenwood.

***Womack, Joel M.**, Pvt. (1844-?) Charleston, 3rd Classman. Exchanged to Co. D (South Carolina Rangers), 5th SC Cavalry 1864 in exchange for M.E. Cohen, Jr. Captured White House June 20, 1864. Escaped from Elmira Dec. 1864. Surrendered Hillsboro.

Yarborough, R.T., Pvt. (1834-?) Fairfield. Enl. June 1, 1864 Winnsboro. WIA Nance's Shop June 22, 1864. Furloughed from Jackson Hospital, Richmond, VA, July 19, 1864. No further record. Merchant at Monticello. Alive 1890; apparently dead by 1900.

NOTE: J.R. Hagood left with the * Cadets but joined the 1st Regiment SC Volunteers.

APPENDIX B

BATTALION OF STATE CADETS

FIELD AND STAFF

White, James Benjamin (Major '49), Commanding Officer (1828-1906) Superintendent, the Citadel. Educator and insurance broker, Marion.
Coffin, Amory, Jr. (2nd Lt. '62), Adjutant (1841-1916) Assistant Professor of French and Drawing, the Citadel. Chief engineer at steel mill, Philadelphia, PA.
Mazyck, Alexander Harris (2nd Lt. '54), Quartermaster (1835-1913) Bursar, the Citadel. Accountant in Charleston.

COMPANY A, THE CITADEL CADETS

FACULTY OFFICERS

Thompson, Hugh Smith (Capt. '56), (1836-1904) Professor of Belles Lettres and Ethics, the Citadel. Educator, State Superintendent of Education, Governor, US Civil Service Commissioner, and Assistant Secretary of the Treasury.
Black, James Ewell (2nd Lt. '57), (1837-1894) Assistant Professor of Mathematics, the Citadel; formerly conscription officer P.A.C.S. Farmer in Spartanburg and insurance agent in Ft. Smith, AR.

CADET OFFICERS

Thomas, Edward (Cadet 1st Lt.), (1843-1895) Fairfield, 1st Class. Railway official in TX, TN, and AR.
Hollingsworth, Stephen Franklin (Cadet 2nd Lt.), (1842-1867) Pickens, 1st Class. Rancher in TX.
Dean, George Roswell (Cadet 2nd Lt.), (1844-1911) Anderson, 1st Class. Physician in Spartanburg.

CADET NON-COMMISSIONED OFFICERS

Gray, James Medicus (Cadet Orderly Sgt.), (1843-1902) Barnwell, 1st Class. Farmer and saw mill and cotton gin owner in Allendale.

Klinck, Gustavus Wickenberg (Cadet 2nd Sgt.), (1844-1916) Charleston, 1st Class. Merchant in Charleston.

DeSaussure, Alexander Baron (Cadet 3rd Sgt.), (1844-1905) Charleston, 1st Class. Railway agent in Lynchburg, VA.

Peronneau, Henry (Cadet 4th Sgt.), (1843-1875) Colleton, 1st Class. Telegraphist in Texarkana, AR.

Pringle, William Ashmead (Cadet 1st Corp.), (1845-1885) Charleston, 2nd Class. Bookkeeper in Charleston.

Murdoch, Francis Johnstone (Cadet 2nd Corp.), (1846-1909) Charleston, 2nd Class. In Salisbury, NC.

Dozier, Melville (Cadet 3rd Corp.), (1846-1936) Williamsburg, 2nd Class. Educator and Chairman, Selective Service Board, Los Angeles, CA.

Spearman, William Robinson (Cadet 4th Corp.), (1843-1876) Newberry, 2nd Class. Brother of John R. Spearman. In Newberry.

Boinest, John Elias (Cadet 5th Corp.), (1845-1896) Charleston, 2nd Class. Bookkeeper in Charleston.

CADET PRIVATES

Barnwell, Joseph Walker (1846-1930) Charleston, 3rd Class. Attorney in Charleston, legislator.

Barre, John J. (1843-1872) Lexington, 3rd Class. In Newberry.

Bartlette, Julius Lyman (1845-?) Sumter, 3rd Class. Bank clerk in Laredo, TX.

Bethune, John B. (1846-?) Spartanburg, 3rd Class. Previous service with Co. K (Spartan Rifles), Palmetto Sharpshooters.

Black, Joseph F., Jr. (1847-1868) Abbeville, 3rd Class.

Bouknight, Joseph Huiet (1841-1911) Edgefield, 1st Class. Planter and bank president in Saluda Co.

Boyd, Thomas B. (1848-1884) York, 2nd Class. Methodist minister in Orangeburg.

Branch, William Tully (1845-1903) Abbeville, 3rd Class. Hotelkeeper and insurance agent in Abbeville.

Breese, William Edmond (1848-1917) Charleston, 4th Class. Banker in Charleston and Asheville, NC.

Brown, Pinckney (1846-1919) Barnwell, 3rd Class. Farmer in Aiken.

Bull, Charles Pinckney (1846-1916) Charleston, 3rd Class. Attorney in New York City.

Carwile, William Edward (1847-1878) Edgefield, 4th Class. Railroad agent and telegraphist, Ridge Spring. Brother of Z.W. Carwile.

Chafee, John William Smith (1848-1907) Charleston, 4th Class. Company president in Augusta, GA. His sister married Theodore G. Croft.

Clark, Robert Knox (1848-1888) Marion, 3rd Class. Farmer and Clerk of Court in Dillon Co.

Coffin, Charles Edmonston (1846-1906) Barnwell, 3rd Class. Banking business in Augusta, GA. Younger brother of Lt. Amory Coffin and 1st cousin of G.M. Coffin.

Croft, George William (1846-1904) Edgefield, 3rd Class. Attorney in Aiken. Legislator and U.S. Congressman. Brother of T.G. Croft.

Croft, Theodore Gaillard (1845-1915) Edgefield, 3rd Class. Physician in Aiken. Prior service as Sgt. Co. C (Croft Mountain Rangers), 16th Regiment SC Infantry. Brother of G.W. Croft; he married sister of J.W.S. Chafee.

Dargan, James Thornwell (1846-?) Richland, 3rd Class. Insurance company president in Atlanta, GA.

Dargan, John Hugh (1846-1877) Darlington, 3rd Class.

DeSaussure, William Peronneau (1847-1936) Charleston, 3rd Class. In Richmond, VA. Brother of A.B. DeSaussure.

Dougherty, John (1846-1892) Charleston, 3rd Class. Cotton broker in Charleston.

Dubose, Hampden Coit (1845-1910) Darlington, 3rd Class. Presbyterian missionary to China.

Duncan, D'Arcy Paul (1846-1921) Spartanburg, 3rd Class. Farmer in Spartanburg Co. Railroad commissioner of SC.

Ervin, Erasmus Ellerbe (1847-1919) Clarendon, 3rd Class. Presbyterian minister in NC, KY, and SC.

Felder, Jacob Stroman (1845-1928) Orangeburg, 3rd Class. Farmer in Orangeburg.

Fike, Claudius Lucius (1845-1894) Spartanburg, 2nd Class. Surveyor in Laurens.

Fishburne, Lawrence Newman (1845-1904) Colleton, 3rd Class. Merchant in Colleton Co. Brother of C.P. and W.J. Fishburne.

Frazier, Wesley W. (1844-?) Abbeville, 2nd Class. Physician at Mechanicsville, Sumter Co., 1890.

Furman, Farish Carter (1846-1883) Greenville, 3rd Class. Attorney, farmer and county judge in Milledgeville, GA.

Furman, John Hudson (1848-?) Greenville, 3rd Class. Mining engineer and world traveler.

Graham, John (1847-?) Beaufort, 4th Class.

Green, Allen Jones (1846-1910) Richland, 3rd Class. Planter, attorney, and judge in Columbia.

Hagood, Lee (1846-1890) Barnwell, 3rd Class. Prior service as courier on Gen. Micah Jenkins' staff. Insurance agent in Columbia.

Harrell, Charles Talley (1847-1907) Darlington, 3rd Class. Cattle dealer in Columbia.

Hayne, Robert Brevard (1848-1883) Charleston, 3rd Class. Clerk, SC Railway in Charleston.

Heyward, Albert Rhett (1846-1910) Charleston, 3rd Class. Planter in Charleston and railway service in Columbia. Brother of J.H. Heyward.

Heyward, James Barnwell (1848-1931) Beaufort, 4th class. Planter at Salkehatchie.

Heyward, Julius Henry (1849-1923) Colleton, 4th Class. Attorney in Greenville. Brother of A.R. Heyward.

Jervey, Lewis Simons (1848-1927) Charleston, 4th Class. Cotton and rice broker in Charleston in partnership with D.H. Bacot.

Johnstone, Sedgewick Lewis Simons (1848-1873) Georgetown, 4th Class.

Lesesne, James Petigru (1848-1892) Charleston, 4th Class. Attorney in Charleston. Drowned in Australia.

Lewis, John Earle (1844-1928) Pickens, 3rd Class. Farmer in Seneca.

Lide, Thomas Parks (1845-1906) Darlington, 4th Class. Baptist minister in Sumter.

Locke, Arthur Hall (1846-1905) Charleston, 2nd Class. Cotton broker and commission merchant in Charleston.

Lockwood, Joshua (1845-1924) Charleston, 2nd Class. Physician and druggist in Charleston.

Lynah, Edward, Jr. (1846-1920) Charleston, 3rd Class. Rice planter in Beaufort Co. Brother of J. Lynah.

Lynah, James (1845-1901) Charleston, 3rd Class. Prominent in shipping and coal mining in Baltimore, MD. Brother of E. Lynah.

Mazyck, Arthur (1848-1914) Charleston, 4th Class. Attorney in Charleston.

McCabe, Benjamin Franklin (1847-1894) Charleston, 2nd Class. Businessman in Charleston and Berkeley Counties.

McCarty, Edward C. (1843-1929) Charleston, 2nd Class. Bookkeeper in Augusta, GA.

McCully, Peter Keys (1845-1917) Anderson, 2nd Class. Prior service in 2nd Regiment SC Rifles. Cotton buyer in Anderson.

Morris, William H. (1845-?) Colleton, 4th Class.

Muldrow, Robert Ellison (1848-1865) Sumter, 4th Class. Died of typhoid fever Apr. 7, 1865.

Parker, William McKenzie (1847-1865) Charleston, 3rd Class. Killed by Federal soldiers in Anderson May 9, 1865.

Pearson, Randall T. (1848-?) Edgefield, 3rd Class.

Perry, Jennings Waring (1846-1886) Colleton, 4th Class. Attorney in Charleston.

Poe, Joseph Taylor (1847-1917) Anderson, 2nd Class. Railroad service in Mobile, AL.

Pringle, James Reid (1846-1920) Charleston, 2nd Class. Cotton and rice factor in Charleston.
Rhett, William Haskell (1844-?) Charleston, 3rd Class. In Brooklyn, NY.
Sams, Mikelle Seabrook (1847-1914) Colleton, 3rd Class. In FL.
Sanders, Lawrence Witsell (1846-1870) Charleston, 2nd Class. Clerk in Charleston.
Simons, Augustus Taveau (1847-1900) Charleston, 4th Class. In Charleston.
Simpson, James Garlington (1846-1926) Laurens, 3rd Class. Farmer in Clinton and attorney, alderman, board of education, mayor, and probate judge in Bolivar, MO.
Smith, John Julius Pringle (1849-1927) Charleston, 4th Class. In Charleston.
Spearman, Frank G. (1844-1928) Newberry, 2nd Class. Property owner in Cross Anchor.
Spearman, John Robert (1841-1922) Newberry, 2nd Class. Farmer in Newberry Co. Brother of W.R. Spearman.
Stewart, John Wistar Simpson (1846-1914) Greenville, 3rd Class. Farmer, surveyor, and mill operator in Greenville Co.
Stone, Eugene Earle (1843-1907) Greenville, 3rd Class. Prior service in 26th SC Infantry. Planter in Greenville Co.
Taylor, David Sloan (1845-1891) Anderson, 2nd Class. In Anderson.
Thomas, Carey Judson (1845-1923) Marlboro, 3rd Class. Prior service in 8th Regiment SC Infantry. In Inverness, FL.
Thomson, Robert (1846-1927) Beaufort, 3rd Class. In Beaufort Co.
Thompson, James (1848-1898) Beaufort, 4th Class. In Blackville.
Tobin, Isidore Lartigue (1847-1909) Barnwell, 4th Class. Prior service in Le Gardeur's Company (Orleans Guard Artillery), Louisiana Artillery. Attorney in Allendale. His sister married Lee Hagood.
Todd, Samuel Ross (1846-1874) Laurens, 3rd Class. In Laurens.
Vernon, W.R. (1844-?) Laurens, 1st Class.
Vinson, John (1846-?) Richland, 2nd Class. Farmer in Fairfield Co.
Waller, Cadmus Garlington (1845-1901) Abbeville, 2nd Class. Merchant in Greenwood and Mayor. Brother of E.H. Waller.
Whaley, Edward Clarence (1847-1907) Orangeburg, 4th Class. Planter on Edisto Island.
Wilson, Franklin Nelson (1844-1905) Williamsburg, 2nd Class. In Clarendon Co.

COMPANY B, CITADEL CADETS

FACULTY OFFICERS

Armstrong, Nathaniel Walker (1st Lt. '51), (1829-1896) Professor of Mathematics and Mechanical Philosophy, the Citadel. Educator and legislator in Alabama.

Lanneau, John Francis (2nd Lt. '56), (1836-1921) Assistant Professor of Mathematics, the Citadel. Prior service as captain of cavalry, Hampton Legion and as engineer officer. Educator in SC, AL, and MO. Professor of physics at Wake Forest.

Cadet Officers

East, Olin Derrick (Cadet 1st Lt.), (1843-?) Laurens, 1st Class. Went west immediately after the war and his family never heard from him again.

White, Sims Edward (Cadet 2nd Lt.), (1844-1881) Charleston, 1st Class. Planter in Berkeley Co.

Sheppard, Orlando (Cadet 2nd Lt.), (1844-1929) Edgefield, 1st Class. Attorney in Edgefield.

CADET NON-COMMISSIONED OFFICERS

Snowden, William Howard (Cadet Orderly Sgt.), (1845-1906) Charleston, 1st Class. Merchant in Charleston and Macon, GA. Brother of T.G. Snowden.

King, James W. (Cadet 2nd Sgt.), (1844-1890) Kershaw, 1st Class. Physician and druggist in Florence.

Baskin, William Peebles (Cadet 3rd Sgt.), (1843-1876) Richland, 1st Class. Planter in Bishopville.

Horsey, Charles W. (Cadet 4th Sgt.), (1845-1878) Charleston, 1st Class. Physician in Fernandina, FL.

Culbreath, James Yarbrough (Cadet 1st Corp.), (1843-1904) Edgefield, 2nd Class. Attorney in Newberry.

Haynsworth, Moses Sanders (Cadet 2nd Corp.), (1845-1928) Darlington, 2nd Class. Farmer in Florence Co.

Horlbeck, John Schernley (Cadet 3rd Corp.), (1845-1916) Charleston, 2nd Class. Pecan grower and brick manufacturer at Boone Hall Plantation near Mount Pleasant.

CADET PRIVATES

Adams, Edgar Sheppard (1848-?) Edgefield, 4th Class. Moved to TX and married there.

Allen, James Pierson (1848-1934) Charleston, 4th Class. Government engineer in Charleston.

Appleby, Felix Vivian (1845-1911) Colleton. Cotton buyer and merchant in St. George.

Boatwright, James Henry "Hal" (1846-1911) Richland, 4th Class. Father was Mayor of Columbia. Dry goods merchant and insurance agent in Wilmington, NC.

Boggs, Thomas E. (1847-1877) 5th Congressional District (Pickens), 4th Class. Farmer in Pickens Co.

Brown, Heyward (1847-1878) Barnwell, 4th Class.

Brown, Lawrence W. (1849-?) Barnwell, 4th Class. Farmer in Lancaster.

Buck, George Olney (1847-1865) Horry, 4th Class. Died of disease Jan. 22, 1865, while Cadets were in service.

Buckingham, William R. (1848-?) Barnwell, 4th Class. Insurance agent in Barnwell.

Cain, Richard Marion (1846-1886) Sumter, 4th Class. Farmer in Sumter Co. Prior service in Co. K, 22nd SC Infantry. Brother of W.O. Cain.

Cain, William O'Dell (1844-1929) Sumter, 4th Class. Farmer in Sumter. Legislator. Brother of R.M. Cain.

Cannon, Lewis Cass (1846-?) Spartanburg, 4th Class. Bank cashier in Spartanburg. Alive 1891.

Cantey, Joseph Samuel (1846-1929) Clarendon, 4th Class. Farmer near Summerton.

Carwile, Zachariah Williams, Jr. (1849-?) Edgefield, 4th Class. Insurance broker and merchant in Augusta, GA. Brother of W.E. Carwile.

Chisolm, Laurens North (1848-1905) Charleston, 4th Class. Cotton and rice factor in Charleston.

Coffin, George Mathewes, Jr. (1847-1934) Charleston, 4th Class. Produce dealer and banker in Charleston. First cousin of Lt. Amory Coffin and C.E. Coffin.

Culbreath, John (1846-1865) Edgefield, 2nd Class. Died of measles April 17, 1865, while Cadets were in service.

Dargan, Kemp S. (1848-?) Richland, 4th Class. Insurance business in Atlanta.

Evans, Calvin L. (1845-1921) Chesterfield, 4th Class. Farmer in Cheraw.

Fell, John Hamlin (1845-1883) Charleston, 4th Class. Clerk in Charleston and Savannah, GA.

Ferrell, George W. (1846-?) 1st Congressional District (Marion), 4th Class. Prior service with Co. H., 8th SC Infantry. Wounded July 1, 1862, at Malvern Hill. Arm may have been amputated. Farmer in Bamberg Co.

Footman, Henry E. (1845-1924) Williamsburg, 4th Class. Prior service in 25th Regiment SC Infantry. School principal in CA and later in commercial interests.

Gantt, Hamilton M. Greenville, 4th Class.

Gantt, **Monroe** (1847-1917) Lexington, 4th Class. Railroad agent and farmer in Aiken.

Goodman, William Pulaski (1845-1873) Edgefield. Rancher in TX; killed by Indians.

Graves, George Crawford (1845-1923) Abbeville, 3rd Class. Farmer in Abbeville Co. near Monterey.

Gwin, Richard A. (1838-?) 5th Congressional District, 4th Class. Prior service with Co. B (Butler Guards), 2nd SC Infantry. Memory Roll says Robert A. Gwin.

Harrison, Isham (1848-1918) Anderson, 3rd Class. In Walhalla.

Hemingway, Allard Belin (1846-1922) Georgetown, 4th Class. Farmer and merchant in Georgetown Co.

Huger, John Chapman (1848-1880) 2nd Congressional District (Charleston), 4th Class. Accountant in Summerville.

Hughes, Samuel Bones (1847-1920) Edgefield, 4th Class. Farmer in Edgefield.

Ingram, John Conyers (1847-1889) Clarendon, 4th Class. Farmer in Sumter.

Janney, Charles F. (1848-1885) Richland, 4th Class. Attorney in Columbia.

Johnson, John (1845-?) Colleton, 4th Class.

Johnson, Thomas Albert (1846-1865) Newberry, 4th Class. Died at Spartanburg of brain fever on March 23, 1865, while Cadets were in service.

Johnson, William Ewing (1847-1910) Kershaw, 4th Class. Dry goods merchant in Camden.

Johnstone, George (1846-1921) Newberry, 4th Class. Attorney in Newberry. Legislator and U.S. Congressman.

Jones, Johnstone (1848-1922) York, 4th Class. Adjutant General of NC and later attorney in CA.

Joye, Edmund Vernon (1847-1891) Charleston, 4th Class. Physician in Athens and Atlanta, GA.

Kennedy, William Watts (1846-?) Laurens, 4th Class. Lawyer in Laurens.

Kershaw, John (1847-1921) Kershaw, 3rd Class. Furloughed January 1865 to join the staff of his father, Maj. Gen. Joseph B. Kershaw, in VA, captured at Saylor's Creek and confined at Fort Warren, MA. Attorney until 1873 when he became Episcopal priest in GA and SC.

Keys, Joseph Whitner (1845-1913) Anderson, 4th Class. In Anderson.

Lamar, Abner Whatley (1847-?) 4th Congressional District (Edgefield). Clergyman in Kershaw.

Lenoir, James Yarborough (1847-?) Sumter, 4th Class. Farmer in Lamar Co., TX.

Lowndes, Richard I'on (1848-1889) Georgetown, 4th Class. Farmer in Georgetown.

Lyons, Jacob "Jake" Cohen, Jr. (1848-?) Richland, 4th Class. Continued his education in Philadelphia. In wholesale pharmaceutical business with his eldest brother in New Orleans.

Magrath, Andrew Gordon, Jr. (1845-1894) Charleston, 2nd Class. Son of the Governor, he was furloughed during the last year of the war to serve as an aide-de-camp to Brig. Gen. James Connor. Attorney and judge in Charleston.

Martin, Robert Hayne (1847-?) Charleston, 4th Class. Merchant in Charleston and Brooklyn, NY.

Matheson, John Stoney (1849-?) Charleston, 4th Class. Purser in the Merchant Marine in Charleston.

McBee, Vardry Echols (1849-1923) Greenville, 4th Class. Railway service in NC and GA. Brother of F.B. McBee.

McGhee, William Zach (1845-1885) 4th Congressional District, 4th Class. Prior service in Co. G, 7th Regiment SC Cavalry. Journalist and teacher in Cokesbury.

McMichael, William Edward (1846-1889) Orangeburg, 4th Class. Deputy Sheriff in Orangeburg Co.

Meng, Lewis (1846-1911) Union, 4th Class. Overseer in cotton mills in Spartanburg and Laurens.

Miller, Daniel A. (1846-?) 6th Congressional District (Fairfield), 4th Class. Prior service with Co. G, 6th SC Volunteers.

Moore, William H. (1847-1921) Abbeville, 4th Class. Farmer in Donalds.

Moore, Matthew Singleton (1849-?) Sumter, 4th Class. Farmer in Waterloo.

Moore, Thomas Thompson (1845-1922) Newberry, 4th Class. Dentist and city alderman in Columbia.

Munro, James (1846-1913) Anderson, 4th Class. In Union.

Noble, Russell (1847-1865) Charleston, 4th Class. Died of disease while Cadets were in service.

Obear, Henry Norwood (1847-1897) Fairfield, 4th Class. Attorney in Fairfield and Columbia.

Palmer, William DeHon (1846-1912) Charleston, 4th Class. Lost hand while Cadets were in service. Planter in Berkeley Co.

Parker, James Rose (1848-1884) Georgetown, 4th Class. Prior service with 1st (Gregg's) Regiment SC Infantry. Planter in Georgetown Co.

Patterson, William Bailey (1845-1864) Charleston, 2nd Class. Mortally wounded at Tulifinny.

Pressley, William Burrows (1847-1930) Williamsburg, 4th Class. Rancher in CA.

Ragin, Henry Lawrence (1845-1906) Clarendon, 4th Class. Prior service in Palmetto Sharpshooters. Postwar, changed his name to Henry Ragin Thomas. Near Williston.

Rivers, Frederick Witsell Fraser (1846-1907) Colleton, 4th Class. Physician in Colleton Co.

Rogers, James Mitchell (1845-1924) Charleston, 1st Class. Merchant in MS, LA, and NC.

Salley, Alexander McQueen (1847-1929) Orangeburg, 3rd Class. Farmer in Orangeburg Co. and sheriff.

Sanders, Cotesworth Pinckney (1846-1919) Colleton, 4th Class. Merchant in Bamberg; attorney in Gaffney and Spartanburg.

Sellers, John Calhoun (1847-1920) Marion, 4th Class. Attorney, farmer, and land surveyor in Marion Co. Legislator and postmaster of Sellers.

Sessions, David Robert (1847-1924) Georgetown, 4th Class. Prior service in Co. B (Brooks Rifle Guards), 10th Regiment SC Infantry. Farmer.

Shuck, John Sexton (1847-1907) Barnwell, 4th Class. Teacher, mercantile business, and newspaper editor in Aiken and Bamberg.

Simons, William Wragg (1846-1913) Charleston, 4th Class. Clerk of Charleston City Council.

Simpson, McNeil Turner (1845-1919) Laurens, 4th Class. Planter and mercantile agent in Laurens Co.

Small, James Hampton (1850-1925) Georgetown, 4th Class. Merchant in Georgetown.

Smith, Henry A. (?-1909) 6th Congressional District, 4th Class. Prior service as Sgt., Co. B, 1st SC Artillery.

Snowden, Theodore Gaillard (1847-1896) Charleston, 4th Class. Brother of W.H. Snowden. Cotton broker in Charleston.

Spann, John Wesley (1846-1917) Lexington, 4th Class. Farmer in Gilbert.

Spearman, John Franklin (1845-?) Newberry, 4th Class. Schoolteacher in Newberry and railroad ticket agent in Columbia.

Stansell, Francis Wardlaw (1845-1875) Barnwell, 4th Class. In Williston.

Thomas, Peyre (1846-1885) Fairfield, 4th Class. Prior service. Physician in TX. First cousin of Capt. J.P. Thomas and brother of Cadets Edward and W.R. Thomas.

Thomson, Arthur W. (1844-?) 3rd Congressional District (Barnwell), 4th Class. Prior service in 1st (Hagood's) Regiment SC Infantry.

Thompson, Waddy, Jr. (1847-1882) Greenville, 4th Class. Physician in Greenville.

Tiedeman, John Carston (1846-1938) Charleston, 4th Class. Wholesale grocer and provision dealer in Charleston.

Vance, James Wistar (1845-?) Abbeville, 4th Class. Physician in Memphis, TN.

Vose, John George (1845-1923) Colleton, 4th Class. City commissioner in Lawrenceville, GA.

Walker, Mendel Lafayette (1845-?) Laurens, 4th Class. Prior service with 5th SC Infantry. Farmer.

Wallace, Edwin Ruthven (1846-1892) Union, 4th Class. Prior service as Sgt., 5th Regiment SC Infantry, severely wounded at Frazier's Farm, VA.

Watson, Artemas Briggs (1847-1912) Edgefield, 4th Class. Methodist Minister in Saluda Co.
Wells, Joseph Seabrook (1848-1883) Beaufort, 4th Class. Commission merchant in Charleston.
Williams, Earle E. (1848-?) Edgefield, 4th Class.
Williman, Walter (1845-1924) Charleston, 4th Class. Bank teller and cashier in Charleston.
Woodward, Alston Parke "Pat" (1847-?) 3rd Congressional District (Beaufort), 4th Class. Prior service as teamster with Co. D, Holcombe Legion. POW Kinston, NC, Dec. 15, 1862. Farmer at Hawthorne in Aiken Co.

COMPANIES A & B, ARSENAL CADETS

FACULTY OFFICERS

Thomas, John Peyre (Capt. '51), Commanding officer (1833-1912) Superintendent and Professor of French, the Arsenal. Educator in NC, Superintendent of the Citadel, legislator, and state historian of SC.
Patrick, John Bellinger (1st Lt. '55), (1832-1900) Professor of Mathematics, the Arsenal. High school principal in Greenville and superintendent of a military academy in Anderson.
Norris, Alfred Junius (2nd Lt. '60), (1833-1900) Professor of Belles Lettres and History, the Arsenal. Attorney and bank president in Edgefield.
Sams, Robert Oswald (2nd Lt. '61), (1841-1930) Assistant Professor of Mathematics and French, the Arsenal. Educator in Spartanburg and Gaffney.
Knight, Benjamin H. (2nd Lt.), (1840-?) Bursar, the Arsenal.
Sams, Melvin Melius (Surgeon), (1815-1900) Physician in Columbia. Father of B.S. Sams.

CADETS (ALL 4TH CLASSMEN)

Adger, Andrew Moffett (1846-1915) Charleston. Prior service with 25th Regiment SC Infantry. Cotton and rice factor and commission merchant in Charleston.
Allston, Charles Petigru (1848-1922) Georgetown. Planter in Georgetown Co.
Allston, Thomas Pinckney (1848-1924) Georgetown. Planter in Charleston and cotton seed oil company owner.
Bacot, Daniel Huger (1847-1920) Charleston. Cotton and rice broker in Charleston in partnership with L.S. Jervey.
Baker, John E. (1846-1912) Charleston. Publisher in Charleston.

Barbot, Charles (1848-1877) Charleston. Accountant in Charleston.

Bates, Benjamin Franklin (1848-?) Spartanburg. Physician in Spartanburg.

Bates, Lucius Bellinger (1846-1930) Orangeburg. Prior service with 2nd SC Artillery. Captured and exchanged 1864. Physician in Newberry and Orangeburg.

Bee, James Moultrie, Jr. (1846-1906) Charleston. Collector in Charleston.

Bettis, John Miller (1848-1916) Edgefield. Brother-in-law of J.H. Bouknight. Merchant in Trenton.

Blair, David G. (1846-?) York. Farmer in Chickasaw Co, MS.

Blakeney, Albert (1848-?) Chesterfield.

Bonney, Francis Broome Lee (1849-?) Kershaw.

Boyd, James S. (1848-1878) Beaufort. Farmer.

Boyle, Woodson Fairfield.

Brooks, Duncan (1848-1872) Greenville.

Brown, Albert Ovid (1845-1865) Anderson. Died of disease Jan. 29, 1865 while Cadets were in service.

Brown, Charles J. (1849-?) Georgetown. Farmer in Bishopville.

Browning, Thomas Smyth (1849-?) Charleston. Farmer at Jedburg in Colleton Co.

Bulow, John Charles (1847-1876) Fairfield. In Summerville.

Butler, William Moses (1847-?) Clarendon. Prior service with Co. F, 5th Bn. SC Reserves. Farmer.

Campbell, Eli Scott (1847-1907) Lancaster. Methodist clergyman in Marion Co.

Carothers, William Meek (1847-?) York. Farmer in Dallas Co., AL.

Carpenter, William Willoughby (1849-1904) Charleston. Merchant in Charleston.

Carriere, Charles Edward (1849-1893) Charleston. Attorney in Charleston.

Chatham, Thomas Sumter (1846-?) Abbeville. Planter in Greenwood Co.

Colclough, John Ashby (1849-1899) Sumter. Planter near Manning.

Cunningham, Robert Noble (1846-1911) Charleston. Farmer near Waterloo in Laurens.

Cunningham, William Arthur (1848-1919) Kershaw. Farmer.

Davant, Augustine D. (1847-?) Beaufort.

Dean, James Lawrence (1847-1919) Anderson. Grocer in Spartanburg and Greenville. Brother of George R. Dean.

Dean, Leonard Yancey (1844-1934) 4th Congressional District. Prior service as Corp. with Co. B (Watson Guards), Hampton Legion. Lost arm at Gaines' Mill, VA. Entered SCMA—detailed to QM Dept. after evacuation of Columbia. Schoolteacher in Edgefield. Cotton weigher and warehouser, insurance adjustor, and fire insurance broker in Eufaula, AL.

Dean, Mills (1847-1897) Spartanburg. Prior service with 22nd Regiment SC Infantry. Attorney in Washington, DC.
de Veaux, Walter Peyre (1847-1892) Charleston. Clerk in Charleston.
Dozier, John Francis (1847-1907) Georgetown. Prior service with 2nd Regiment SC Cavalry. Planter in Georgetown Co.
Edgerton, Joseph Ives (1848-1870) Charleston. Clerk in Charleston.
Elliott, Henry De Saussure (1848-1907) Beaufort. Prior service with Elliott's Company (Beaufort Volunteer Artillery), SC Artillery. Attended College of Charleston. Became truck farmer and master of tugboats for Port Royal Sound.
Epps, John Law (1848-1916) Newberry. Farmer, schoolteacher, judge, and county treasurer in Newberry.
Evans, Benjamin Albert (1847-1902) Lancaster. Prior service with Co. C, 5th SC Reserves. Farmer in Jefferson.
Fishburne, Cotesworth Pinckney (1846-1909) Colleton. Farmer in Ashepoo. Brother of W.J. and L.N. Fishburne.
Fishburne, William Josiah (1848-1927) Colleton. Attorney in Walterboro; legislator.
Fisher, Walter E. (1849-?) Charleston. Clerk in Charleston. Alive in 1902.
Gaillard, Benjamin Sloan (1848-1910) Anderson.
Gaillard, Louis Leroy (1847-1925) Anderson. Farmer in Anderson.
Galluchat, Joseph, Jr. (1847-1886) Sumter. Attorney in Manning.
Gannon, Michael John (1845-1883) Charleston. Marble and stone business in Charleston.
Gantt, Earle Pickens. Prior service with Co. I, 1st SC Regulars. Merchant in High Falls, Oconee Co.
Geiger, William A. (1848-?) Lexington.
Grady, William Sims (1848-1927) Greenville. Cotton broker in Greenville.
Graham, Michael Willis (1847-1889) Barnwell. In Barnwell.
Graham, Thomas William (1849-1905) Horry. Planter in Horry County.
Grant, George (1849-1865) Horry. Left Cadets in early 1865 to enlist in Co. B, 18th SC Artillery BN. Never heard from after Bentonville.
Gray, Charles Jacob (1845-1920) Barnwell. Farmer and saw-and-grist-mill operator in Hampton Co.
Harp, William I. (1848-1888) Newberry. Clerk in retail store in Newberry.
Hart, Thomas W. Darlington. Farmer.
Henderson, Robert Harllee (1847-1869) Marion.
Heyward, Robert Barnwell (1848-1918) Charleston. Rice planter near Charleston.
Hodges, John Lawrence (1848-1907) Marlboro. Planter in Bennettsville.

Hubbell, Edward S. (1847-1890) Orangeburg. General merchandise clerk and insurance company president.
Hughes, Beatty F. (?-1901) Union. Prior service with Co. G, 6th SC Cavalry.
Ingram, William D. (1847-?) Chesterfield.
Johnson, Benjamin Jenkins, Jr. (1845-1929) 3rd Congressional District (Pickens). Farmer.
Johnson, David (1847-1894) Union. Judge in Spartanburg.
Johnstone, Francis Withers (1847-1929) Spartanburg. Railway service in Panama and Mexico.
Lanneau, Charles Blum (1846-1937) Charleston. Physician in Charleston and Darlington, SC and Savannah, GA.
Larissey, Henry Mood (1848-?) Colleton.
Latta, Robert James (1847-1919) York. Railroad surveyor in York.
Latimer, William C. (1847-1910) Abbeville. Merchant in Yorkville.
Lee, George Washington (1846-1902) Sumter.
Lewis, John Baylis (1848-1929) Anderson. Prior service with 1st Regiment SC State Troops. Merchant in Belton.
Lipscombe, Francis Wilkinson Pickens (1848-?) Newberry.
Lorick, William Washington (1848-1886) Lexington. Farmer in Lexington.
Lowry, James Ernest (1849-1945) York. Druggist in York.
Madden, Patrick Henry (1848-1914) Lancaster.
Mangum, Johnnie C. (1847-1865) 1st Congressional District (Chesterfield). Prior service with Co. E, 8th SC Infantry and Co. F, 26th SC Infantry.
Martin, William Evans (1848-?) Barnwell. Planter in Hampton Co.
Matthews, Charles Graves (1848-1908) York. Cotton and naval stores factor and commission merchant in Charleston.
Maxcy, Jonathon (1846-1891) Richland. Farmer in Sumter Co.
McBee, Frank Butler (1847-1922) Greenville. Brother of V.E. McBee. Lawyer in Greenville.
McConnell, William Evans (1848-1914) Greenville. Cotton mill employee in Williamston.
McCue, General George Washington (1846-?) Barnwell.
McCullough, David Shields (1848-1895) Greenville. Farmer, livestock dealer, and race-horse breeder in Darlington.
McCullough, John James (1846-1907) Williamsburg. Prior service with 4th Battalion SC Reserves. Farmer in Anderson.
McKay, John Coachman (1848-1872) Charleston. Graduated College of Charleston 1868.
McKewn, George Robert (1846-1916) Orangeburg. Prior service with Co. I (Orangeburg Artillery), 2nd SC Artillery. In Orangeburg.

Miles, David Franklin (1846-1926) Marion. Physician and planter, Marion Co.; legislator and longtime County Clerk.

Miller, William Gray (1845-1911) Pickens. Prior service with Buist's Company (Palmetto Guards Artillery), SC Artillery. Railway service in Summerville.

Miller, William Martin (1846-1918) Laurens. Farmer in Cross Hill.

Mims, Mark Abney (1846-1919) Edgefield. In Ridge Spring.

Nichols, E.C. "otherwise known as E.C. Jones" so called in honor of his stepfather, Gen. James Jones, Chairman of the Board of Visitors. (1847-1929) Richland. Postwar, adopted the name Edward Joseph Jones. Farmer.

Norris, James Pope (1848-1925) Edgefield. Prior service with Co. B, 2nd Artillery, Furniture dealer in Columbia.

O'Brien, Andrew Flynn (1845-1890) 2nd Congressional District (Colleton). Prior service as Orderly Sgt., 1st (Gregg's) Regiment SC Infantry. Lost right arm at Spotsylvania Court House, VA. Worked for SC Railway in Charleston, later an attorney.

O'Dell, William Taylor (1847-1933) Pickens. Farmer near Liberty; state senator.

Owens, B.H. (1843-?) 1st Congressional District. Prior service with Zimmerman's Company (Pee Dee Light Artillery), SC Artillery. WIA Chancellorsville.

Owens, Eli L. (1848-1918) Barnwell. In Columbia.

Paine, Edward Tattnall, Jr. (1848-1898) Charleston. In New York City.

Parrott, J.W. (1847-?) Darlington. Prior service with Ward's Battalion, SC Reserves. In Effingham.

Parrott, Thomas Hardee (1847-1929) Darlington. Farmer at Swift Creek.

Pearson, Philip (1849-1896) Richland.

Pitts, Robert M. (1847-?) Sumter. Farmer in Sumter.

Powell, William B. (1849-1924) Richland. Physician in Columbia.

Prentice, Robert J. (1848-?) Colleton.

Prioleau, Edward Harleston (1847-1928) Charleston. Ship broker and commission merchant in Charleston.

Rawls, Benjamin Andrew (1848-?) Prior service with 3rd Regiment SC Reserves. Supposedly captured and paroled near Greenville in April 1865. Mercantile interests in New York and Columbia; city alderman.

Reed, Walter F. Colleton. Prior service with Capt. Charbonnier's Company (Pickens Rifles) SC Militia. Planter in Charleston Co.

Reid, Samuel Henry (1846-1913) Chesterfield. Received appointment but did not report as he was a prisoner. Carried on roster of Cadets at war's end. Farmer in Cheraw.

Reeves, James B. (1849-?) Charleston. Insurance agent in Charleston.

Reynolds, John Schreiner (1848-1909) Charleston. Historian, attorney, and legislator. Prior service with Co. H, 3rd SC Troops.

Richardson, John Madison (1848-1907) Edgefield. Farmer in Anderson.

Ripley, John Calhoun (1849-1884) Charleston. Building materials dealer in Charleston.

Robinson, James Kirk, Jr. (1847-1866) Charleston.

Rogers, John Terrell (1846-1912) Marlboro. Farmer in Society Hill.

Ryan, Thomas A. (1848-1866) Charleston. Farmer near Moncks Corner.

Sams, Barnwell Stanyarne (1845-1928) Beaufort. Son of Dr. M.M. Sams.

Sams, Joseph Edings (1848-1865) Charleston. First cousin of R.O. Sams. Died in service Mar. 22, 1865.

Sanders, W.A. (?-1891) 6th Congressional District. Prior service with 2 Co. I, 6th SC Infantry. WIA Campbell's Station. Lost an arm. Lawyer in Chester, 1890.

Schipman, James Harris (1847-1884) Charleston. Left to join Co. F, 6th SC Cavalry. Merchant and turpentine dealer. He changed his name to James John Schipman.

Sheppard, Lafayette (1847-1911) Edgefield. Prior service with Rhett's Company (Brooks Light Artillery), SC Artillery.

Sheppard, Walter Scott (1848-1893) Edgefield. Physician in Greenwood.

Sigwald, Edward C. (1848-1867) Charleston. Watchmaker in Charleston.

Silcox, Ferdinand Augustus (1846-1897) Charleston. Factor and commission merchant in Charleston.

Simons, Keating Lewis, III (1847-1917) Charleston. Planter in Berkeley County.

Sistrunk, George (1844-?) Spartanburg.

Small, James C. Georgetown.

Smith, Thomas Ogier (1849-1891) Charleston. Clerk in Charleston.

Smyth, Joseph Ellison Adger (1847-1942) Charleston. Prior service as Sgt., 3rd Regiment SC State Troops. Wealthy industrialist in Anderson and Greenville.

Stackhouse, James (1849-1919) Marion. Dealer in livestock and farm implements, Marion. Mayor and State Senator.

Stephenson, Daniel H. (1849-?) Chester. Bookkeeper in Columbia.

Stephenson, Henry McNeil (1848-1928) Chester. Farmer at Hazlewood.

Stewart, James Mushatt (1847-?) Fairfield. Farmer. Attended USC and UVA.

Strauss, Henry Clay (1848-1912) Abbeville. Clerk in Charleston and York. Dry goods merchant.

Strohecker, Thomas Hamlin (1847-?) Charleston. Graduated College of Charleston 1870. Clerk in Charleston.

Sullivan, George Washington, Jr. (1848-1928) Laurens. Prior service as Orderly Sgt., 1st Regiment SC State Troops. Farmer and merchant in Anderson Co. and State Senator.

Taylor, Charles G. (1848-?) Richland.

Thomas, William Rosborough (1848-1899) Fairfield. Manufacturing executive in New York City. Brother of Cadets Edward and Peyre Thomas. First cousin of Capt. J.P. Thomas.

Vance, Samuel Watson (1847-1901) Pickens. Insurance broker in Pickens and Greenwood Co.; state civil servant.

Villepigue, J. Frederick (1848-1898). In Macon, Ga.

Walker, George O. (1845-1897) Edgefield.

Walker, George Williams (1848-1911) Union. Methodist minister and college president in Augusta, GA.

Waller, Edward Henry (1848-?) Abbeville. Brother of C.G. Waller.

Ward, Theodore O. (1846-?) 5th Congressional District (Pickens District). Prior service with 22nd Regiment SC Infantry. Physician in Reidville.

Waring, Edward Perry (1848-1916) Charleston. Agent for SC Railway in Charleston.

Wienges, Jacob Conrad (1848-1895) Charleston. Clerk for SC Railway in Charleston.

Williams, Archibald Campbell (1847-1912) Colleton. Left in Feb. 1865 and joined Co. F (St. Peter's Guards), 3rd SC Cavalry. Teacher in Verdier Township.

Williams, William (1848-?) Colleton.

Willingham, Thomas Henry, IV (1849-1909) Barnwell. Attorney in Macon, GA.

Wilson, Edward Morton (1847-1897) Charleston. Bookkeeper in Charleston.

Wilson, Matthew Harvey (1848-1911) Abbeville. Farmer in Abbeville.

Withers, Andrew Springs (1848-1907) York. In York.

Witherspoon, Charles LeRoy (1844-1890) Williamsburg. Prior service with Co. C (Manning Guards), Hampton Legion. Farmer in Clarendon Co.

Youmans, Augustus Marion (1846-1894) Beaufort. Attorney in Hampton Co.; legislator.

APPENDIX C

OUR SOUTHERN FLAG

I

Up! Up with our flag and fore'er may it be
High, floating in pride o'er the land of the free,
And beneath its bright folds how proudly we'll fight,
For God and for justice, for truth and for right!
Oh, long shall it wave o'er the loyal and brave,
For the chivalric hearts of a patriot band
By their honor have sworn its glory shall stand,
And ever shall wave o'er our dear native land.

Chorus

Yes, we've lifted our flag; we've raised it at last,
We've nailed it on high at the top of the mast!
And grandly it flashes and proudly it blows,
As sternly it dashes defiance to foes.

II

May it jauntily flaunt and joyously wave
O'er the peaceful homes of the happy and brave,
Where the heart's own beautiful loved ones abide,
But where furious war rolls its bloodflowing tide!
May it triumphantly stream with a meteor's gleam,
And nerve every soul for the desperate fight,
And glow with a luminous glory all bright,
An emblem of truth and an emblem of might!

Chorus

III

There are hands that are willing and arms that are strong,
And souls that are dauntless to battle gainst wrong;
They've hearts that are loving and loyal and stout,
And from mountain to sea hath gone forth the shout,
From the Palmetto boys, with a loud ringing noise
That our flag forever and ever shall be
Wide streaming in glory and waving o'er thee,
Dear, loved Carolina, the home of the free.

Chorus

— Samuel L. Hammond

"The Southern Flag" was written by Capt. Samuel L. Hammond while he was on duty on James Island during the firing on the *Star of the West*. "The Southern Flag" is dedicated to the Citadel Cadets, and right worthy are these gallant young soldiers of the handsome compliment. Capt. Hammond fell at the head of his company at Walthall Junction in 1864. In the same engagement, his two brothers were killed upholding the cause fought for by their ancestor, Col. Samuel Hammond, of the Revolution.*

_____

* *Tri-Weekly Southern Guardian*, May 4, 1861.

BIBLIOGRAPHY

PUBLISHED BOOKS

Bachman, Catherine L. *John Bachman.* Charleston: Walker, Evans & Cogswell Co., 1888.

Barlow, Albert R. *Company G, A Record of the Services of One Company of the 157th N.Y. Volunteers in the War of the Rebellion.* Syracuse, NY: A.W. Hall, 1899.

Bell, Louise M., ed. *Rebels in Grey.* Seneca, SC: United Daughters of the Confederacy, 1984.

Blackford, Susan Leigh. *Letters From Lee's Army.* New York: Charles Scribner's Sons, 1947.

Boatner, Mark M. III. *The Civil War Dictionary.* New York: David McKay Co., Inc., 1959.

Bond, Oliver J. *The Story of The Citadel.* Richmond, VA: Garrett and Massie, Inc., 1936.

Bowen, James Riley. *Regimental History of the First New York Dragoons.* Lyons, MI, 1900.

Brooks, Ulysses R. *Butler and His Cavalry in the War of Secession 1861-1865.* Columbia, SC: State Company, 1909.

Brooks, Ulysses R. *Stories of the Confederacy.* Columbia, SC: State Company, 1912 (hereafter Stories)

Calhoun, Charles M. *Liberty Dethroned: A Concise History of Some of the Most Startling Events Before, During, and Since the Civil War.* Greenwood, SC, 1903.

Capers, Brig. Gen. Ellison. *Confederate Military History.* Vol. 5, edited by Gen. Clement A. Evans, Blue and Gray Press. (hereafter CMH).

Cauthen, Charles E. *South Carolina Goes to War, 1860-1865.* Chapel Hill, NC, 1950.

Chapman, John A. *History of Edgefield County.* Easley, SC: Southern Historical Press, 1976 reprint.

Clark, Walter, ed. *Histories of the Several Regiments and Battalions from North Carolina.* Goldsboro, NC: Nash Brothers, 1901.

Crawford, Samuel Wylie. *The Genesis of the Civil War: The Story of Fort Sumter, 1860-1861.* New York, 1887.

Davies, Henry E. *General Sheridan.* New York: D. Appleton & Co., 1895.

Denison, Frederic. *Shot and Shell*. Providence, RI: J.A. & R.A. Reid, 1879.

Devereux, Margaret Green. *The Land and the People (An American Heritage)*. New York: Vantage Press, 1974.

Dickert, D. Augustus. *History of Kershaw's Brigade*. Dayton, OH: Morningside Press, 1973.

Dictionary of American Biography. New York: Charles Scribner's Sons, 1928.

Doubleday, Abner. *Reminiscences of Forts Sumter and Moultrie in 1860-61*. New York: Harper & Brothers, 1876.

Emilio, Luis F. *A Brave Black Regiment*. Boston: Boston Book Co., 1891.

Fisk, Joel C. and Blake, William H.D. *Condensed History of the Fifty-Sixth Regiment New York Veteran Volunteer Infantry*. Newburgh, NY: Newburgh Journal Printing House, 1906.

Fletcher, A. *Within Fort Sumter*. New York: N. Tibbals & Co., 1861.

Freeman, Douglas Southall. *Lee's Lieutenants*. New York: Charles Scribner's Sons, 1946.

Grant, Ulysses S. *Personal Memoirs of ------*, 2 vols., New York: Charles Webster and Co., 1886.

Green, Edwin L. *A History of the University of South Carolina*. Columbia: State Co., 1916.

Hagood, Johnson. *Meet Your Grandfather*. n.p. n.d. (hereafter Meet)

Hagood, Johnson. *Memoirs of the War of Secession*. Columbia: State Co., 1910.

Harris, William A. *The Record of Fort Sumter*. Columbia, SC: S.C. Printing Office, 1862.

Hartness, George Bowman. *By Ship, Wagon and Foot to York County, SC*. Columbia, SC: Privately published, 1966.

Harwell, Richard & Racine, Phillip N., ed. *The Fiery Trail*. Knoxville, TN: University of Tennessee Press, 1986.

Hayes, James P. *James and Related Islands*. Charleston, SC: Walker, Evans & Cogswell Co., 1978.

Hyde, William L. *History of the One Hundred and Twelfth NY Volunteers*. Fredonia, NY: W. McKinstry & Co., 1866.

Isham, Asa B. *An Historical Sketch of the Seventh Regiment Michigan Volunteer Cavalry*. New York: Town Topics Publishing Co., 1894.

Johnson, John. *The Defense of Charleston Harbor*. Freeport, NY: Books for Libraries Press, 1970.

Johnson, Robert U. and Buel, Clarence C., eds. *Battles and Leaders of the Civil War*. New York: Century 1887-1888. (hereafter B&L)

Jones, Katherine. *When Sherman Came: Southern Women and the "Great March."* Indianapolis: Bobbs-Merrill Co., 1964.

Journal of the Conventions of the People of South Carolina, Held in 1860, 1861, and 1862... (hereafter Journal)

Journal of the South Carolina Executive Councils of 1861 and 1862. South Carolina Archives Department, Columbia, 1956. (hereafter Executive Council)

Kennedy, Gayle. *My Kennedy Ancestors of Fairfield County, SC.* Spartanburg, SC: author, 1969.

Kidd, James H. *Personal Recollections of a Cavalryman with Custer's Michigan Cavalry Brigade in the Civil War.* Ionia, MI: Sentinel Printing Co., 1908.

LaBree, Benjamin, *Camp Fires of the Confederacy.* Louisville, KY: Courier-Journal Printing Co., 1899.

Law, John Adger, ed. *Citadel Cadets, the Journal of Cadet Tom Law.* Clinton, SC: PC Press, 1941.

Long, E.B. *The Civil War Day by Day.* Garden City: Doubleday & Co., 1971.

Manning, William Harris, Jr., and Edna A. *Papers,* 15 volumes. South Caroliniana Library.

Marshall, Vera Lee Kearl. *Proud to Remember.* Provo, UT: Brigham Young University Press, 1963.

Marszalek, John F., ed. *The Diary of Emma Holmes.* Baton Rouge, LA: LSU Press, 1979.

May, John A. and Faunt, Joan Reynolds. *South Carolina Secedes.* Columbia, SC: University of South Carolina Press, 1960.

McDaniel, Ruth Barr, compiler. *Confederate War Correspondence of James Michael Barr and Rebecca Ann Dowling Barr.* Taylors, SC: Faith Printing Co., 1963.

McElroy, John. *Andersonville.* Toledo, OH: D.R. Locke, 1879.

McGrath, Franklin, ed. *The History of the 127th New York Volunteers.* New York, 1898.

McMaster, Elizabeth Waring. *Girls of the Sixties.* Columbia, SC: State Printing Co., 1937 (hereafter Girls).

Moore, Frank, ed. *Fort Sumter Memorial.* Edwin C. Hill, New York, 1915.

Moore, Frank, ed. *The Rebellion Record.* 11 Vols. New York: G.P. Putnam, 1861-1868 (hereafter Record).

Myers, Frank M. *The Comanches: A History of White's Battalion, Virginia Cavalry.* Marietta, GA: Continental Book Co., 1956.

Neuffer, Claude Henry, ed. *The Christopher Happoldt Journal.* Charleston: Charleston Museum, 1960.

Obear, Katherine Theus. *Through the Years in Old Winnsboro.* Reprint Company, Spartanburg, SC, 1980.

Oliphant, Mary C. Simms; Odell, Alfred Taylor; and Eaves, T.C. Duncan. *The Letters of William Gilmore Simms.* Columbia, SC: USC Press, 1955.

Official Records of the Union and Confederate Armies in the War of the Rebellion. Washington, DC, 1880-1901 (hereafter OR - refers to Series I, unless otherwise noted).

Official Records of the Union and Confederate Navies in the War of the Rebellion. Washington, DC, 1894-1922 (hereafter Naval OR).

Preston, Noble D. *History of the Tenth Regiment of Cavalry New York State Volunteers.* New York: D. Appleton and Co., 1892.

Reynolds, Emily B. & Faunt, Joan R. *Biographical Directory of the Senate of the State of SC 1776-1964.* Columbia, SC: Archives & History, 1964 (hereafter Senate).

Ripley, Warren. *Siege Train.* Columbia, SC: Charleston Library Society by University of South Carolina Press, 1986.

Roman, Alfred. *Military Operations of General Beauregard.* 2 Volumes. New York: Harper & Brothers, 1884.

Scarborough, William K., ed. *The Diary of Edmund Ruffin.* Baton Rouge; LSU Press, 1972.

Sheridan, Philip H. *Personal Memoirs of Philip H. Sheridan.* New York: Charles L. Webster & Co., 1888.

Sherman, William T. *Memoirs of General William T. Sherman.* 2 Volumes. New York: D. Appleton & Co., 1875.

Smith, Daniel Elliott Huger, ed. *Mason Smith Family Letters.* Columbia, SC: University of South Carolina Press, 1950.

Smythe, Mrs. A.T.; Poppenheim, Miss M.B.; and Taylor, Mrs. Thomas. *South Carolina Women in the Confederacy.* Columbia, SC: State Co., 1903-1907.

Snowden, Yates. *History of SC.* 5 Volumes. New York: Lewis, 1920.

Thomas, John Peyre. *History of the South Carolina Military Academy.* Charleston: Walker, Evans and Cogswell Co., 1893.

Wells, Edward L. *A Sketch of the Charleston Light Dragoons.* Lucas, Richardson and Co., Charleston, 1888.

Wells, Edward L. *Hampton & His Cavalry in '64.* Richmond, VA: B.F. Johnston Publishing Co., 1899.

Wells, Edward L. *Hampton & Reconstruction.* Columbia, SC: State Co., 1907.

White Family.

Wiles, Dr. A.G.D. *The Boys Behind the Guns.* n.p., n.d.

Williams, Ben Ames, ed. *A Diary from Dixie.* Cambridge, MA: Harvard University Press, 1949.

Woodward, C. Vann and Muhlenfeld, Elisabeth. *The Private Mary Chesnut.* New York: Oxford University Press, 1984.

ARTICLES AND JOURNALS

Adger-Smyth-Flynn Family MSS, South Caroliniana Library

Adjutant General's Ledger

Adjutant General of South Carolina, General Orders.

Aiken MSS, South Caroliniana Library.

Arsenal Cadet.
Association of Graduates.
Barnwell MSS, South Carolina Historical Society.
Bartlette MSS, South Caroliniana Library.
Board of Visitors Minutes, 1861-1865.
Boatwright Family Papers
Boy Soldiers of Tulifinny
Burke MSS, The Citadel Archives.
Campbell MSS, South Caroliniana Library.
Charles MSS, South Caroliniana Library.
Charleston Yearbook, 1892.
Citadel Magazine.
Citadel News.
Coffin MSS, The Citadel Archives.
Compiled Service Records, Battalion of State Cadets (hereafter CSR-Cadets).
Compiled Service Records, 6th South Carolinia Cavalry (hereafter CSR).
Confederate Veteran (hereafter CV)
Dozier MSS, South Caroliniana Library.
Dubos, Charles vs. U.S.
Furman MSS, South Caroliniana Library.
Kershaw, John. "Reminiscences of Citadel Life 1864-65," The Sphinx, 1911, 148.
Lee's Official Dispatch, June 29, 1864.
Lewis, J. Baylis, "Their First and Last Fight."
Lewis, J. Baylis. "Arsenal Cadets Before Sherman."
Lowry MSS, South Caroliniana Library.
McDowell MSS, South Caroliniana Library.
McMaster MSS, South Caroliniana Library.
Obear MSS, South Caroliniana Library.
Patrick MSS, South Caroliniana Library.
Price MSS, South Caroliniana Library.
Reports and Resolutions of the General Assembly.
Robinson, Joseph M. The Defense of the Charleston and Savannah Railroad.
Sams, "First Shot"
Sams MSS, South Caroliniana Library.
Sams, R.O. MSS, The Citadel Archives.
Sease, Eunice P. Some Reminiscences of a Confederate Soldier, Edwin Calhoun, Company C., 6th Cavalry, CSA.
Sellers MSS, The Citadel Archives.
The Shako. "The Firing on the Star of the West," March 1967, p. 8.
Sherfessee MSS, South Caroliniana Library.
Simkins, MSS, The Citadel Archives.
Sims, William Gilmore, Unpublished Letter.
Smith, S. Porcher, South Caroliniana Library.
Smythe Family Correspondence, South Caroliniana Library.

South Carlina Historical and Genealogical Magazine (hereafter SCHGM).
Southern Bivouac.
Southern Historical Society Papers, Vol. II, p. 275 and Vol. IX, p. 171.
The Sphinx.
Stokes MSS, South Caroliniana Library.
Sullivan, G.W. Pickens Sentinel, March 9, 1921.
Teague MSS, South Caroliniana Library.
Thomas, John Peyre, Letter to R.J. Davant, Chairman of the Board of Visitors, December 6, 1865.
Thomas, John Peyre. Report to Board of Visitors. October 31, 1865.
Thomas, John Peyre. Scrapbooks, South Caroliniana Library (hereafter Thomas Scrapbooks).
Thurston MSS, The Citadel Archives.
United Daughters of the Confederacy Scrapbooks, SC Confederate Relic Room (hereafter UDC).
Unpublished account. The Citadel Archives.
Vandiver, Mrs. J.R. Pickens Sentinel, February 24, 1921 & March 9, 1921.
Walker, C. Irvine. Reminiscences of Days in the Citadel 1858-1861. The Citadel Archives.
Welch, Sgt. S.E. "The Citadel Cadets and the 'Star of the West'."
White, John B. Report to the Board of Visitors, Hillsboro, NC, December 12, 1865.
Who Burnt Columbia?
Williams, Ben. "A Confederate Soldier's Memoirs," The Sunday News.
Williams, Ben. "A Gallant Soldier's Story." The Sunday News.
Wilson, James H. "The Cavalry of the Army of the Potomac," Papers of the Military Historical Society of Massachusetts, Vol. XIII, 1913, p. 57.

NEWSPAPERS

Charleston Daily Courier.
Charleston Mercury.
Charleston Tri-Weekly Courier.
Charleston News and Courier.
Daily South Carolinian.

Harper's Weekly.
Frank Leslie's Illustrated.
The State.
Sunday News.
Sunny South.
Tri-Weekly Southern Guardian.

INDEX